THE SUPREME COURT AND RELIGION

THE SUPREME COURT IN AMERICAN LIFE

SAMUEL KRISLOV, *General Editor*

SAMUEL KRISLOV

The Supreme Court and Political Freedom

ARTHUR SELWYN MILLER

The Supreme Court and American Capitalism

MARTIN SHAPIRO

The Supreme Court and Administrative Agencies

ROBERT SCIGLIANO

The Supreme Court and the Presidency

JOHN R. SCHMIDHAUSER and LARRY L. BERG

The Supreme Court and Congress

RICHARD E. MORGAN

The Supreme Court and Religion

The Supreme Court and Religion

RICHARD E. MORGAN

THE FREE PRESS, New York

Collier–Macmillan Limited, London

For EVA CORLISS MORGAN

Printed in the United States of America

The Free Press
A Division of The Macmillan Company
866 Third Avenue, New York, New York 10022

Collier-Macmillan Canada Ltd., Toronto, Ontario
Library of Congress Catalog Card Number: 72-80077

printing number
1 2 3 4 5 6 7 8 9 10

Contents

Preface

What excuse could there be for another book about the religion clauses of the First Amendment? There are two, in fact. The first is that, despite the number of titles, almost everything now available on the subject is badly out of date. The second is that, even allowing for their lack of currency, the books on religion and the public order constitute a disappointing literature. There are a few "straight histories" and recitations of court decisions which offer little political or legal analysis, and there are a number of lawyers' briefs urging particular interpretations of the First Amendment language. The journal literature on the subject is far superior, but it is not easily accessible to university students and is not accessible at all to that beau ideal of authors, the general reader.

This is the modest target at which I have aimed—to produce a short volume which would be up-to-date and involve the reader at the level of analytical sophistication currently achieved in scholarly (learned-journal) discussions of religion and the Supreme Court.

Of course I did not produce a manuscript and describe the arguments of others without adding arguments and comments of my own. My fondest hope is that some readers may find these stimulating. My more modest hope is that those who find these offerings stupid will feel the volume to be useful despite them.

In the course of ten years' work in the area of religion and American law, I have incurred debts far too numerous to list. This particular effort was improved by my Bowdoin colleague James E. Bland, who read the first two chapters, and by my friend Arthur E. Sutherland of the Harvard Law School, who read the first five. Jesse Choper of the Law School of the University of California at Berkeley, read the entire manuscript and saved me from numerous errors. I thank them and confer the conventional absolution for what now appears.

In the preparation of the book, Gladys McKnight was tirelessly patient in typing and retyping my ghastly copy. Two student assistants, Timothy J. Parsons and C. Mitchell Goldman, were also great helps.

A grant from the Bowdoin College Faculty Research Fund is acknowledged. It enabled me to have the considerable secretarial services of Cynthia F. Pyle, in New York, in the summer of 1970.

My largest debt of the years spent with the religion clauses is acknowledged by the dedication.

R. E. M.

Introduction

This account of the work of the Supreme Court of the United States in interpreting the religion clauses of the First Amendment is intended to serve two purposes. First, it is meant to provide a short description—a large-scale roadmap if you will—of an intrinsically important area of American constitutional law. Second, it is meant to suggest something of the political setting in which the Supreme Court works and the difficulty of deciding hard-fought constitutional issues in ways which are both doctrinally coherent and politically acceptable.

The tension between doctrinal consistency and political acceptability is the distinctive tension in which the Justices of the Supreme Court must operate; and while one or the other concern predominates in the work of particular Justices on particular issues, neither value can be ignored by too many of the members of the Court over too long a time. The authority of the Supreme Court in the American political system is dependent on a broadly shared perception of the Court's decisional process as different from that of legislatures, executives, and administrative agencies.[1] Not only must the Justices reach tolerable adjustments of intensely conflicting social interests and demands, but they must rationalize and explain these outcomes. It is all very well in the American political culture for a legislature, in the course of allocating public resources, to bestow a bit here and a bit there in accordance with the momentary play of political forces. Over the long haul, however, this approach will not be tolerated from a court—especially not from the Supreme Court of the United States as it goes about the task of developing that very special body of principles we call constitutional law. Judicial policy-makers must struggle explicitly to relate particular decisions to other previous decisions, and suggest how future conflicts of a similar sort shall be resolved.

When a commentator taxes the Supreme Court for incoherence in its explanations (or failure to attempt to explain) he is passing something more than an esthetic judgment. When the Court fails in its distinctive task—rationalizing, reconciling, and explaining its policy initiatives—there are at least potentially important costs. The legitimacy of a Court decision (the extent to which it is perceived as a proper command from an authority competent to issue it) is obviously important in securing compliance with the decision; it is also important to the long run "standing" of the Court in the eyes of the various publics which compose the American political nation. To garble or waffle the explanation of a departure in constitutional law is to weaken its force and diminish the capital of public regard which sustains the Court as an institution.

It is for this reason, and not from a compulsion to pick nits and spin intricate verbal webs, that so much attention is devoted in the pages that follow to the difficulties of rationalization which the Justices have encountered in construing the religion clauses. To describe only the play of forces operating on the Court, and the consequences of outcomes in particular cases, is to present a misleading half-picture of the functioning of the Court in the American system.

But a final word of caution. The Court must rationalize

and explain the way it resolves conflicts and makes policy, yet to expect that the Court can ever perform this task perfectly is naive. While it is the proper business of those who make their living following and commenting on the work of the Court to criticize its doctrinal performance, this criticism should be tempered always by a sympathy for the Justices as they attempt to decide in ways which satisfactorily adjust social conflicts. It may be necessary, on occasion, for Court majorities to resort to ambiguity and non-sequitor. The policy which could be best rationalized simply may not constitute an acceptable accommodation of social interests. How much resort to ambiguity can be forgiven is a matter of intense debate among lawyers and political scientists,[2] and it is not part of my purpose here to contribute to that debate. The point is that the Court's work with the religion clauses is an excellent illustration of *why* the debate over the importance of doctrinal consistency *is* fully as important as the debates over whether the policy outputs in particular areas are wise or acceptable.

NOTES

1. The extent to which this is a mass perception, as opposed to an elite perception, is unclear. But it is also rather unimportant. An elite perception which is common to a large number of otherwise differing elites is as politically significant as a mass perception. In fact, most of what we refer to in common parlance as "public opinion" is elite perception. See generally V. O. Key, Jr., *Public Opinion and American Democracy* (New York: Knopf, 1961), pp. 535–558, and Walter F. Murphy and Joseph Tanenhaus, "Public Opinion and the United States Supreme Court," in Joel B. Grossman and Joseph Tanenhaus, eds., *Frontiers of Judicial Research* (New York: Wiley, 1969).

2. Classics in the debate over doctrinal consistency (or "craftsmanship," as it is often called) are Herbert Wechsler, "Toward Neutral Principles of Constitutional Law." This paper was delivered as the Oliver Wendell Holmes Lecture at the Harvard Law School in 1959, and appeared in Wechsler's collection *Principles, Politics, and Fundamental Law* (Cambridge: Harvard University Press, 1961); Alexander M. Bickel, *The Least Dangerous Branch* (Indianapolis: Bobbs-Merrill, 1962); and Gerald Gunther, "The Subtle Vices of the Passive Virtues—A Comment on Principle and Expediency in Judicial Review," 64, *Columbia Law Review,* 1 (1964).

I

Religion and the Law in Early America

It is impossible to portray the difficulties which the Supreme Court has encountered in attempting to interpret and apply the religion clauses of the First Amendment without the aid of an historical backdrop. Certain aspects of the early American experience are crucial to an understanding of the forces which have operated on the Court, forcing it to involve itself with potentially divisive questions of religion and the law. In addition, the constitutional and statutory language with which the Court must work[1] is far from self-defining, and reference to historical materials is one of the ways in which the justices give it meaning. The inherited attitudes of the early settlers, the nature of colonial religious and legal practices, religious "settlement" at the federal constitutional convention, and the framing of the First Amendment are all matters which need concern us.

The English Inheritance

The most important characteristic of the immigrants who settled the Atlantic littoral of the North American continent was that they were English. This is not to ignore the scattering of Scots, Swedes, French Huguenots, and Germans; nor is it to contradict altogether the rhapsodic observations of some contemporary observers such as Crévecoeur[2] on the tolerant and cosmopolitan behavior of what they took to be history's first polyglot national community. It is simply to recall that the cultural baggage of the vast majority of those who managed the affairs of the towns and colonies was English.

By cultural baggage I mean two things: first, a set of fears and hatreds having their roots deep in the English past, and second, certain specific religious ideologies—Quakerism, Puritanism, Brownism, Anabaptism, orthodox Anglicanism—which had been developed in the context of English society and politics and were seeking room to develop in the American wilderness. Both historically rooted demonology and the explicit ideologies had profound political implications—not only for the narrow question before us here—the relationship of religion to the public order—but for the broader questions of how the state itself should be organized and the relationship of individual men to it. Let us examine demonology and ideology in turn.

Demonology

The English Reformation was less bloody than those on the Continent, but it engendered in English Protestantism an abiding hostility to Roman Catholicism. There were comparatively few Protestant martyrings during the brief reign of the Catholic Mary (1553–1557), but the stench of burning flesh at Smithfield carried pungently down the centuries.[3]

Periodic domestic alarms during the late sixteenth and early seventeenth centuries reenforced the hostility of Anglicans to Rome and of Puritans to both Rome and Canterbury. Beginning in 1559 with the Acts of Supremacy and Uniformity, a series of statutes was enacted, aimed at excluding Catholics from positions of social or political power—from law, government, and the universities. Priests were banned from the realm on pain of death, and "Papists" were formally required to attend Anglican services.

What Ray Allen Billington[4] called "quasi-historical propaganda" was widely circulated depicting the barbarous and repressive practices of Rome, and it is interesting that while England had never really felt the lash of the Inquisition, that very fact seemed to make its history and legend more vivid and morbidly fascinating for Englishmen. On November 5, 1606, a day set for the opening of Parliament, a cache of gunpowder was discovered in a cellar under the House of Lords. A desperate band of English Catholics had intended the explosion as the start of a counter-reformation, and in later years the anniversary of their failure became a national holiday on which effigies of Guy Fawkes, one of the conspirators, were burned amid great gaiety. This was followed, in the 1630's, by the High Church purges of Archbishop William Laud, which sent shockwaves through Puritanism on both sides of the Atlantic.

The extent to which the English Revolution of 1640 was a function of religious fervor is a matter of sharp debate among historians.[5] Whether the basic causes were economic, social, or religious, however, the religious rhetoric in which the verbal dimension of the struggle was carried on left its mark on English culture. As Michael Walzer has written, "it was only the Lord which secured the righteousness of the Saints, and they set the Lord in opposition to all the 'man-made' customs and comfortable traditions of their native land."[6] After the Restoration had renewed fears of a Catholic infiltration and the anti-Catholic rantings of Titus Oates had aroused rumors of Jesuit intrigues—"traitor" and "Papist" became synonymous terms. J. H. Plumb has written that

> By 1688 conspiracy and rebellion, treason and plot, were a part of the history and experience of at least three generations of Englishmen. Indeed, for centuries the country had scarcely been free from turbulence for more than a decade at a time.[7]

And whether Puritan or Anglican, those who suffered this instability had reason to ascribe it to the wiles of Rome and Roman princes or to a Canterbury too Romish in its ways.

It should be emphasized that English anti-Catholicism became, during this same period, closely bound up with English nationalism. The threat of Catholic military conquest was as recurrent as the fear of Catholics boring from within. England's national identity had been redefined when Henry VIII led the country out of the Universal Commonwealth of Rome, and the threats of the Armada and successive French and Spanish plots to install Catholic pretenders made hatred of the Pope an article of English patriotism. As Roland H. Bainton put it

> Englishmen would not tolerate Catholics because they did not trust Catholics to be tolerant of Protestants. However much a Catholic might aver his tolerance, the suspicion could not be allayed that if he were given power he would revert to the Inquisition and the stake.[8]

And Billington concluded

> The settlers who came to America, reared in this atmosphere of intolerance, carried with them to the new land the same hatred of Popery which characterized the England of that day. In America natural conditions intensified this attitude even though there were almost no Catholics in the colonies. . . . The isolation of the people, the introspection to which they reverted in their wilderness homes, the distance which separated the colonies from the mother country and from Europe, all fostered the bigotry which they had brought from the old world.[9]

Ideology

As for particular Protestant ideologies they all, with the exception of orthodox Anglicanism, contained an implicit notion of the state as an inferior and potentially dangerous institution. At first blush this suggestion may seem to contradict the conventional wisdom concerning early American Protestantism, and it is worth pausing a moment to understand what is involved in the argument.

It is true that Calvin, Luther, and the Fathers of the Anglican Church all emphasized man's duty to obey the state.[10] It is also true that the Puritans of Massachusetts Bay spoke respectfully of the importance of civil government and the role of the magistrate. And it is finally true that these same Massachusetts Puritans, along with other early American Protestant sects, attempted in various ways to use the machinery of the state to enforce religious orthodoxy. How, then, can it be said that American Protestants were ideologically indisposed toward the state?

First, the English political experience which we have just reviewed resulted not only in an abiding antipathy to Roman Catholics, but also (at least among non-Anglican Protestants) in a reaction against the English state as an institution—a reaction which altered Protestant attitudes despite the teaching of Calvin and Luther on the importance of the state and the duty of Christians to cooperate with it. The American historian, Roy F. Nichols, in his masterful essay on self-government in the United States, *American Leviathan,*[11] traces the course of the English Protestant struggle and emphasizes its importance for the development of American political and social patterns. Beginning with the infiltration of Protestant ideas and teachers from the low countries in the early sixteenth century, through the Marian excesses, to the efforts of Elizabeth I to construct a settlement which would end religious feuding which threatened political stability, Nichols stresses that the radical Protestant cause was both anti-Catholic and suspicious of the existing governmental order. Throughout the reigns of Elizabeth, James, and Charles, it was the government of the realm which was perceived as the barrier in the road to radical Protestant ascendency. The governmental apparatus, at a minimum, sought to enforce conformity to the Anglicanism of the Thirty-Nine Articles, and there was always the danger of it falling again under the awful power of Rome—of a Catholic monarch coming to the throne. Here are the clear beginnings of that antipathy toward the state which became by the late eighteenth century such an obvious feature of non-Anglican Protestantism in America and has had such a profound effect on our constitutional development.

Second, and again despite statements of early Protestant theoreticians favorable to the state, there is an individualistic bias inherent in Protestantism which disposes the believer to regard *all* social (human) institutions as potentially dangerous. After all, the most basic assertion of the early Protestant rebels was the direct relationship between man and God. Individualism and privatism are inherent in this theology, even though they may be temporarily obscured, as in the first few decades of the Massachusetts Bay Colony. In contrast to the temporal preoccupations of Rome, Protestant concerns were distinctly other-worldly. Norman St. John-Stevas has pointed out the disparity between the Protestant view of man and his institutions as utterly fallen and the Catholic view of an imperfect man whose life on earth and whose civil institutions are worthy partners and not corruptors of the Church.[12] For Catholicism, civil government is a natural and blessed, not just a necessary, institution; cooperative arrangements are desirable. For radical Protestants (with the world an inn and the Devil the innkeeper), cooperation between the Church and a government was always a little uneasy—with the state held at arm's length. One of the ablest American students of Puritanism, Edmund S. Morgan, captured this disdain for the merely secular in his work on *The Puritan Family:*

> There was a type of man whom the Puritans never tired of denouncing. He was the good citizen, a man who obeyed the laws, carried out his civil obligations, never injured others. Puritans called him a "civil man", and admitted that he was "outwardly just, temperate, chaste, careful to follow his worldly business, will not hurt so much as his neighbour's dog, payes every man his owne, and lives of his owne; no drunkard, adulterer, or quareller; loves to live peaceably and quietly among his neighbours." This man, this paragon of social virtue, the Puritans said, was on his way to Hell, and their preachers continually reminded him of it.[13]

The truly important activity of the community was churchly. Social peace was also important, but it was principally secured by God's law and only incidentally by man's.

Third, the use by the early colonists (especially those of Massachusetts Bay) of the state machinery to enforce religious orthodoxy, the so-called experiments in theocratic government, did not contradict Protestant wariness of the state but, indeed, were profound expressions of it. This has been the source of much historical confusion, but the key lies in distinguishing between wariness toward the state and toleration of religious diversity. The wariness existed among early non-Anglican Protestants, but there was little diversity and no toleration. When wariness exists without toleration and diversity, it is both sensible and possible to subordinate the state and use it to support the church. But when there are diverse positions competing for adherents within the community there must be strict separation. In the absence of religious homogeneity it is impossible to subordinate the state, and the only way to protect the competing sects against this external enemy is to dissociate the two spheres to the greatest extent possible. If this is not done, the state will be "captured" by one sect and used to improve its position vis à vis the others. Early American Protestants did not begin with a fully formed ideology of separation. The ideology was a combination of negativism toward the state and denominational toleration, and while the first was part of the English inheritance and present at the outset, the second developed slowly through the late seventeenth and eighteenth centuries.

The process by which toleration developed and became engrafted on the early doctrine of institutional separation, and the way the new fused doctrine was reenforced by the general hostility of Protestantism to state power, is a complicated one. I have attempted to trace it elsewhere,[14] and for our purposes it is enough to note that the process was not "complete" until well into the nineteenth century, and even then it impressed itself to varying degrees on different Protestant denominations:

> Strict separation is, of course, only one strand in the tangled weave of Protestant doctrine, and it varies in its prominence throughout the whole. Baptists are more conscious of separationist doctrine than Episcopalians, and Congregationalists fall somewhere in the middle. Yet even today, when other doctrines of American Protestantism are eroding and many church members are embarrassed by the old theologies, the strict separation remains a powerful notion around which broad Protestant support can be mobilized.[15]

Sidney E. Mead, following Roger Williams, has called this mature separationism "the lively experiment," and sees it as a distinct contribution of American Protestantism to religious and political thought.[16] Its essence is a concern to protect the church *from the state*.[17]

COLONIAL PRACTICES

Much has been made over the years of differences in religious practices between the colonies, and there were some. But it is important to note that these differences were of style and idiom of worship, not in the relationship of religion to the public order. In this respect the development of the various colonies and regions was really quite similar.

Massachusetts

The reason, to repeat, that Massachusetts Bay is so baffling to modern students is because we find it difficult to see in early Puritan practices the seed of the later Protestant doctrine of strict separation of church and state—the seed which needed the development of toleration to germinate. At first glance there does not seem to be anything resembling either separation or toleration in early Massachusetts. As Perry Miller put it

> The government of Massachusetts, and of Connecticut as well, was a dictatorship, not of a single tyrant, or of an economic class, or of a political faction, but of the holy and regenerate. Those who did not hold with the ideals entertained by the righteous, or who believed God had preached other principles, or who desired that in religious belief, morality, and ecclesiastical preferences all men should be at liberty to do as they wished—such persons had every liberty, as Nathaniel Ward said, to stay away from New England. If they did come, they were expected to keep their opinions to themselves; if they discussed them in public or attempted to act upon them, they were exiled; if they persisted in returning, they were cast out again; if they still came back,

> as did four Quakers, they were hanged on Boston Common, and from the Puritan point of view it was good riddance.[18]

Technically speaking there was an established church; government taxed for it and religious offences were civil crimes. Yet, even here, it is quite misleading to say that in Massachusetts (or anywhere else in New England) the state was "simply the police department of the church."[19] John Cotton reminded his followers that "it was toleration that made the world anti-Christian," but John Winthrop was wont to criticize clergy for intruding into "affairs of the state, which did not belong to their calling." Also, it is easy to overdo the degree of institutional fusion of church and government in the so-called theocracies. Edmund Morgan has pointed out that

> The only [formal] connection they retained between the church and the state lay in the provision, adopted in Massachusetts in 1631, that only church members could become freemen and thus be entitled to vote and hold office. . . . the officers of government were kept distinct and separate from the officers of the churches. There were no church courts: the clergy held no place in the legislature; and although no law prevented it, clergymen were not elected to public office.[20]

Certainly a partial theory of separation was operating here, and care was taken not to reproduce the intermingling of religious and governmental structures which characterized the despised Roman or the erring English churches. The one thing which makes the theocracies seem so contradictory of the anti-statism and separationism apparent in later Protestant thought was the short-lived practice of using the state to enforce religious conformity. The arrival of more diverse sorts of people through the seventeenth century, the need to dampen and contain religious hostilities in order to further commercial development and attract more settlers, and the fear that repression directed against Quakers and Anglicans would result in abolition of separate colonial entities and the creation by Britain of a New England-wide jurisdiction ruled from Whitehall (with an Anglican establishment), all contributed to the growth of toleration and, following on its heels, strict separation.

Massachusetts adopted the Halfway Covenant after 1657, and this admitted to church membership children of the baptized even though they had not experienced a traditional conversion. This step served to considerably broaden citizenship. By 1721, Perry Miller tells us, Increase Mather and his son Cotton

> participated in the ordination of a Baptist minister in Boston . . . and preached a sermon on the need for harmony between differing sects. . . . by that time much water had gone under the bridge, the old charter had been revoked, there was danger that the Church of England might be made the established church of the colonies, theology had come to be of less importance in men's minds than morality, the tone of the eighteenth century was beginning to influence opinion—even in Boston. Increase was old and weary. Puritanism, in the true sense of the word, was dead.[21]

Connecticut

In Connecticut, which had closely paralleled Massachusetts in religious attitudes and church-state practices, the Saybrook Platform of 1708 recognized the full citizenship and freedom of worship of dissenting Protestant sects. Thus, early in the new century, did the theocratic pretensions of the Fundamental Orders meet the same fate as those of the Cambridge Agreement.

Rhode Island

It is fair to say that the settlement along Narragansett Bay was an exception to most colonial rules concerning toleration and the relationship of religion to the public order. Not only was Roger Williams committed to toleration of all varieties of Christians, he was acutely anxious to protect the churches from the state and to segregate spiritual and temporal authorities. The "lively experiment" became the doctrinal pacesetter and model for American Protestant development during the eighteenth century. Over the years it has had a profound impact on Protestant thought, and Williams has become something of a Protestant saint while only the scholars read Ward, Cotton, Hooker, and the Mathers. That Williams was not altogether a "modern" in his views on the necessity of governmental enforcement of morality need not detain us here.[22]

The Middle Colonies

New York, from the time of its seizure from the Netherlands, had an established Anglican Church under the Bishop of London. There is little evidence that this bore heavily on dissenters in any respect other than taxation. Prayers in the Reformed churches continued to be offered for the Stadlholder of Amsterdam rather than the King of England as head of the "established Church" and no one seemed to take this deviance as raising grave issues. Roman Catholics were, of course, civilly disabled, but this was the practice throughout the colonies, including vaunted Rhode Island.

The rather easy-going Anglicanism of New York was also the style in New Jersey, but in Pennsylvania we encounter a somewhat different set of practices. While superficially similar to Rhode Island with its recognition of all Christians,[23] William Penn's polity was in fact much more committed to punishing sin and backing up the Quaker oligarchy than either Roger Williams' "lively experiment" or the Anglican regimes. There are some striking similarities between Pennsylvania and Puritan New England, but tolerance and separation came on about the same schedule and for the same reasons on the Delaware as on the Charles.

Maryland's church-state arrangements also present a problem of interpretation. The standard textbook version is that the colony was founded by Lord Baltimore as a haven for English Catholics and that the colony enjoyed a period of virtually complete tolerance before Protestants gained the upper hand in the 1650's and imposed disabilities on Catholics. While it is certainly true that the original Maryland practice went beyond any other colony in including Catholics as full citizens, it is also true that even under the Calverts the criminal law was used to punish blasphemers, Sabbath breakers, and so on. And after the Protestant take-over there is very little to distinguish Maryland from the other middle colonies.[24]

The Great Awakening

This widespread evangelical movement had the effect of stimulating toleration and separationism among American Protestants. It had its beginnings in the middle colonies in 1734, but quickly spread to New England, where it found its most influential preacher, Jonathan Edwards. The movement did two things: it reemphasized the individual and private character of the Protestant religious experience, and it contributed to the fragmentation of existing churches and sects into numerous new bodies. Edwin Scott Gaustad, in his study of *The Great Awakening in New England,* concludes that "pietism does not deliberately or necessarily hack away at organizational unity; yet, the integrity of the institution is manifestly secondary to the integrity of the spirit."[25] While these new sects were anything but tolerant in their beginnings, their very existence contributed mightily to religious diversity which, over time, brought toleration and separationism. As Anson Phelps Stokes put it

> Edwards, perhaps far beyond all men of his time, smote the staggering blow which made ecclesiastical establishments impossible to America, although it is unlikely that he meant to do anything of the kind.[26]

The Quebec Act

Another important series of eighteenth-century events supplied a fillip to American anti-Catholicism. This began in 1754 with the French and Indian War (the Seven Years' War on the other side of the Atlantic) and culminated in 1774 in the

Quebec Act. After all the inherited and patriotic No-Popery of the colonists had been aroused by the barbarous aggressions of the Romish French and their wily Indian allies, the imperial government at Westminster saw fit to recognize the Catholic faith in Canada, and prohibit colonial expansion into these territories—a Papist polity on America's back doorstep! Generations of Americans who had never seen a Catholic, and for whom the inherited demonology might have been fading, felt confirmed in their hatred of Rome, and the stage was further set for periodic outbursts of anti-Catholic feeling throughout the nineteenth century. The furor over the Quebec Act was one of the major precipitating events of the Revolution, and it served to link more firmly American nationalism and No-Popery.

Virginia: Enlightenment and Revolution

Virginia's was the most vigorous Anglican establishment among the colonies, and it took a good deal to bring it down. Catholics were disabled in various ways, especially after the onset of the French and Indian War, and despite a steady migration of Protestant dissenters onto the Piedmont frontier, the hold of the tidewater Episcopalianism remained firm. There was less enforcement of morals than in Puritan establishments (Anglicans, if nothing else, were worldly), but taxation for the church was rather stiff. The growth of toleration and separationist sentiment in Virginia was accelerated by two developments which deserve special attention. They had impacts throughout the colonies, but the effects on church-state arrangements in Virginia were so dramatic that they are best treated in this context.

The first accelerating factor was the Enlightenment. Thus far we have discussed separationist sentiment only in terms of Protestant doctrine. While one stream of American thought on the separation of church and state does flow from Roger Williams, and other devout Protestant dissenters, another equally important stream flows from the secular thought of the Enlightenment and from its foremost American examplar, Thomas Jefferson. It was this stream which swelled in Virginia in the later eighteenth century. Where Roger Williams sought to preserve the churches from the state, Jefferson and those of similar persuasion sought to preserve the state from the mischievous effects of religion. Peter Gey has called the Enlightenment the rise of "modern paganism" and his description of the attitude of the philosophes toward Christianity is wonderfully helpful in understanding Jefferson, Madison, Mason, and the other Virginians who mounted the most important early American campaign for separation outside of Rhode Island, and one which was to have far more influence on U.S. Constitutional law after 1787.[27] As Gey remarks,

> Sometime in the first century of our era, an insidious force began to insinuate itself into the mentality of the Roman Empire. Slyly exploiting men's fears and anxieties and offering grandiose promises of eternal salvation, Christianity gradually subverted the self-reliant paganism which had sustained the ruling class. . . . Christianity claimed to bring light, hope, and truth, but its central myth was incredible, its dogma a conflation of rustic superstitions, its sacred book an incoherent collection of primitive tales, its church a cohort of servile fanatics as long as they were out of power and of despotic fanatics once they had seized control.[28]

For the early American secularist such as Jefferson, taxation to support churches (any one or all of them) was unconscionable coercion. No one should be deprived of a farthing which would go to the support of a religious activity of which he disapproved or toward which he was indifferent. And the effect of religious involvement in public affairs was mordant. In education the secularists were especially concerned to prevent any intermingling; it was obvious to them that learning and religion were incompatible.[29] It should be emphasized that the "agreement" between secular separationism and dissenting Protestant separationism has always been limited and uneasy. Certainly spokesmen from the two camps can agree on particular policies and institutional arrangements, but their basic motivations are quite opposite; and the Protestant, despite his ingrained suspicion of the state, is much more likely to give way to the temptation to use it for his purposes if the situation seems advantageous—especially by promoting public pronouncements of support and encouragement for the deity. Many Protestants by the end of the eighteenth century had come to pride themselves on their toleration of other Protestant sects, and they wanted government to keep hands off the churches, but there remained a readiness to give Christianity a little boost over unbelief. Nonetheless, because of the frequent agreement on specifics (disestablishment in these early days) the secularist and the radical Protestant could make common cause, and it was in Virginia that secularism established itself first as a political force.

A second factor accelerating the development of toleration and separationism in Virginia and throughout the colonies was the Revolution and the decline of Anglicanism. Throughout this discussion, Anglicanism has been rather ignored. There are two reasons for this: first, Episcopalianism (as later Americans called it) is not of a piece, ideologically, with radical or dissenting Protestantism, and second, the events of this Revolutionary period so weakened it that it never again exerted much influence in American culture or politics. This is the case despite the fact that by the end of the nineteenth century the Episcopalian flock was heavily monied and upper class. American Protestanism, as a social force, has been dissenting Protestantism. To this day, Episcopalians are looked upon by strict separationist Protestants as very unsound—descended from a state church, lacking the essential hostility to the state, far too ready to compromise with Roman Catholicism.[30] In any case the impact of the break from Britain on the American Church was devastating. The Anglican clergy, in the Northern colonies, was largely Tory, and large segments of it were driven into exile. Even in the Southern colonies the taint of treason lingered for generations, and Anglican establishments in America were doomed.[31] New York's went in 1777 as did Georgia's, South Carolina's and North Carolina's (such as they were) in 1776, and Virginia's in 1784.

In this same year a bill was introduced into the General

Assembly which would have committed Virginia, which had just disestablished Anglicanism, to provide support for "Teachers of the Christian Religion"—each ratepayer in this multiple-establishmentarian arrangement could select the church to which his compulsory payment would go. This set the stage for articulation of a secularist theory of religious freedom and separation of church and state which within a few short years came to underpin and inform the religion clauses of the new First Amendment. Opponents of the bill succeeded in having it postponed until the following session and Colonel George Mason and others prevailed on young James Madison to prepare a pamphlet opposing the measure. This appeared as *A Memorial and Remonstrance* to the members of the General Assembly. It took the giant step of arguing that disbelief should enjoy the same rights as belief, and that the state's role was properly neutral. Furthermore, Madison wrote, "it is proper to take alarm at the first experiment on our liberties," and though the sums involved be small the coercion involved for the dissenter or the unbeliever is no less real. Organized society was exempt from the demands of all the churches even as it was exempt from the demands of one. A single establishment was not to be replaced by a multiple establishment.

The bill was defeated, and Madison and Jefferson took advantage of the wave of feeling the issue had raised to press through to passage, in late 1785, the Act for Establishing Religious Freedom which Jefferson had originally drafted in 1777. This established that individuals could not be taxed to support any sort of religious activity, nor could their citizenship be in any way impaired because of their views concerning the Almighty. The years 1786–1787 saw Anglican forces in Virginia attempting a comeback, but these efforts were finally defeated by the coalition Madison and Jefferson had built up.

When the Constitutional Convention convened in Philadelphia in the spring of 1787, the Virginia battles were fresh in delegates' minds, and the Madisonian-Jeffersonian theory of separation and religious liberty was enjoying great vogue.[32] Because of its importance in the process of constitution-making it is worth repeating that the theory was essentially secularist, even though it sought, and to some extent won, favor among more radical Protestants.

THE FRAMING OF THE CONSTITUTION AND THE BILL OF RIGHTS

For someone interested in the relation of religion to the public order in America the most important thing about the federal Constitution of 1787 is what is *not* in it. The records of the Continental Congress are liberally sprinkled with references to God, the Creator, Jesus Christ, and the Christian religion. The Declaration of Independence of 1776 (a document intended to have propagandistic rather than formal legal impact) opens by invoking "Nature's God." The Constitutional text (which *has* ultimate legal significance) contains only three references to the deity, and two of these are quite remote: (1) the clause exempting Sundays as days to be counted in determining the period of time within which the President must exercise his veto; (2) the dating of the document as "in the year of our Lord one thousand seven hundred and eighty seven," and (3) the crucial clause of Article VI prescribing religious tests for office. The absence of any positive reference to God was not accidental. It was, Stokes tells us, much remarked on at the time and blamed by that dour Federalist Timothy Dwight, President of Yale, on Jefferson.[33] A great deal had happened in America between the rhetoric Declaration and carefully carpentered compromises of the Constitution, not the least of which was the battle just recounted in Virginia.

Now it is quite true, as is often pointed out in this connection by those who wish more accommodation between church and state, that the Philadelphia Convention did not concern itself greatly with religion because it was assumed by all hands to be a state matter, inappropriate for intermeddling of any sort by the federal government. Nonetheless, the disposition of the delegates with regard to religion and the public order was signaled in several tell-tale ways. Under Washington's chairmanship there were no invocations, and when Benjamin Franklin (himself no orthodox Christian) moved that the meeting pray for divine guidance, he was defeated. And when Madison and Charles Pinckney proposed a national university it was to be without "distinctions . . . on account of religion." This proposal found support among some of the more influential delegates (James Wilson and Gouverneur Morris) and its defeat seems to have resulted more from an indifference to a national university than to its proposed non-religious character.

As every schoolboy knows the charter proposed by the Philadelphia Convention was greeted in the state ratifying conventions with demands for a bill of rights which would specifically prohibit the new federal government's engaging in certain sorts of activities. Included was a demand for some more precise circumscription of the federal government's power with respect to matters of religion. Madison was ready. He introduced into the First Congress a draft of the First Amendment which guaranteed that

> The civil right of none shall be abridged on account of religious belief or worship, nor shall any national religion be established nor shall the full and equal rights of conscience be in any manner, or on any pretext, infringed.
>
> No state shall violate the equal rights of conscience, . . .

The continuing question is what Madison intended by this language, and what Congress, when it completed its deliberations, thought it was recommending to the state as constitutional law. Was it the "intent" of these "Framers" to prohibit federal establishment of a particular religion, or to prescribe impartial federal support to all religions, or simply to keep the national Congress from interfering with state establishments? Tank cars of ink have been spilt in debating this question, and we cannot presume to settle the matter here. The best that can be done is to lay out the record and suggest where the weight of evidence seems to lie.

Madison's initial draft was referred to a special committee of the House chaired by John Vining of Delaware. If any records of the committee's deliberations were kept they have not been preserved to us, but on August 15, 1789, the committee reported the following language: "no religion shall be established by law, nor shall the equal rights of conscience be abridged." In debate on the floor of the House some fears were voiced that this language was too sweeping. Madison responded that the provision meant that "Congress should not establish a religion, enforce the legal observation of it by law, nor compel men to worship God in any manner contrary to their conscience." But on August 20, on the motion of the Federalist partisan Fischer Ames of Massachusetts, the House approved a further altered version: "Congress shall make no law establishing religion, or to prevent the free exercise thereof, nor to infringe the rights of conscience."

On September 3, the Senate took up the House draft and defeated a number of attempts to introduce "clarifying" language to the effect that all that was being excluded was a federally established church. The version which finally achieved Senate approval declared: "Congress shall make no law establishing articles of faith or a mode of worship, or prohibiting the free exercise of religion."

Because of conflict between the House and Senate versions of the proposed amendment, it was necessary to refer the matter to a conference committee. This was composed of Oliver Ellsworth of Connecticut, Charles Carroll of Maryland, and William Patterson of New Jersey for the Senate, and Madison, Vining, and John Sherman of Connecticut for the House. It was this body which produced the final language, the focus for all the conflict that was to come: "Congress shall make no law respecting an establishment of religion, or prohibiting the free exercise thereof: . . ."[34]

Now several things seem clear but they do not all point in quite the same direction:

1. Madison used the same language in his original House draft that he had used in 1787 in his Memorial and Remonstrance, and that document opposed multiple as well as single

establishments. By "full and equal rights of conscience" Madison meant that nobody's tax money should be spent in furtherance of any religious purpose.

2. Madison did offer on the floor of the House to accept language which would have proscribed only single establishments.

3. The version passed by the House was deliberately ambiguous. The question of single versus multiple establishments was skirted.

4. The Senate was disposed toward precluding both single and multiple establishments, but also adopted language which admitted of different interpretations (establishing articles of worship).

5. The Conference Committee could have left the Senate version alone had it wished to preclude only single establishments. It chose instead to substitute broader language.

6. Whatever the intention of various legislators at various stages on the question of single or multiple establishments, one element of Madison's original package found no favor whatever: the proposal to extend a federal guarantee of religious freedom and separation of church and state to the states. The new amendment was to protect against actions of the central government, and the established churches which still existed in some states were to be undisturbed.

7. "Freedom of conscience" as used by Madison and some others referred specifically to the question of whether or how one believed in God. It did not mean that the federal government could not force people to do things or to pay taxes for things which offended them, only that people could not be coerced into making or contributing to any profession of belief regarding a Supreme Being.[35]

What then can one conclude? In answering it is important to remember that the "Founding Fathers" or "Framers" were not holding a series of seminars on the ideal polity, but were involved in deadly hard politicking to get results that they wanted in the face of opponents who are not called Founding Fathers because they allowed themselves to be out-maneuvered. John P. Roche has likened the leadership of the Philadelphia Convention to a "reform caucus"[36] and that would apply as well to leaders of the First Congress. We know what Madison and the hard-line separationists wanted. We know that they gave considerable ground in debate. But finally, we know that they kept the soft-line opposition from getting the explicit single-establishment provision it wanted, and that the Conference Committee version left plenty of room for a hard-line interpretation: to wit, that "respecting an establishment of religion" meant no governmental aid to or involvement with religion, and "prohibiting the free exercise thereof" meant no interference with verbal expressions of belief. Thus while it is impossible to refer to any "intent" of the Framers of the First Amendment, the evidence establishes at least a presumption in favor of the hard-line, Madisonian position.[37]

CONCLUSION

The new nation, on the threshold of the new century, harbored a long tradition of anti-Catholicism. It had bred a radical Protestantism which, on the basis of an ingrained suspicion of the state, was developing a doctrine of the separation of church and state but was still subject to occasional relapse into theocratic ways. A bridgehead of secularism was firmly established in the upper (and governing) classes and this secularism required a stricter separation than the Protestant varient. The new national charter had been amended so as to prevent the central government from interfering with religious belief and the Amendment also seemed to go some way toward enjoining national governmental aid to religion. The states, meanwhile, remained free to interfere and aid according to their respective lights.

NOTES

1. Alexander M. Bickel has called constitutional language the "fuel on which the Court's engine runs."

2. See J. Hector St. John Crévecoeur *Letters from an American Farmer* (London: Davis in Russell Street, 1782).

3. See Roger Lockyer, *Tudor and Stuart Britain, 1471–1714* (New York: St. Martin's Press, 1964), pp. 120–130.

4. Ray Allen Billington, *The Protestant Crusade, 1800–1860* (Chicago: Quadrangle Books edition, 1964), p. 2.

5. See Christopher Hill, *Puritanism and Revolution* (New York: Schocken Books edition, 1964), pp. 3–31.

6. Michael Walzer, *The Revolution of the Saints* (Cambridge: Harvard University Press, 1965), p. 130.

7. J. H. Plumb, *The Origins of Political Stability, England 1675–1725* (Boston: Houghton Mifflin, 1967), p. 1.

8. Roland H. Bainton, *The Travail of Religious Liberty* (New York: Harper Torchbooks edition, 1958), p. 230.

9. Billington, *op. cit.*, p. 4.

10. On the influences of Calvin and Luther on Puritan thought see William Haller, *The Rise of Puritanism* (New York: Harper Torchbooks edition, 1957).

11. Roy F. Nichols, *American Leviathan* (New York: Atheneum, 1963), pp. 11–30.

12. Norman St. John-Stevas, *Life, Death and the Law* (New York: Meridian Books edition, 1964), p. 31.

13. Edmund S. Morgan, *The Puritan Family* (New York: Harper Torchbooks edition, 1966), p. 1.

14. Richard E. Morgan, *The Politics of Religious Conflict* (New York: Pegasus, 1969), pp. 20–26.

15. *Ibid.*, p. 22.

16. Sidney E. Mead, *The Lively Experiment* (New York: Harper and Row, 1963). See also Alan P. Grimes, *Equality in America* (New York: Oxford University Press, 1964), pp. 3–40; and Edmund S. Morgan, *Roger Williams, The Church and the State* (New York: Harcourt, Brace and World, 1967).

17. On this point see especially Mark deWolfe Howe, *The Garden and the Wilderness* (Chicago: University of Chicago Press, 1965). Of this work, more later.

18. Perry Miller, *Errand into the Wilderness* (Cambridge: Harvard University Press, 1956), p. 143.

19. Alan Simpson, *Puritanism in Old New England* (Chicago: Phoenix Book edition, 1961), p. 40. Simpson's essay seems to me to reflect the confusion between nascent separation and toleration. For an exploration into the historiography of Puritanism in America, see Richard Schlatter, "The Puritan Strain," in John Higham, ed., *The Reconstruction of American History* (New York: Harper Torchbooks edition, 1962). On the slow growth of toleration see John P. Roche, "American Liberty: An Examination of the 'Tradition' of Freedom," in Milton Konvitz and Clinton Rossiter, eds., *Aspects of Liberty* (Ithaca: Cornell University Press, 1958), pp. 129–162.

20. Edmund S. Morgan, *Puritan Political Ideas, 1588–1794* (Indianapolis: Bobbs-Merrill, 1965), p. xxxi.

21. Miller, *op. cit.*, p. 146.

22. See especially Edmund S. Morgan, *Roger Williams: The Church and State* (New York: Harcourt, Brace and World, 1967), pp. 115–135.

23. Arthur E. Sutherland, *Constitutionalism in America* (New York: Blaisdell, 1965), p. 284.

24. Anson Phelps Stokes and Leo Pfeffer, *Church and State in the United States* (New York: Harper and Row, revised one-volume edition, 1964), pp. 11–13.

25. Edwin Scott Gaustad, *The Great Awakening in New England* (New York: Harper and Brothers, 1957), p. 125.

26. Stokes and Pfeffer, *op. cit.*, p. 26. Especially good on the Awakening is Alan Heimert, *Religion and the American Mind* (Cambridge: Harvard University Press, 1966).

27. On the various intellectual influences on the framing of the Constitution see also Gordon S. Wood, *The Creation of the American Republic* (Chapel Hill: University of North Carolina Press, 1969).

28. Peter Gey, *The Enlightenment: An Interpretation* (New York: Knopf, 1966), p. 207.

29. On this point see Leonard W. Levy, *Jefferson and Civil Liberties: The Darker Side* (Cambridge: Harvard University Press, 1963), pp. 3–15; and Robert M. Healy, *Jefferson on Religion in Public Education* (New Haven: Yale University Press, 1962).

30. Richard E. Morgan, "Backs to the Wall: A Study in the Contemporary Politics of Church and State," unpublished doctoral dissertation, Columbia University, 1967.

31. See generally, Carl Bridenbaugh, *Miter and Sceptre: Transatlantic Facts, Ideas, Personalities, and Politics, 1689–1775* (New York: Oxford University Press, 1963).

32. See Merrill Jensen, *The New Nation* (New York: Knopf, 1950), pp. 130–134. On the cooperation between Madison and Jefferson during the Virginia battle see Adrienne Koch, *Jefferson and Madison: The Great Collaboration* (New York: Knopf, 1950), pp. 26–31.

33. Stokes and Pfeffer, *op. cit.*, p. 90.

34. The quotations here are from the "record" as it appears in the *Annals of Congress* (Washington: Gales and Seaton, 1934).

35. In discussion of the *Second Amendment,* Madison argued that "no person religiously scrupulous shall be compelled to bear arms." This suggestion found little favor with the Congress, but if one emphasizes Madison's views, as I do, in giving meaning to whatever language Congress finally voted, a case might be made for bootlegging *this* Madisonian sentiment back into the free-exercise clause of the First Amendment. To do so, however, requires quite an inferential leap, and in any case the suggestion indicates only Madison's opposition to compulsory military service for the conventionally religious, and is not an espousal of a general "right" of conscientious disobedience.

36. John P. Roche, "The Founding Fathers: A Reform Caucus in Action," 55 *American Political Science Review* 799 (1961).

37. For a similar inference see Madison's biographer, Irving Brant, *The Bill of Rights* (Indianapolis: Bobbs-Merrill, 1965), p. 406.

2

The Nineteenth-Century Experience

In law school casebooks on American constitutional law the section on the religion clauses of the First Amendment characteristically begins with the decision in the case of *Everson* v. *Board* in 1947. This marks the first full-dress attempt by the Supreme Court to interpret the establishment clause; it is of crucial importance, and we shall presently pay it considerable attention. But the Court's experience with religion and the law did not begin in 1947 or even in the twentieth century. Throughout the nineteenth century conflicts involving churches and religious doctrine were finding their way into lower courts and occasionally to the Supreme Court. Disputes over the ownership of church property arose frequently and had to be dealt with within the new state and federal constitutional strictures. Claims to First Amendment protection for unorthodox religious practices were made and gave rise to the first interpretation by the Court of the free-exercise clause. The system of free public education was developed and a powerful attempt was made to alter the First

Amendment's religion clauses in order to forestall an imagined Roman Catholic threat to that system. These things are also necessary parts of our backdrop.

JEFFERSON AND MADISON IN OFFICE

Initial governmental practices within a new polity, and the utterances of its early leaders, inevitably come to constitute important precedents. There are a few such initiatives and utterances in the American formative experience which later became ammunition for arguments in the courts in church-state and free-exercise cases.

The Federalist administrations of Washington and Adams saw modest efforts by the chief executives to use religious appeals to strengthen the new national government. Marcus Cunliffe and Seymour Martin Lipset have reminded us that Washington, by manipulating the trappings of monarchy—and assuming an almost God-like position in popular affections—served to reenforce the legitimacy of the federal structure.[1] A "divine service" was included as part of the pageantry of the first inauguration, and Washington set aside November 26, 1789 as a day of national prayer and thanksgiving "to the Lord and Ruler of Nations." And the first President issued several other proclamations with a religious character, including a day of thanksgiving in February 1795, for the successful suppression of the Whiskey Rebellion. John Adams' efforts were more limited, but did include proclaiming May 9, 1798 as a day of national fasting and prayer that the nation might "be delivered from all dangers which threaten it."[2] (Radical French political ideas were, it seems, what the President principally had in mind.)

With the accession of the Democratic Republicans to power, however, things changed rather dramatically. Probably the most quoted single document in the American church-state literature (after the text of the First Amendment itself) flowed from Jefferson's pen New Year's Day 1802—his letter to the gentlemen of the Danbury, Connecticut Baptist Association in response to their expression of affection and support for him and his separationist policy. "I contemplate with reverence," he said,

> that act of the whole American people which declared that their legislature should "make no law respecting an establishment of religion, or prohibiting the free exercise thereof," thus building a wall of separation between church and State.

Here Jefferson's selective capitalization is expressive, and it is no wonder that those who have, over the years, sought cooperative arrangements between government and religious enterprises have recoiled from the sentence. They have argued that as a practical matter it is impossible for church and state never to be involved—religious bodies must register deeds and need police and fire protection just as do other institutions. They have also pointed out that "wall of separation" is a metaphor, and that great doctrines of constitutional law should not be built upon metaphors but upon careful compromises of the competing social interests which have come into conflict. They have further suggested that Jefferson has been highly overrated as a Founding Father, and that his occasional rhetorical flourishes need not be accepted as definitive glosses on constitutional provisions. All these things are true, of course, but they do not alter one wit the radical separationism of the Third President or his vast influence in American thought.[3] One commentator has gone so far as to suggest that "Jefferson shifted verbal gears" by referring to a separation of "church" and state rather than "religion" and state[4]—the inference being that Jefferson did not mean to exclude intermingling of religion and the state as long as the agency of a church was not involved. "The point," says this author, "is a nice one and has escaped, so far as I know, the generality of historians and legal exegetes." (For precisely the reason, one suspects, that the Will o' the Wisp has thus far escaped detection by radar.)

Nor does the character of the record change greatly with the accession of Mr. Madison. Jefferson had broken with the Federalist practice of proclaiming national days of prayer, explaining that "fasting and prayer are religious exercises; the enjoining them an act of discipline." Such an act, he explained, was placed beyond the federal government by the establishment clause. Madison did relent sufficiently on several occasions to make proclamations, but was uneasy and apologetic about it and condemned the appointment of chaplains for the House and Senate.

In summary, Cannon Stokes' minimal generalization is certainly correct: that of the first four Presidents of the United States, two were approving of ceremonial invocations of nondenominational religion and two were not.[5]

STATE CONSTITUTIONAL PROVISIONS

Stressing that Madison's attempt to bring the states within the explicit preview of the First Amendment had failed, Professor Wilbur Katz concluded: "It seems undeniable that the First Amendment operated, and was intended to operate [only] to protect from congressional interference the varying state policies of church establishment."[6] While it is highly doubtful that this was *all* the establishment clause was "intended" to do, it certainly did at least that. No congressional interference was ever attempted. Most of the state constitutions adopted upon independence and shortly thereafter contained some provisions for freedom of worship, but several continued to recognize established churches—in the sense that public monies were provided for the support of ministers—and in other states Protestantism or "piety" was a requirement for holding office.[7] These official acknowledgements of religion were prised out of state constitutions piecemeal through the first half of the nineteenth century. If there had been any doubt that the substantive prohibitions of the federal First Amendment (whatever they were) did not extend to the states, it was removed in 1833 by Justice Marshall's opinion for the Supreme Court in *Barron* v. *Baltimore* reaffirming that the Bill of Rights applied only to the federal government.

The old Anglican colonies rid themselves of establishments earliest, with Virginia completing the process, as we have noted, in 1786, Georgia in 1790, and South Carolina in 1790. New York had done the job in 1782, and North Carolina in its original constitution in 1776. Of the middle colonies, Pennsylvania and Maryland clung to provisions requiring belief in God as a condition of public office. Indeed, Maryland's provision was retained into modern times to become the object of a Supreme Court challenge in the case of *Torcaso* v. *Watkins*,[8] about which more later. Delaware broke cleanly from all religious ties, but New Jersey restricted full civil rights to Protestants until 1844. In New England, Rhode Island had little to disestablish or eliminate, and the former Congregationalist colonies slowly changed. In Massachusetts the Third Article of the Declaration Rights of the Constitution of 1780 authorized towns to maintain "public Protestant teachers of piety, religion, and morality, in all cases where such provision shall not be made voluntarily."[9] This was not repealed until 1833. Connecticut exempted dissenting Christian sects from taxation for the Congregational establishment in 1784, but the end of the old "standing order" did not come until 1818. And while New Hampshire had long been free, as a practical matter, for religious pluralism, Arthur Sutherland points out that from 1784 "to the present time her Constitutions have purported to empower the legislature" to authorize

> The several towns, parishes, bodies-corporate, or religious societies within this state to make adequate provision at their expense for the support and maintenance of public protestant teachers of piety, religion and morality; . . .[10]

In the new states of Vermont, Kentucky, and Tennessee the pattern was a guarantee of freedom of worship combined with some requirement of piety for office holders. In none of the states was there any great staying power in establishments of religiously restrictive rules for the enjoyment of civil rights. And Sutherland is surely right that "by 1800 imposed orthodoxy and subvention were both reduced to feeble remnants."[11] This resulted from the interplay of ideas with changing social conditions referred to in Chapter 1 (the development of Protestant toleration and separationism), and not from the force of the federal Constitution.[12] Today, most state constitutions contain provisions, of varying strengths, for freedom of worship and enjoining separation. Most of them also contain vestigial references to God, reminders of the former establishmentarian arrangements.[13]

THE CHURCH PROPERTY CASES

When a religious congregation for some reason disintegrates, and multiple groups emerge out of the single old one, who owns the real estate and personalty which were previously enjoyed in common? Given the schismatic character of American Protestantism during the late eighteenth and early nineteenth centuries this question was of much more than passing interest. Courts grappled with it frequently and it was capable of generating considerable political heat—as in New England where the Unitarian heresy disrupted Congregational churches by the hundreds between 1800 and 1830.

One approach to the problem, taken by the British courts which found themselves facing the same sort of problem at about the same time, was to hold that the donors who originally gave or paid for the land, built the buildings, paid the preacher, and so on, had created implied trusts. That is, the donors had intended that their gifts be employed to advance the particular religious views to which the congregation was committed *at the time* the gift was made. It thus became the duty of the court in the event of a schism to discover which of the contending factions adhered most closely to the doctrines which the donors had sought to support. But not only did this "implied trust" approach have the disadvantage of involving judges in drawing nice theological distinctions. It also had the embarrassing potential of awarding large amounts of property to numerically tiny factions—as finally happened in 1904 when the properties of the Free Church of Scotland, including 800 churches, three universities, and a considerable treasury were turned over to a claimant "convention" made up of thirty or so small Highland congregations.[14] Furthermore, what happened when the doctrinal question was a very close one, or when some non-doctrinal factor has caused the split and there was little or no distinction between the views of the factions? Courts were left resting decisions on discriminations which unkind critics called artificial.

In the same year that the British embarked on the implied trust approach (1813), the Supreme Judicial Court of Massachusetts struck out on another tack. A majority of the members of an Episcopalian congregation in Boston had voted to go Unitarian, and the court held that the use of property must be governed by majority rule within the congregation and refused to consider the question of doctrine.[15] This approach, grounded in the New England tradition of congregational autonomy, had a rough and ready democratic quality to recommend it. The difficulty, of course, was that not all denominations were organized along congregational lines. What about the hierarchical churches, such as the Episcopal, where governing authority was located in conventions, boards, and bishops? Were the governmental habits of one New England sect (the Congregationalists) to be written into law and were hierarchies to have nothing to say if a majority within a member parish wished to secede, taking the property with it?

And even in New England the simple majority-rule doctrine proved not without difficulty. In 1800, the Supreme Judicial Court of Massachusetts had held that the voting units of the established Congregational Church were not the actual membership of the individual church—the congregation in fact—but the citizens of the more comprehensive governmental unit, the town. Thus a band of strict, church-going Congregationalists were turned out of their building in Dedham by the votes of a lot of luke-warm Unitarians who never went near the place but were voters of the town—[16] part of the congregation in law. Thus "democracy" worked crazily for what was supposedly the most democratically organized denomination. Admittedly this particular anomaly resulted from a vestigial establishmentarianism, it was not the less painful.

Neither the simple majority rule nor the English implied trust approach (with which some American courts also experimented) really fitted the emerging American disposition concerning the relation of religion to the state: both involved serious interventions by the courts in the affairs of the churches. A way out of the difficulties was not mapped, however, until 1871 when the Supreme Court decided *Watson* v. *Jones*.[17]

The case involved the Walnut Street Presbyterian Church in Louisville, Kentucky. Presbyterianism, along with other American denominations, had been split by the Civil War between northern and southern branches and the Walnut Street congregation of Louisville, in a border state, was bitterly divided. A majority of the congregation voted to continue with the northern controlled General Assembly and a minority voted for affiliation with the new "Presbyterian Church of the Confederate States." The minority faction seized physical control of the building and the Kentucky courts upheld its claim on an implied trust argument —that the General Assembly had departed from original Presbyterian doctrine by passing a resolution condemning slavery. The Kentucky judges held this act (and the agreement of the majority of the congregation with it) to have been in violation of the religious doctrine supported by the original donors of the property of the Walnut Street Church. Pure Presybyterian doctrine, the Kentucky judges suggested, forbade church intermeddling in civil affairs.

The disappointed northern faction then began a second action in a federal court, based on diversity of state citizenship—some few of the loyalists must have resided on the Indiana side of the Ohio River—and in due course the U.S. Supreme Court, speaking through Mr. Justice Miller, rejected Kentucky's resort to the implied trust approach, pointing to its British origins and suggesting the approach presumed intimacy between religion and public authority which was distinctly un-American. The only question which it is proper for courts to answer in such cases, Miller argued, was the limited one of who, under the existing rules of the particular denomination, held the general governing power. When that agency was identified its decision regarding the use of the property would be enforced. Previous Presbyterian practice located such authority in the General Assembly, and whoever the Assembly said "owned" the Walnut Street Church, did.

While there is no well-developed common law of voluntary associations in America (and even less when Miller wrote in 1871) the approach taken in *Watson* had the general effect of placing religious associations on a legal plane with other private groupings—when disputes came to the courts, judges would examine the organization's internal government, determine who had the general power to decide things. This approach did involve courts in exploring church rules, but at least avoided decisions based on constructions of religious doctrines or decisions enforcing congregational majority rule in denominations which did not accept that principle.

Watson, it must be noted, was not a constitutional decision. The First Amendment was not formally involved, and Miller's new approach to church-property disputes might best be characterized as a rule of federal common law. But the spirit of the First Amendment clearly animated Miller's writing. He sought to lessen the likelihood of courts being drawn into religious controversies, and to ensure that should judicial intervention become necessary, courts would deal with the sorts of questions they were most competent to handle—making findings of fact—and would be kept out of theological swamps. Although technically applying only in federal courts, *Watson* has become, over the years, the prevailing American approach despite repeated attempts to substitute the theory of implied trust.[18]

Of course, restricting themselves to ascertaining the authoritative decision-making body was not always an easy matter for the courts. Perhaps the most publicized application of the *Watson* rule came after World War II, in a dispute over the ownership of the St. Nicholas Russian Orthodox Cathedral in New York City. A conflict had developed within Russian Orthodoxy between the Communist dominated Patriarch of Moscow (the supreme ecclesiastical authority) and a group of the American faithful seeking to separate from the established hierarchy and to take with it St. Nicholas Cathedral. The Patriarch refused to surrender his claim to ownership, and in 1945 the New York

State Legislature stepped into the dispute, passing an act sustaining the American group and declaring it the owner of the Cathedral on an implied trust theory—those who gave the property had not envisioned a Communist-dominated Patriarch. The New York Court of Appeals sustained the Act. In 1952, in *Kedroff* v. *St. Nicholas Cathedral,*[19] the United States Supreme Court disallowed New York's intervention into the matter on *First Amendment grounds* (establishment clause). The Court, relying on *Watson,* suggested that the Moscow-based hierarchy was the traditional governing authority within the organization of Russian Orthodoxy, and was entitled to determine the use of the Cathedral.[20] The case for the break-away American faction could hardly have been more politically appealing, but the Justices resisted the temptation to which the New York legislators had succumbed. Thus, almost a century after its original announcement, the *Watson* approach was elevated by the *Kedroff* decision to constitutional stature, and became a part of the law of the First Amendment. Its most recent major application can be seen in the case of *Presbyterian Church in the U.S.* v. *Blue Hill Memorial Church,* which involved the secession from the denomination of an individual congregation and was decided by the Supreme Court in January of 1969[21] in favor of the pre-existing governing authority (the Presbyterian Church) and against a break-away congregation.

THE ABERRATIONAL JUSTICE STORY

It would do less than justice to the variety of nineteenth-century judicial expressions concerning religion and the law to pass on without noting the strong accommodationist position taken by one of America's greatest early constitutional lawyers, Joseph Story—Harvard Law School Professor, compiler of a learned and influential set of commentaries on the federal Constitution, and Associate Justice of the Supreme Court.

Story came to the Court as a Jeffersonian appointee, and stayed to second John Marshall, Jefferson's bitter enemy, as an expositor of Federalist (nationalist) constitutional theory. He also adopted a view of the proper relation of government to religion which was greatly at odds with that of the President who had nominated him. Quite simply, Story thought it was a proper function of both state and federal governments to give support and encouragement to the Christian religion, up to and including even-handed financial support of all denominations, and he saw nothing in the religious clauses of the First Amendment to prevent such accommodations. Government was not bound to give financial support, it could if it wished; but it was positively bound to prevent disrespect or disturbance of Christian practice. He was a multiple establishmentarian and favored some residual duty in government to encourage Christian piety. Story's disposition in these matters was manifested on three interesting occasions.

The first was the case of *Terrett* v. *Taylor,* decided by the Supreme Court in 1815.[22] In 1776 the Virginia Legislature had passed an act incorporating all Episcopal parishes in Virginia and confirming all titles to property they then held. These parishes owned buildings, of course, but also glebes (tracts of undeveloped land originally bestowed by the crown). In 1801, at the end of the process of religious disestablishment, the Legislature declared its 1776 act null and void, held the Episcopal churches disincorporated, and no longer seized their glebes. The new law directed that these glebes be sold by the overseers of the poor in each county and the proceeds used to help the needy. The justification for this action was that strict separation of church and state, now written into the Virginia Constitution, required it. The case at bar involved an Episcopal parish in Alexandria. This city had been part of Virginia in 1776 but by 1815 was within the District of Columbia. Story, writing for the Court, was thus a *federal* judge interpreting *Virginia* law. He examined the relevant provisions of the Virginia Constitution and found them not to require what the state legislature had held them to require; he further concluded that the titles held by the parishes could not be disturbed anymore than could the titles held by other sorts of corporations and voluntary associations. More interesting than

Story's holding, however, is his view of the limited effect of Virginia's religion clauses—which roughly paralleled those of the federal Constitution:

> Consistent with the constitution of Virginia the legislature could not create or continue a religious establishment which should have exclusive rights and prerogatives, or compel the citizens to worship under a stipulated form or discipline, or to pay taxes to those whose creed they did not conscientiously believe. But free exercise of religion cannot be justly deemed to be restrained *by aiding with equal attention the votaries of every sect* to perform their own religious duties, or by establishing funds for the support of ministers, for public charities, for the endowment of churches. . . .[23]

A second statement of Story's views came in 1833 with the publication of *Commentaries on the Constitution.* In Volume III, the Justice turned his attention to the religion clauses of the First Amendment. "How far any government has a right to interfere in matters touching on religion," he began, "has been a subject much discussed by writers upon public and political law." Recalling the divine provenance of Christian principles, Story argued that:

> It is, indeed, difficult to conceive, how any civilized society can well exist without them. And at all events, it is impossible for those who believe in the truth of Christianity as a divine revelation to doubt that it is the especial duty of government to foster and encourage it among all the citizens and subjects. This is a point wholly distinct from that of the right of private judgment in matters of religion, and of the freedom of public worship according to the dictates of one's conscience.[24]

Harking back to the adoption of the First Amendment, Story asserted that if the religion clauses had been understood as an attempt to level all religions and make them a matter of indifference to the federal government, the clauses would have met with "universal disapprobation."

A third occasion for Story's expression of his truncated

notion of the separation of church and state arose late in his career in connection with the famous will of the wealthy Philadelphia merchant, Stephen Girard. That doughty old entrepreneur left two million dollars to the Mayor and aldermen of Philadelphia for the erection and maintenance of a school for "poor, white, male orphans." After specifying the construction, financing, and curriculum of the prospective institution, Girard further commanded the trustees that no minister of religion be allowed so much as to set foot on its campus. Some of Girard's heirs, French nationals, seized upon this exclusionary provision, among others, in an attempt to break the will in the federal courts and retrieve the two million from the city. Daniel Webster argued the case before the Supreme Court for the heirs, suggesting that the common law of Pennsylvania and the United States incorporated the Christian religion, and that a will so evidently hostile to that religion was contrary to public policy and could not be probated—just as a will establishing a school for the training of pickpockets or smugglers could not be probated. But this argument went too far even for Story. Noting that Girard had not excluded ministers out of hostility to religion but to protect tender minds from the cacophony of doctrine which is American Christianity, Story distinguished the case before him from a hypothetical one in which a school was proposed which would denigrate or oppose Christianity. In arriving at his holding, however, Story did agree with Webster that the Christian religion was part of the common law of Pennsylvania, and in two rather chilling sentences alluded to the residual power which he saw in the state to suppress heresy.

> It is unnecessary for us, however, to consider what would be the legal effect of a device in Pennsylvania for the establishment of a school or college, for the propagation of Judaism, or Deism, or any other form of infidelity. Such a case is not to be presumed to exist in a Christian country; . . .[25]

Story offered, thus, a rather fully formed theory of accommodation between the Christian churches and the various governments within the United States. The most interesting thing about it is its aberrational quality. As we shall see, it never led anywhere. Could latter accommodationists have marshalled sufficient support in courts or legislature for their plans of supportive cooperation between government and the churches in America it would have been perfectly possible to reach back to Story for historical support. This has not been done, however, and the Story approach sits high and dry, out of the mainstream of American constitutional law.

THE POLYGAMY PROBLEM

The judicial encounters which we have thus far examined have involved the religion clauses of the First Amendment only obliquely. Neither *Terret,* nor *Girard,* nor *Watson* turned on a clear free-exercise or no-establishment ground. The first such test before the Supreme Court arose under the free-exercise clause and presented a claim for protection of what, to American Victorians at least, seemed a most unorthodox exercise of religion—the practice of polygamy.

The followers of the prophet Joseph Smith, organized as the Church of Jesus Christ of the Latter-Day Saints, had not been accepted into the American Protestant consensus in the years after the Angel Mordecai revealed himself to Smith at Palmyra, New York. Moving West, the Mormons encountered resistance from their neighbors in Ohio, Missouri, and Illinois, and finally, under Brigham Young's leadership, organized a strong community around the Great Salt Lake in the Utah Territory. Unhappily, the community did not long remain in isolation. Non-Mormon "gentiles" began to enter Utah, especially in the decade following the Civil War, and relations were exacerbated by Young's announcement, in 1853, of the doctrine of plural marriage. Lurid reports spread during the 1870's, the attention of the nation was engaged, and Congress, exercising its power over territories, legislated against polygamy:

> Every person having a husband or wife living, who marries another, whether married or single, in a Territory, or other place

> over which the United States have exclusive jurisdiction, is guilty of bigamy, and shall be punished by a fine of not more than $500, and by imprisonment for a term of not more than five years.[26]

One George Reynolds was duly convicted under this provision, and in 1878 his case reached the Supreme Court. He argued that his conviction for an act commanded by the religious doctrine to which he subscribed constituted a denial of free exercise in contravention of the First Amendment.[27]

Chief Justice Morrison Waite wrote for the Court. Conscious that his was the first construction of the meaning of the free-exercise clause, Waite marshalled Madison's "Memorial and Remonstrance," Jefferson's letter to the Danbury Baptists (which he accepted as an "authoritative" gloss on the religion clauses), and all the state constitutions in support of his conclusion that

> Congress was deprived of all legislative power over mere *opinion*, but was left free to reach *actions* which were in violation of social duties or subversive of good order.[28]

Thus if the Congress acted to forestall behavior which it would ordinarily have the power to prevent, if it has acted in furtherance of a valid "secular objective," the fact that someone's behavior was religiously motivated was no grounds for exemption from the effect of the rule.[29] Only belief, not behavior, was protected. In the case of polygamy, Waite had no difficulty in finding a valid social interest which Congress was properly protecting. Monogamous marriage, after all, was an important sort of civil contract:

> Upon it society may be said to be built, and out of its fruits spring social relations and social obligations and duties, with which government is necessarily required to deal. . . . Professor [Francis] Lieber says, polygamy leads to the patriarchal principle and which, when applied to large communities, fetters the people in stationary despotism, while that principle cannot long exist in connection with monogamy.[30]

And the "Feds" were not finished with the refractory Mormons. In April of 1889, Samuel D. Davis was indicted in the

Third Judicial District of the Territory of Idaho for falsely swearing, for the purpose of becoming a registered voter, that he was not associated with any organization which advocated the practice of polygamy. The Idaho Territory, in short, had disenfranchised Mormons, and Davis was a Mormon and lied about it. Here there was no "action" or behavior, but mere membership. The case reached the Supreme Court in the same year, and Associate Justice Stephen Field spoke for the Court. With a reference to Waite's opinion in the *Reynolds* case, he brushed aside Davis' free-exercise claim and reasserted the secular regulation rule with a flourish:

> There have been sects which denied as part of their religious tenets that there should be any marriage tie, and advocated promiscuous intercourse of the sexes as prompted by the passions of its members. And history discloses the fact that the necessity of human sacrifices, upon special occasions, had been a tenet of many sects. Should a sect of either of these kinds ever find its way into this country, swift punishment would follow the carrying into effect of its doctrines, and no heed would be given to the pretence that, as religious beliefs, their supporters could be protected in their exercise by the Constitution of the United States.[31]

To outlaw polygamy clearly was proper, and the territorial legislature of Idaho just as clearly had power, delegated to it by Congress, to prescribe qualifications for voters in such a way as to best secure obedience to its laws. There was nothing unreasonable in Idaho's concluding that persons who associated themselves with an organization advocating crime were not suitable members of the electorate.

Finally, toward the end of the Court term of 1889 came the decisions in *Mormon Church* v. *United States* and *Romney* v. *United States*.[32] These cases were decided together and the history of the litigation is somewhat complex. Since 1862 Congress had been threatening to move against Mormon Church property if the sect did not give up its vile connubial practices. In 1887 Congress finally did so—disincorporating the Mormon Church in the Utah Territory and appropriating all Church property except that used for strictly liturgical purposes. Both the Church and an individual member (of a famous Mormon family) sued. This time it was Justice Joseph Bradley who dealt with the free-exercise argument: "No doubt the Thugs of India imagined that their belief in the right of assassination was a religious belief."[33] Bradley went on to assert that in a situation where the law of the land had been systematically defied by a charitable organization, it was quite within the reach of Congress, which possessed plenary power over the territories, to declare property of that organization without a legal owner, to assume control over it, and acting as a trustee, devote it to some other charitable purpose. For the first time in a Mormon case there was a dissent (by Chief Justice Fuller, joined by Justices Field and Lamar), but it was on grounds of insufficiency of congressional power, not deprivation of free-exercise. The dissenters did not for a moment question the secular regulation approach; they only doubted whether the national government, a government after all of specifically enumerated powers, was competent to take over property even in the territories. The concern of the dissenters was to keep Congress within the confines of Article I, sec. 8, and was not anchored in any way in the First Amendment.

This seems a quaint, far-off controversy from the vantage of the 1970's, and yet the polygamy problem established what was to be the controlling interpretation of the free-exercise clause down to the 1940's. The secular regulation "rule," of course, did not spring full blown from the Reynolds case; as early as 1828 it had been suggested by one of the most influential of early state court judges and constitutional commentators, John B. Gibson of Pennsylvania,[34] and the Supreme Judicial Court of Maine had employed it in 1854 to enforce Bible-reading—which was intended to inculcate morality and was thus held a secular regulation.[35] The distinction between belief and behavior was one with which nineteenth-century judges and public men were comfortable, but it took the Mormons to put the question of the meaning of free-exercise squarely before the Supreme Court and to fix the secular reguiation rule into the body of constitutional law. In the latter years of the nineteenth and the early twentieth centuries the rule was applied by lower courts to sustain regulations which touched, among others, the Salvation Army, soliciting, palmists, and preachers who caused disturbances by shouting during services. The only instance of a religious claim being granted against a valid secular regulation occurred in California in the early 1920's when a local school board made social dancing part of a required physical education course and ran into the Protestant fundamentalist nonconformance of the Hardwicke family. The opinion of the middle-level appeals court which decided the case does suggest that the Hardwicke children were to be exempted because the requirement of social dancing infringed on their "freedom of religion," but the reasoning is not sufficiently clear for the case to constitute a clear exception to the dominant persuasion. It may, however, be read as a tell-tale sign of the erosion which was to overtake the rule later in the century.[36]

PROTESTANTS ON THE OFFENSIVE

While the Supreme Court was dealing with polygamy during the 1870's, 80's, and 90's, another dispute was shaping up which, by the middle of the new century, would put the establishment clause squarely before the justices. This was the conflict over public aid for church-related schools—or, to put the matter bluntly, aid to Roman Catholic parochial schools. By the 1960's, as we shall see, other denominations were experimenting with their own schools and there was a fair sized Lutheran educational establishment; but the Catholic educational effort has always accounted for over ninety per cent of America's church-related schools, and from the 1840's to the present, they have been a source of bitter political and inter-faith tension. In the beginning the combustible ingredients of the conflict were an ascendant American Protestantism, an assertive and "foreign" Catholic community, and an emergent system of public education.

Nineteenth-Century Protestantism

We left American Protestantism, in the wake of the Great Awakening of the eighteenth century, after tracing the development of the notion of toleration and the doctrine of the separation of church and state. The early decades of the nineteenth century saw another wave of evangelism break over the nation with revivalistic activity concentrated this time along the frontier in the Mississippi and Ohio Valleys.[37] The growth of the "newer" denominations—Baptists and Methodists—increased, and the slight lapse in interest and attendance at churches which had occurred around the turn of the century was reversed. Not only was America a Protestant nation, it was militantly so, with rates of participation far outstripping, so far as we can tell, anything known in Europe. Seymour Martin Lipset has done an excellent job of marshalling the evidence on this point, including the observations of the most important foreign commentators on the nineteenth century American scene,[38] and Lipset concludes, regarding the growth diversity of early nineteenth century American Protestantism, that

> The "religious fecundity" of American Protestantism seems to be an outgrowth of the intertwining of the democratic value of free expression of all political ideas with the Protestant stress on the obligation to follow individual conscience. The norms of political tolerance and religious tolerance have been mutually reinforcing. The special pressure on churches to proselytize *and* to tolerate each other, brought about by "voluntarism," is reinforced by another trait of American society—its geographic, occupational, and class mobility.[39]

Thus the denominations flourished, with a brisk interchange of members and multiplication of offshoots, all the while recognizing one another's essential legitimacy.

The glaring exception to this, however, was the Church of Rome. The 1830's and 1840's saw a change in the composition of the stream of immigration to the United States. Irish and German Catholics began to appear in substantial numbers and to cluster in the new nation's rapidly growing cities. American Protestants had little previous *experience* with Catholics. There was the inherited demonology, and there had been a few aristocratic Marylanders who attempted, tactfully, to stay out of the line of Protestant fire and not to attract attention. The new arrivals were something else again.

Varieties of Anti-Catholicism

Duff Cooper once remarked of England that there were only two religions—Catholicism, which was wrong, and the rest, which didn't matter. In America the "rest" mattered terribly. Protestants took themselves seriously, and they saw in the "wrong" a very grave challenge. The notions of denominationalism and tolerance which developed within Protestantism in the late eighteenth century were only slowly and grudgingly extended to Catholicism in the twentieth. The legacy of English No-Popery was powerful and an outburst of animus greeted the new arrivals in the 1830's.

The most interesting thing about this first surge of nineteenth century religious bigotry was the intimate linkage of anti-Catholicism to xenophobia in the package which scholars have come to call "nativism." The No-Popery of the English and colonial past certainly had had an anti-foreign dimension—largely francophobic—but in nineteenth century nativism the foreigner was the newly arrived immigrant who was often seen as a soldier under the command of the Roman general staff which remained safely in the European rear. Billington concludes that "the advent of the foreign immigration on a large scale was probably the important causal force" leading to the outbreak of the 1830's.[40] And John Higham has also argued that nativism was a compound:

> Historians have sometimes regarded nativism and anti-Catholicism as more or less synonymous. This identification, by oversimplifying two complex ideas, does little justice to either. Many social and religious factors . . . have contributed powerfully to anti-Catholic feeling . . . anti-Catholicism has become purely nativistic, however, and it has reached its maximum intensity only when the Churches' adherents seemed dangerously foreign agents in the national life.[41]

The nineteenth century was pockmarked by this virulent fusion of hostility to the newcomer and inherited No-Popery. There were mob outrages such as those which ended in the burning of the Ursuline Convent in Charlestown, Massachusetts, in August of 1834, and led to street fighting in Philadelphia in May of 1844. Perhaps the most popular preacher of the era, Lyman Beecher, published a sermon in 1835 entitled *A Plea for the West* in which he exhorted Protestants to resist the Pope's plan to take over the Mississippi Valley; and in the same year the inventor, Samuel F. B. Morse, published his vastly influential *Foreign Conspiracy Against the Liberties of the United States.* There were fraternal and "civic" associations such as the American Protestant Association of the 1840's, the Order of United Americans of the 1850's, and the Order of United American Mechanics which survived from its founding in 1845 into the middle of the twentieth century! Finally there were the overtly political manifestations of nativism in political party organization beginning with the scattered Native American successes in the 1840's to the powerful Know-Nothing party which developed considerable strength in Congress in the late 1850's (principally from northeastern and border states), and brought out 800,000 votes for its presidential candidate, Millard Fillmore, in 1856.[42]

The most important post-bellum manifestation of the nativist impulse was the infamous American Protective Association. Founded in 1887, it reached its peak in the middle 1890's with a formal (secret) membership of about 1,000,000 and a trail of fellow travelers (organized in affiliated "patriotic societies") which may have numbered as many as two and one-half million.[43]

By the middle of the twentieth century the nativist impulse had faded, but the Protestant fear of Catholic subversion survived it. An excellent example of contemporary non-nativist anti-Catholicism is the organization called Americans United. Founded in 1947, in a period of Protestant reaction to a more militant stand by the Catholic hierarchy on aid to parochial schools and American diplomatic representation at the Vatican, the group has pursued a strict separationist line and argued that the principal danger to traditional American arrangements in that regard is the hierarchy of the Roman Church. Other Protestant organizations, such as the Baptist Joint Committee on Public Affairs and the Seventh-Day Adventist Religious Liberty Association, have taken generally the same line. The most important Protestant formation, the National Council of Churches (an alliance of denominations claiming 42 million members) was quite critical of Catholic policy and activities in the 1940's and 1950's, but has relaxed its attitude in recent years in the name of ecumenicity and in order to make common cause with Catholic organizations on issues of race relations and social welfare.[44]

It is important to remember that nineteenth century nativist outbursts and twentieth century anti-Catholic upsurges have been cyclical.[45] Both Billington and Higham have noted this, and suggested a relationship between such eruptions and economic depressions. While this seems to work well for the late nineteenth century, it is less persuasive for the anti-bellum period and not at all right for the twentieth century. It is probably closer to the truth that while essentially "bad times" occasionally lent force to anti-foreign feelings, the outbursts were in fact WASP (and by mid-twentieth century WASP and Jewish) responses to either sudden swellings of Catholic ranks or to some Catholic initiative which was perceived as threatening the church-state status quo. And such a Catholic initiative did come in the 1840's. It was occasioned, in turn, by the rise of the American public school.

Catholic Claims in Education

Until well into the nineteenth century elementary education in America was afforded privately if at all. It was not until the 1830's that most states and municipalities began to provide from tax funds for the schooling of the young. Massachusetts established the first state board of education in 1837 with Horace Mann as its secretary. What Mann did in Massachusetts eventually became the model for the nation, and this included purging of the schools of all specifically sectarian influences. Mann was very fearful of Roman Catholicism and argued that if its teaching were to be kept out, Protestant sectarianism must be kept out as well. He urged, rather, that non-controversial biblical and moral teachings be made the basis of instruction.[46] In the transition from private to public patterns, however, many of the new governmentally funded schools prescribed for their students heavy doses of Protestant piety, and even the supposedly non-controversial biblical and moral teachings created problems for Catholics. Readings from Protestant King James versions of the scriptures was the usual sticking point.

The first major dispute developed in New York City. There in the early 1840's the Public School Society, a private, Protestant-dominated group, was charged with disbursing from the public, tax-raised common school fund. The schools the Society supported were effectively Protestant; Catholics did not send their children to them, choosing to maintain their own schools without public aid.

In his annual message to the Legislature on January 7, 1840, Whig Governor Charles Seward, in a plày for the votes of Catholic Democrats, suggested that perhaps the Catholic schools in the City had some claim upon the common fund. Thus encouraged, the City's Catholic leaders, under the leadership of fiery Bishop John Hughes, launched into three years of bruising political combat, both in the City and in the State Legislature, to end the reign of the School Society and have Catholic schools incorporated in a new scheme of publicly funded education. This campaign, which included endorsing and opposing candidates for office, evoked Catholic sympathy all along the Eastern Seaboard and provoked a withering Protestant-nativist response.

The result was the establishment of a public elective Board of Education in New York City, and the reduction of overt Protestantism in the schools. Catholics, however, were specifically and forcefully denied participation in the new scheme, and bitterness on both sides was greatly increased. The Catholic resort to electoral politics in this struggle supplied nativists ammunition which kept them going through the 1850's.

The Civil War saw a diminution of nativist sentiment. Catholic fought alongside Yankee in the Union Army, and two-thirds of General Thomas Meagher's Irish Brigade fell in the attack on the Sunken Road at Fredericksburg. Whether fellow-feeling was bred of common adversity or whether animosities were simply displaced by more pressing wartime concerns, the heat was off Catholics in the mid-1860's.

This experience again encouraged Catholic leaders and, as Higham put it,

> About 1869 . . . Catholics in many parts of the Northeast and midwest opened a campaign to eliminate the Protestant tinge the Bible-reading gave to the public schools, to secure for their own parochial schools a share of the funds that the states were providing for education, and to get for Catholic charitable institutions public subsidies comparable to those traditionally awarded to Protestant charities.[47]

It is interesting that in the area of charitable institutions Catholics did make substantial progress in securing public support. In education, however, they received another stinging rebuke.

The Blaine Amendment

Protestant fears of a Catholic grab of school funds, brought about by the bloc voting of Catholic Democrats in the large cities, intensified during the early 1870's. In 1875 the faltering Grant Administration, stained by scandal and casting about for a way to recoup for the Republicans before the 1876 election, took up the issue. In an address to the veterans of the Army of the Tennessee, meeting in Des Moines, the President exhorted his former comrades to

> Encourage free schools, and resolve that not one dollar appropriated for their support shall be appropriated to the support of any sectarian school. Resolve that neither the State nor nation, nor both combined, shall support institutions of learning other than those sufficient to afford every child growing up in the land of opportunity a good common-school education, unmixed with sectarian, pagan, or atheistical dogmas. Leave the matter of religion to the family altar, the church, and the private school supported entirely by private contributions.[48]

Rutherford B. Hayes, then running for Governor of Ohio, lambasted the Democrats as Catholic coddlers. And that prince of Republican opportunists, James G. Blaine of Maine, Minority Leader of the House, introduced an amendment to the Constitution which would have altered and added to the First Amendment as follows:

> No State shall make any law respecting an establishment of religion or prohibiting the free exercise thereof; and no money raised by taxation in any state for the support of public schools, or derived from any public fund therefor, nor any public lands devoted thereto, shall ever be under the control of any religious sect, nor shall any money so raised or lands so devoted be divided between religious sects or denominations.[49]

This tactic was not original with Blaine. Several states had already modified their constitutions in a similar fashion, specifically proscribing aid to church-related schools. The Blaine Amendment passed the House by a thumping 180–7, with 98 members not voting, but in the Senate, Democrats moved to weaken the language, and the final version failed slightly of obtaining the necessary two-thirds.[50] It had been a near thing, however, and it is clear that this attempt to modify the federal First Amendment provided impetus for many states to write such bans in their constitutions—provisions which came to be known in their turn as "Blaine Amendments" although the Plumed Knight had nothing directly to do with their adoption and had, in fact, been gathered to his fathers before some states acted.[51]

Perhaps the best known Blaine Amendment is New York's. Introduced at the state constitutional convention in 1894, in response to a new round of Catholic school-fund initiatives in the Empire State, it has been the focus of bitter controversy ever since.[52] In 1967 another New York constitutional convention proposed a charter without the "Blaine"; it aroused a storm of criticism and was rejected by the voters.[53] On January 7, 1970, one hundred and thirty years to a day after his predecessor, Charles Seward, had done the same thing, Governor Nelson Rockefeller, in *his* annual message to the Legislature, suggested more public aid for church-related schools and called for the repeal of the "Blaine." Certainly Rockefeller's motivation was similar to that of Seward (there are still those Catholic Democrats in New York City); whether the result will be a similar defeat for Catholics only time will tell. In any case, the issue must be one of the longest-lived in American politics.

CONCLUSION

The nineteenth century saw the first exposition by the Supreme Court of the free-exercise clause, and it saw successive reaffirmations (albeit not in formal, constitutional terms) of a national policy of strict separation of church and state—despite arguments and political initiatives to the contrary. The new American Catholic community succeeded in securing some occasional public support for its charities, and succeeded in diluting somewhat the Protestant character of religious exercises in the public schools (this through political pressure rather than judicial decision). On the whole, however, Protestant America (which conceived itself as "America period") was implacably hostile to Catholicism and particularly to its schools. In the words of Josiah Strong, a leading *liberal* Protestant and participant in the founding of the Federal Council of Churches (predecessor of the National Council):

> Manifestly there is an irreconcilable difference between papal principles and the fundamental principles of our free institutions. . . . it is as inconsistent with our liberties for Americans to yield allegiance to the Pope as to the Czar.[54]

NOTES

1. See in this regard Marcus Cunliffe, *George Washington, Man and Monument* (New York: Mentor Books, 1960); and Seymour Martin Lipset, *The First New Nation* (New York: Basic Books, 1963), pp. 15–60.
2. Quoted in Stokes and Pfeffer, *op. cit.,* p. 88.

3. One attempt to put all the attacks together is Joseph F. Custango, "Thomas Jefferson, Religious Education and Public Law," 8 *Journal of Public Law* 81 (1959).

4. The point is Charles Wesley Lowry's. It came to my attention in John H. Laubach, *School Prayers: Congress, the Courts and the Public* (Washington: Public Affairs Press, 1969), p. 18; it was originally developed in 13 *Journal of Public Law* 454 (1964).

5. Stokes and Pfeffer, *op. cit.,* p. 39.

6. Wilbur G. Katz, *Religion and the American Constitution* (Evanston: Northwestern University Press, 1964), p. 9.

7. On early Maryland see Thomas O'Brien Hanley, *Their Rights and Liberties* (Westminster, Maryland: The Newman Press, 1959). On Massachusetts see Jacob C. Meyer, *Church and State in Massachusetts From 1740 to 1833* (Cleveland: Western Reserve University Press, 1930). New York has been elegantly done by John Webb Pratt in *Religion, Politics and Diversity* (Ithaca: Cornell University Press, 1967).

8. 367 U.S. 488 (1961).

9. Quoted in Sutherland, *op. cit.,* p. 274.

10. *Ibid.,* p. 275.

11. *Ibid.,* p. 299.

12. It is interesting to note that Vermont has continued into modern times its ancient practice of leasing state lands and turning the income over to town selectmen for distribution to the various "religious societies." New York *Times,* August 21, 1966.

13. For early constitutions see F. N. Thorpe, *Federal and State Constitutions, Colonial Charters and Other Organic Laws.* For a contemporary catalogue see Chester James Antieau, Phillip Mark Carroll, and Thomas Carroll Burke, *Religion Under the State Constitutions* (Brooklyn, N.Y.: Central Book Co., 1965).

14. The case was *General Assembly of Free Church of Scotland* v. *Overtown.* [1904] A.C. 515 (Scot.). The decision was reversed by act of Parliament a year later. For a useful review of this subject see Note, "Church-Property Disputes," 75 *Harvard Law Review* 1142 (1962).

15. *Rector of King's Chapel* v. *Pelham,* 9 Mass. 501 (1813).

16. *Baker* v. *Fales,* 16 Mass. 488 (1820).

17. 13 Wall. 679 (1871).

18. This occurred especially in cases where the majority of a congregation, within a congregationally organized denomination, voted to convert the common property to a clearly nonreligious use over the protest of a religious minority. Cf. *Hensel* v. *Purnell* 1F.2d 266 (1924). Many states have sought to regularize the legal status of churches through the adoption of religious corporation acts. These acts attempt, in regard to ownership of property, to allow for the needs of churches with differing ecclesiastical organizations. Some states, for instance, allow for the incorporation of a Roman Catholic bishop as a corporation sole in order that he may "own" all church property within his diocese and thus fulfill the requirements of that most hierarchical of major American denominations.

19. 344 U.S. 94 (1952).

20. See also *Kreshik* v. *St. Nicholas Cathedral,* 363 U.S. 190 (1960). Here New York's courts attempted, futilely, to do for the American faction what the Supreme Court had said New York's legislature could not do.

21. 393 U.S. 440 (1969). The decision of the Fourth Circuit Court of Appeals is at 167 2E2d, 658 (1969). Decided *per curium* on January 15, 1970 was *Maryland and Virginia Churches of God* v. *Church of God at Sharpsburg, 396* U.S. *367.* This cited *Blue Hill* and is notable for a brief but interesting concurrence from Mr. Justice Brown. Brennan carefully distinguished between the question of who exercises general governing power within a denomination, and the question of who the rules or "laws" of the denomination say exercises control over property. Only the first question is permitted to courts. It, Brennan argues, is an objective question in the sense that an outside observer can look around and see who has been doing most of the governing. The second question involves court interpretation and construction of church rules. This is too close to interpreting and construing doctrine. The property follows the general governing authority no matter what the rules may say.

22. 9 Cranch 43 (1815).

23. *Ibid.,* p. 49 (italics mine).

24. Commentaries on the Constitution (Boston: Hilliard, Gray, and Co., 1833), Volume III, p. 722.

25. *Vidal* v. *Girard's Executors,* 2 Howard 127 (1834).

26. *Revised Statutes of the United States,* sect. 5352.

27. *Reynolds* v. *United States,* 98 U.S. 145 (1878).

28. *Ibid.,* p. 164 (italics mine).

29. The phrase is David Manwaring's. See his *Render Unto Caesar* (Chicago: University of Chicago Press, 1962).

30. 98 U.S. 145, 165 (1878).

31. *Davis* v. *Beason,* 133 U.S. 33, 343 (1889).

32. Decided together at 139 U.S. 1 (1889).

33. *Ibid.,* p. 49.

34. In dissent in *Commonwealth* v. *Lesher,* 17 S.&R. 155 (Pa. 1828).

35. *Donahue* v. *Richards,* 38 Me. 379 (1854).

36. *Hardwicke* v. *Board of School Trusteees,* 54 Cal. App. 696 (1921).

37. For a brief description see Russell B. Nye, *The Cultural Life of the New Nation* (New York: Harper & Row, 1960), pp. 216–234. On the competitive, sectarian qualities of nineteenth century Protestantism see Walter Brownlow Posey, *Religious Strife on the Southern Frontier* (Baton Rouge: Louisiana State University Press, 1965).

38. Chapter 4, "Religion and American Values," in Lipset's *The First New Nation* (New York: Basic Books, 1963).

39. *Ibid.,* pp. 166–167 (author's italics.).

40. Billington, *op. cit.,* p. 33.

41. John Higham, *Strangers in the Land* (New Brunswick, N.J.: Rutgers University Press, 1955), p. 5.

42. On the Native American and Know Nothing parties see Billington, *op. cit.;* W. Darrell Overdyke, *The Know-Nothing Party in the South* (Baton Rouge: Louisiana State University Press, 1950); and Sister M.

Evangeline Thomas, *Nativism in the Old North-West, 1850–1860* (Washington, D.C.: Catholic University Press, 1936).

43. Donald L. Kinzer, *An Episode in Anti-Catholicism: The American Protective Association* (Seattle: University of Washington Press, 1964).

44. See Morgan, *op. cit.*, pp. 49–54.

45. Very roughly the mid-1830's, the early 1840's, the mid-1850's, the mid-1870's, the late 1880's to mid-1890's, the early 1920's and the late 1940's. The 1940's we shall discuss in Chapter IV. The upsurge of the early 1920's was spearheaded by the Ku Klux Klan; see David M. Chalmer's *Hooded Americanism* (Chicago: Quadrangle Books edition, 1969).

46. See Laubach, *op. cit.*, p. 25.

47. Higham, *op. cit.*, p. 28.

48. Quoted in Anson Phelps Stokes, *Church and State in the United States* (New York: Harper and Bros., 1950), Vol. II, p. 722.

49. *Ibid.*, p. 723.

50. There has been occasional suggestion that the failure of passage of Blaine's Amendment is evidence that the establishment clause *itself* does not bar aid to church-related schools. This seems quite wrong. Blaine himself saw his language as extending to the States what already operated against the national government. At least a few of those Senators who voted against the Amendment did so because they thought that the establishment clause, as it stood, prohibited such aid. Stokes, *op. cit.*, Vol. II, p. 727. The original amendment is at 4 *Congressional Record* 5580 (1876).

51. See Antieau, *et. al.*, *op. cit.*, pp. 23–50; and Stokes, *op. cit.*, pp. 489–495.

52. On its adoption see Pratt, *op. cit.*, pp. 225–258.

53. On the defeat of the proposed constitution of 1967 see Morgan, *op. cit.*, pp. 98–127.

54. Quoted in Edwin Scott Gaustad, ed., *Religious Issues in American History* (New York: Harper Forum Books, 1968), pp. 201–202. In fairness, it should also be noted that at the same time majority Protestants were castigating Catholics for breaking the supposed "wall" between church and state, a small minority group of Protestants was seeking to have Christianity constitutionally recognized as the national religion. The so-called "Christian Amendment" movement enjoyed some brief notoriety in the late nineteenth century, and even survived into the twentieth. See H.J. Res. 103, 87th Cong., 1st Sess., 1961.

3

The "Witnesses" and Free Exercise

As we have seen, the development of the free-exercise clause began in the nineteenth century and a particular theory of its meaning—the secular regulation rule—had been set into the structure of constitutional law by the beginning of the new century. In the 1880's and 1890's, as public attention began to focus on the "establishment-type" questions raised by Catholic claims for school funds, and as the establishment clause continued to await fundamental exposition by the Supreme Court, the free-exercise clause, at least, seemed to possess a core meaning. But the twentieth century was to bring successive challenges to this "settled" doctrine. The first came from conscientious objectors, the second, and far more important, came from the Jehovah's Witnesses.

THE EARLY C.O.'s

The First World War saw the development of substantial pacifist sentiment in America, much of which was religiously motivated. Ministers, and indeed whole sects such as Quakers and Adventists, argued that the federal conscription of individuals into military activity which violated their religious scruples was an infringement of the free-exercise clause. This argument was summarily rejected by the Supreme Court the first time it was aired in the Selective Draft Law Cases of 1918,[1] but it reached the Court again in several important cases during the interwar years.

The first of these, *United States* v. *Macintosh,* decided in 1931, involved the claim by an applicant for naturalization to a right of religiously motivated selective conscientious objection to war. He was willing to participate if a war was "necessary," but demanded that he be the ultimate judge of necessity. He would not unqualifiedly promise to bear arms against all enemies. The Court had previously held that a consistent religiously motivated pacifist (who would not fight at all) could be constitutionally excluded from citizenship for refusing that promise,[2] and had no trouble in concluding, through Justice Sutherland, that the American "government must go forward on the assumption, and safely can proceed upon no other, that unqualified allegiance to the Nation and submission and obedience to the laws of the land, as well those made for war as those made for peace, are not inconsistent with the will of God."[3] Anyone was free to disagree, of course, but should he attempt to act on the disagreement he would be in contravention of a valid secular regulation and unprotected in his disobedience by the free-exercise clause.

The second case was harder. In *Hamilton* v. *Regents,* in 1934,[4] a handful of religiously motivated students at the University of California at Berkeley refused to participate in an ROTC program required, in accordance with the common practice of state universities at that time, of freshmen and sophomores. They were duly dismissed and sued for reinstatement, arguing that the requirement of military instruction, when it violated religious conscience, was a denial of free-exercise. This time Mr. Justice Butler wrote for the Court, and made the position even clearer: there was no First Amendment right to be exempted from the secular requirement of military service because of religious scruples. The right to believe, to expound and to teach were secured, but the free-exercise clause would not protect action or refusals to act which were otherwise illegal. The object of the free-exercise clause was what the nineteenth century judges had said it was—to preclude persecution of belief, not to protect behavior. The right to exemption from military service on grounds of conscience, to the extent it existed, was a matter of legislative grace (of which more later) and since the California Legislature had provided no exemption from the requirement of ROTC instruction at Berkeley, there was nothing for the dissenting students to do but comply or forfeit the privilege of a California-financed baccalaureate. The secular-regulation rule continued undiluted.

ENTER THE WITNESSES

Changes began, however, with the entrance onto the constitutional stage of a group which was to trigger numerous important utterances by the Supreme Court during the thirties and forties—the Watch Tower Bible and Tract Society, commonly known as the Jehovah's Witnesses.

This aggressively missionary sect had its beginnings in the 1870's in Pittsburgh, Pennsylvania, in a small Bible class under the direction of Charles Taze Russell. It grew as a powerful grassroots movement and by the late 1930's, under "Judge" Joseph Franklin Rutherford, its militant preaching activities reached throughout the United States and several foreign countries. Each Witness saw himself as a minister with an evangelical mission. Satan was locked in struggle with Jehovah, the True God, and it was the duty of the faithful to do constant battle against Evil. This took them into the streets and onto doorsteps, trying to disseminate the literature in which the message was principally contained. In addition, Witnesses believed that to salute the American flag was to worship a graven image in contravention of the Biblical commandment. It was inevitable that any such group would run afoul of the law.

What was perhaps most remarkable about the Witnesses

was the way in which the group approached its legal problems. Rather than stoically taking its lumps and waiting for inevitable vindication in the Kingdom of God, the group's leaders organized a highly professional legal operation to challenge convictions of Witnesses before the Supreme Court on constitutional grounds. David Manwaring, the closest student of the group's litigious activities, explains that

> The growing flood of arrests led in 1935 to the re-establishment of the legal department, which had lain dormant since Rutherford's accession to the presidency. Olin R. Moyle, himself a Witness, who had already won several . . . [Witness] cases, was brought in from Wisconsin to serve as full-time legal counsel. The legal department was and is decentralized, consisting of the chief counsel, several assistants and clerical help in Brooklyn, and a large number of attorneys—all Witnesses—scattered about the country.[5]

During Moyle's tenure in the office as Witness chief counsel, he attempted to develop sympathetic working relationships with other groups—such as the American Civil Liberties Union and the Workers' Defense League—which were interested in the same constitutional points the Witnesses were raising. In 1938 Moyle was dismissed after a dispute with Judge Rutherford, and Rutherford took over the legal department himself with the aid of a serious young lawyer named Haydon Covington. The coming of Covington signaled the end of efforts at cooperation and coordination with other groups, but Covington went on, in his loner fashion, to compile one of the most impressive personal records of constitutional advocacy in American history.[6]

The first major victory for the Witnesses came in a case involving the speech guarantee of the First Amendment. In March of 1938, Chief Justice Charles Evans Hughes delivered the opinion for the Court in *Lovell* v. *City of Griffin*.[7] Here a Witness had been convicted of distributing leaflets in a small Georgia town in defiance of an ordinance requiring a permit from the City Manager for such distributions. The ordinance prescribed no standards for the Manager in issuing the permits, nor were any application or appeal procedures set. Hughes held the regulation unconstitutional on its face. While municipalities have an interest in keeping their streets free from litter, he suggested, they are limited by the speech clause of the First Amendment in the ways they go about it. An unfettered grant of discretion to an official would never pass constitutional muster; only a permit ordinance with clear standards and procedures would stand a chance.

Lovell was followed the next year by *Schneider* v. *Town of Irvington,*[8] a case to which was joined three others, involving not Witnesses but political radicals and union picketers. At issue again were permit requirements. Irvington, New Jersey, required that anyone canvassing or distributing materials door-to-door obtain a permit from the Chief of Police. The procedure for obtaining the permit involved being fingerprinted and photographed, and the Chief was free to deny the permit if he judged the applicant not to be "of good character." Associate Justice Owen Roberts disposed of this and the three similar cases with a reference to *Lovell* and a reminder of the importance in a democratic polity of "liberty to communicate." These permit cases were occasion for important Supreme Court statements on the meaning of the free-speech clause, but the real Jehovah's Witnesses breakthrough in the free-exercise area was yet to come.

CANTWELL v. *CONNECTICUT*

Cantwell[9] was decided in 1940 and again Justice Roberts spoke for the Court. The situation also resembled the previous Witness cases. Newton Cantwell (Sheridan could hardly have chosen a better name) and his sons Jesse and Russell were offering Witness literature for sale on Cassius Street in New Haven. The population of the Street was heavily Roman Catholic, and the Cantwells' sales approach was hardly calculated to win friends. Their technique was to approach one or more individuals and request permission to play a phonograph record. If permission was given the record was played, and it included a vitriolic attack on the Church of Rome as the Scarlet Woman and the Whore of Babylon. The episode at issue in the litigation was one in which the record had been played to two men who in turn had threatened Jesse Cantwell with violence, causing him to pack up and move away along the Street. The Cantwells were convicted as a result of the encounter with the threatening Catholics, all three for violating a Connecticut statute which forbade public solicitation for a religious or philanthropic cause without prior certification by the state; in addition, Jesse was convicted of the common law crime of disturbing the peace.

Incorporation of the Religion Clauses

The first innovation contained in Roberts' opinion concerned the application of the religion clauses of the First Amendment to the actions of states (and those creatures of states, municipalities).

It had, of course, been a perfectly fixed principle of constitutional law during the nineteenth century that the provisions of the federal Bill of Rights (the first eight amendments to the Constitution of the United States) applied only to the national government.[10] State courts might read the federal provisions into state law if they chose or state constitutions might include provisions similar to the federal document. But it should be recalled that the polygamy cases forced an early interpretation of the free-exercise clause precisely because the practice took place in territories and the prosecuting agent was the *federal government* (Congress) and not a state. In the early decades of the twentieth century there were suggestions that the due process clause of the Fourteenth Amendment (which came into effect in 1867) extended the provisions of the First Amendment to the states. The breakthrough came in 1925 when the Supreme Court, in affirming the conviction of a political radical under the New York Criminal Anarchy Act, announced that it was "assumed" that the speech, press, and assembly clauses of the First Amendment applied to the states.[11] In the jargon of lawyers they were "incorporated" into the due process clause of the Fourteenth. But what about the religion clauses? Did the 1925 breakthrough mean that *all* of the First Amendment now operated through the Fourteenth, or only the speech, press, and assembly clauses?

This question had been put to the Court in *Hamilton* in 1934, but the Justices, in deciding that case against the student pacifists, managed to avoid giving a clear answer. Roberts, however, gave such an answer in *Cantwell:*

> The First Amendment declared that Congress shall make no laws respecting an establishment of religion or prohibiting the free exercise thereof. The Fourteenth Amendment has rendered the legislatures of the states as incompetent as Congress to enact such laws.[12]

Here was unambiguous incorporation of the religion clauses, and it was of the first technical importance. Yet Roberts' second substantive innovation may, in the long run, prove almost as significant.

The Erosion of Secular Regulation

At the time no one seemed to notice this second innovation in Justice Roberts' opinion—his departure from the accepted distinction between protected belief and unprotected action. It only becomes clear that something of consequence has happened in *Cantwell* when one remembers the confidence with which nineteenth century judges had relied on the belief-action distinction. By contrast hear Roberts:

> Thus the Amendment embraces *two* concepts—freedom to believe and freedom to act. The first is absolute but, in the nature of things, the second cannot be. Conduct remains subject to regulation for the protection of society. The freedom to act must have appropriate definition to preserve the enforcement of that protection. In every case the power to regulate must be so exercised as not, in attaining a permissible end, unduly to infringe the protected freedom.[13]

Action was no longer wholly unprotected, and the state, in exercising its legitimate power to regulate, must take care not "unduly to infringe" on individual behavior which was in exercise of a religion. Of course the implication of this innovation was ambiguous. Was government only to avoid careless restriction of religious behavior? Or did the requirement extend to a governmental showing that a certain limitation of religious action was necessary to effect an otherwise valid governmental purpose? In any case, however, the erosion of secular regulation rule had begun.

Since the question of what has happened to the secular regulation rule will recur throughout this book, it is useful once more to state the issue involved as simply and starkly as possible: is the free-exercise clause to be interpreted as affording protection to certain sorts of behavior, above and beyond the protections of behavior afforded by other constitutional protections such as the speech, press, and assembly clauses? Before Roberts wrote in *Cantwell* the answer was a confident no; after *Cantwell* the best that could be said is that one did not really know.

In the actual case at bar, Roberts held all convictions of all *Cantwells* to have been unconstitutional. Those based on the permit statute went down on a now familiar distinction. The Connecticut requirement that those who would solicit for religious purposes present themselves for examination by the state officials was a reasonable one. The difficulty lay in the discretionary power accorded state officials to deny the permit. Without the permit solicitation was impossible, and this put the officials in the position of deciding absolutely which religious groups were going to solicit and which were not. Connecticut, Roberts held, had an interest in guarding against the perpetration of frauds within her borders, but the means which she chose in this instance (empowering an official to determine whether the applicant was a bona fide religious group) was a denial of free-exercise. What Justice Roberts did not tell us was how the case would have gone had the solicitation been for a non-religious purpose. Would the permit scheme then be acceptable? Could Connecticut subject non-commercial but secular solicitation to burdens not permitted on religious solicitation?

Of Jesse Cantwell's second conviction, the misdemeanor of

breaching the peace of Cassius Street, Roberts had less trouble and spoke more coherently. Jesse simply had not disturbed the peace by playing his record after obtaining permission. Religion and politics are naturally topics which stir strong feelings, and the mere fact that such feelings are stirred in someone cannot be made to constitute a breach of the peace. Should a state attempt to do so, it will fly in the face of the First Amendment. Interestingly, Roberts disposition of this second count relied as much on the speech clause as on the free-exercise clause. It is quite clear that it is expression that was being protected, and that religious and non-commercial secular expression were seen to stand on an equal footing. There was no hint that the free-exercise clause conveyed some special protection.

Because of the holding on the first count, however, the cat of free exercise had at least one paw out of the secular regulation bag.

RELIGION DOOR-TO-DOOR

In addition to proselytizing in the streets, it became the practice of Witnesses in the late 1930's to saturate neighborhoods and whole towns with workers who, under the direction of an organizer called an "area servant," moved from door-to-door offering literature for sale. Or, to be precise, contributions were requested in return for various pieces of literature according to a fixed schedule. Numerous communities felt disturbed and threatened by these campaigns and either enacted new ordinances or applied old ones in attempts to discourage the Witnesses. Four cases were decided by the Supreme Court in the spring of 1943 which dealt with such "crash" canvassing, and the majority opinions reflect the weakening of the secular regulation rule which had been signaled by Roberts in *Cantwell.*

In *Jones* v. *Oplika,*[14] *Murdock* v. *Pennsylvania,*[15] and *Douglas* v. *Jeannette*[16] the issue was a tax levied by municipalities upon all those who sold anything door-to-door. The Witnesses, predictably, had not paid and were convicted for the omission. *Douglas* was decided against the Witnesses on technical grounds, but in *Jones* and *Murdock* the convictions were overturned and the ordinances held unconstitutional as applied to Witnesses. The key opinion for the majority was written by Associate Justice William O. Douglas and it is particularly interesting.

Asserting that the practice of carrying the gospel directly into homes through "personal visitations" was a traditionally accepted technique of evangelism and thus an exercise of religion, Douglas concluded that it "has the same claim to protection as the more orthodox and conventional exercises of religion" such as preaching in churches.[17] The tax, he said, "restrains in advance the exercise of those constitutional liberties of press and religion and inevitably tends to suppress their exercise."[18] The Court was only restoring "to their high, constitutional position the liberties of itinerant evangelists who disseminate their religious beliefs and the tenets of their faith through distribution of literature."[19] Douglas did not go so far as to suggest that the door-to-door activities of the Witnesses were absolutely unregulatable by municipalities, but there was little in his opinion to indicate what restraints might be imposed. While making reference to the free-exercise clause, Douglas was careful to link it always with the speech clause, referring to them almost as if they were interchangeable parts.

The fourth case decided that spring, *Martin* v. *Struthers*,[20] involved a somewhat different fact situation. The city of Struthers, Ohio, a mill town in which many workers on night shifts slept during the day, enacted an ordinance prohibiting door-to-door canvassing of any kind, and the Witnesses ran afoul of it. Here Mr. Justice Hugo Black spoke for the Court. This was not, Black pointed out, a garden variety "Green River"[21] ordinance aimed exclusively at commercial solicitation, but a prohibition of all uninvited approaches no matter the motive. Phrasing his opinion more in free-speech than in free-exercise terms, Black noted that the "freedom to distribute information to every citizen wherever he desires to receive it is clearly so vital to the preservation of a free society that, putting aside reasonable police and health regulations of the time and manner of distribution, it must be fully preserved."[22] It might be possible, Black continued, to enact an ordinance which punished those who approached doors after explicit warning by the occupant that approaches were not desired, but a blanket restriction was unconstitutional. Mr. Justice Frank Murphy added a concurrence which stressed the free-exercise clause and attacked the ordinance as over-broad. There were three dissents in this group of cases and all are worth noting.

Justice Stanley Reed attacked what he took to be Douglas' free-speech argument by suggesting that the real contention of Witnesses in the tax cases (which the Court had inadvertently approved) was that the sale of a book could not be taxed. This he concluded was patently absurd—the First Amendment's speech clause had never been conceived as exempting all those associated with publishing the written word from paying taxes. The Witnesses might be subjective evangelists, but objectively they were "book agents." The mere fact that the materials were of a religious nature did not make the transaction any less commercial. Nowhere, Reed pointed out, had Douglas, or the Witnesses, offered any indication that the tax was excessive or involved more than the cost to the community of administering the ordinance regulating door-to-door selling. There was no power to deny licenses absolutely as had been the case in *Cantwell,* and as a secular regulation the ordinance was eminently reasonable.

Mr. Justice Felix Frankfurter was even more precise, and more worried about Douglas' invocation of the free-exercise clause. No tax, he argued, can "be invalidated merely because it falls upon activities which constitute an exercise of a constitutional right."[23] Nothing in the Constitution, he concluded, "exempts persons engaged in religious activities from sharing equally in the costs of benefits to all, including themselves, provided by the government." Frankfurter's dissent was, in fact, a firm reassertion of the secular regulation doctrine, and it is especially remarkable in that it contained the first suggestion that a contradiction between the free-exercise and establishment clauses would arise if the secular regulation approach were abandoned:

> To say that the Constitution forbids the states to obtain the necessary revenue from the whole of a class [those who evangelize by selling literature door-to-door] that enjoys these benefits and facilities, when in fact no discrimination is suggested as between purveyors of printed matter and purveyors of other things, and the exaction is not claimed to be actually burdensome, is to say that the Constitution requires not that the dissemination of ideas shall be free, but that it shall be subsidized by the state. Such a claim offends the most important of all aspects of religious freedom in this country, namely, that of the separation of church and state.[24]

Mr. Justice Robert Jackson bore the burden of dissent from the decision in the *Martin* case. At some length he described the canvassing practices of the Witnesses, stressing the value of domestic privacy which the municipality was attempting to protect. The right of the occupant to be left alone was no less worthy of governmental protection than the right of the itinerant preacher to propagate the faith. What was needed in *Martin* was a delicate balancing of competing claims, an issue which could not be resolved by a simple-minded identification of door-to-door canvassing with a minister preaching to a congregation which had assembled voluntarily. The question was too difficult "to be disposed of by a vague but fervent transcendentalism."[25] Like Frankfurter, Jackson saw a contradiction of the establishment clause in any special exemption of religiously motivated behavior from otherwise valid secular regulations. Religious and non-religious behavior enjoyed the freedom of expression guaranteed by the speech, press, and assembly clauses, but beyond that Jackson

> had not supposed the rights of secular and non-religious communications were more narrow or in any way inferior to those of avowed religious groups.[26]

As with *Cantwell,* it is difficult to say that these cases represent a clear departure from the secular regulation rule. In the majority opinions the speech and free-exercise grounds are muddled together. There were, however, hints that the free-exercise clause should be read to protect behavior that would not otherwise be protected by the speech clause. The fact that two of the dissents indicated a concern that this might be the effect of the decisions is, while not conclusive, worthy of note. Further, the Court lent credence to the view that *Martin* and the rest created a special religious exemption when, in 1951, it decided the case of *Breard* v. *City of Alexandria*.[27] Here an opinion by Mr. Justice Reed upheld an ordinance of the City of Alexandria, Louisiana, which banned all door-to-door soliciting, against the claim of a salesman for a line of national magazines. The salesman argued that the ordinance restricted free speech, but only Black and Douglas agreed. Would the outcome have been different, and controlled by *Martin,* had the magazines been religious and the salesman a believer? Would free-exercise have protected what speech would not? Again it is possible to evade the question by regarding *Breard* as a case of commercial activity not entitled to the protection of any part of the First Amendment. But whichever way the Reed opinion in *Breard* is turned, it seems to sit awkwardly alongside *Martin.* The only way of distinguishing them cleanly is to assume that the latter established a free-exercise right for religiously motivated persons to ring doorbells which those pursuing ordinary free speech errands must leave alone.

THE FLAG SALUTE CASES

The Witnesses vexed authorities almost as much with their refusal to salute the American flag as they did with their itinerant evangelism. At the same time the Supreme Court was wrestling with challenged permit systems, license fees, and prohibitions on door-to-door solicitation, it was forced to juggle the superheated issue of "disrespect" to the flag. War clouds were gathering; dictatorships were on the march; there was the natural upsurge of patriotic feelings. And while Witnesses were being jailed and fined for passing out leaflets in the streets, they were occasionally tarred and feathered because their children refused to take part in school flag-salute exercises.

The development of the flag-salute cases, their argument before the Supreme Court, the decisions and their impact have been carefully chronicled by David Manwaring [28] and it is not necessary to cover the ground in any detail here. Suffice it for our purposes that the question of whether it was constitutional for a state to require a school child to recite the pledge, on pain of expulsion or worse, was twice considered by the Justices. The first time the Court sustained the requirement, the second time the Court reversed itself and disallowed it.

The first case, *Minersville School District* v. *Gobitis,*[29] came out of the hard-coal country of Pennsylvania and attracted national interest on its way to the Supreme Court. It was decided in the spring of 1940, just two weeks after *Cantwell* and three years before the doorbell cases. The Gobitis children, Witnesses, refused to salute and the predominently Roman Catholic community did not like it. The school board expelled them. The case began its way up the appellate ladder under the direction of Moyle and was finished in the Supreme Court by Rutherford and Covington. *Amicus curiae* (friend of the court) briefs were submitted by the American Civil Liberties Union and the Bill of Rights Committee of the American Bar Association. Both of these are interesting.

The ACLU brief purported to stick by the secular regulation approach and quoted *Reynolds* with approval. Conduct could be regulated in aid of legitimate legislative purpose; belief was absolutely protected. What was involved in *Gobitis,* of course, was not a regulation of conduct but the imposition of a *belief*. This was not the practice of polygamy or refusal to be vaccinated or any other behavior which the State had the right to punish in reasonable furtherance of the community interest. This was precisely the realm of ideas which the free-exercise clause had historically been considered as protecting. By thus characterizing the facts the ACLU drafters sought to make a favorable decision easy for the Court.

The American Bar Association brief took quite a different tack. Forsaking the secular regulation doctrine, it called for an *ad hoc* balancing of the competing claims of government to regulate and the individual to believe *and* behave in such manner as his sincere religious convictions might direct. How important is the interest of the individual? How important is the interest of the legislature and are there other ways in which that interest could be satisfactorily secured without limiting religiously motivated behavior? This, as we shall see in Chapter VI, was an approach which came to prove very attractive to the Supreme Court in the late 1960's.

Mr. Justice Frankfurter delivered the opinion of the Court, and followed the strict secular regulation line. Requiring children to salute the flag was in no way to foist a religious belief on them. The exercise was purely secular, and the only question to be answered was whether it was a reasonable exercise of Pennsylvania's legislative power. After reviewing the interest which any polity has in fostering patriotic regard for itself, Frankfurter concluded that a pledge of allegiance was an unreasonable means to this end, and thus was a valid secular regulation. "The religious liberty which the Constitution protects has never excluded legislation of general scope not directed against doctrinal loyalties of particular sections."[30]

Mr. Justice Stone, in what became one of the most quoted and acclaimed dissents of the 1940's, insisted that nothing could constitute greater coercion of belief than requiring individuals to perform an act—such as speaking words—which is to him profane. The old distinction between belief and action seemed meaningless to Stone. He agreed with the ACLU brief that belief was involved in the *Gobitis* case, but he was not forthcoming with a crisply articulated alternative to the secular regulation role. The sense of Stone's opinion seems to be that secular regulations should override religious claims only when the most important social values such as monogamous marriage or the prevention of the spread of disease are involved, and in this he moved toward or perhaps beyond the balancing approach urged by the ABA.

The reaction by the law reviews and by professional commentators on the work of the Court was highly unfavorable to the Frankfurter opinion in *Gobitis*. As Manwaring points out,

Frankfurter's workmanlike assertion of what, before *Cantwell,* had been fairly settled law was often distorted into an assertion that national unity was more important than religious scruples.[31] Stone was praised for expressing in his dissent the essential general spirit of the First Amendment—the only compliment possible under the circumstances since he had offered no coherent argument based either on the speech clause or the free-exercise clause, although mentioning both frequently.

A decision which draws as much fire as *Gobitis* is not likely to endure for the ages, and in 1943 a somewhat altered Supreme Court (Stone had succeeded Hughes as Chief Justice and Jackson and Wiley Rutledge had replaced Stone and James F. Byrnes respectively) heard oral argument in a second flag-salute case. The arguments came on the heels of the decisions in the tax and doorbell-ringing cases, and the disposition of the Justices there gave clear indication of how the flag-salute issue would go the second time around. *West Virginia State Board of Education* v. *Barnette*[32] was decided finally on June 14, 1943, and Justice Jackson wrote for a Court divided six to three.

The briefing of this second case had occasioned one innovation. The ACLU, loyal to the Witnesses' cause despite repeated rebuffs by Rutherford, came in with a proposed theory of free-exercise which clearly surpassed the *ad hoc* balancing process which had been suggested by the ABA in *Gobitis.* Borrowing from the constitutional law of free-speech, the Union suggested that unless the exercise of religion (and this was, presumably, anything a person was sincere about) constituted a clear and present danger to the community, it could not be regulated no matter how worthy and reasonable the legislative purpose. Thus the free-exercise clause was to be interpreted in a fashion to parallel the speech guarantee, but while the latter had not been interpreted up to that time as protecting anything by expression (verbal behavior), the free-exercise clause *would* protect non-verbal action, if religiously motivated, up to the clear and present danger threshold. The ACLU theory went well beyond what was needed for the case at bar, where, after all, it was essentially verbal activity which was at stake. It might have been supposed that a speech argument, employing the established clear and present danger test, would have served just as well. But the ACLU was seeking the *obliteration* of the secular regulation rule and the establishment, in one stroke, of a new constitutional bridgehead for the protection of individuals against government.

Jackson did not rise to this bait. As might have been expected from his opposition to the *Martin* decision, he was not enthusiastic about extending the free-exercise clause. In fact, he excluded consideration of religious freedom from his opinion as irrelevant to the disposition of the case, and, as Manwaring had suggested, was unwilling to "jettison" the secular regulation rule.[33] He took the case on freedom of speech grounds, and rather than asking whether it was constitutional for West Virginia to require the Barnette children to salute the flag, he asked whether the state could compel anyone, religious or indifferent, to do so. The flag salute requirement moved the government into an area of basic belief which was beyond the competence of the state. The opinion neatly disposed of the obnoxious practice without accelerating the slippage of the secular regulation rule.

Not all the majority Justices were satisfied. Justices Douglas and Black concurred, and seemed to adopt the vaulting approach of the ACLU brief. Since the "little children" had done nothing to disturb "domestic tranquility" or to erode the nation's "martial power in war," they deserve protection under the free-exercise clause. While not formally adopting a clear and present danger test for free-exercise, the opinion comes close. Justice Murphy also concurred, and also seemed to want something close but not quite a clear and present danger test. He asserted a right to free-exercise protection of behavior which operated "except insofar as essential operations of government may require it for the preservation of an orderly society—as in the case of compulsion to give evidence in court."[34]

Justice Frankfurter dissented alone and bitterly, suggesting that his colleagues acted beyond their warrants as judges by not deferring to legislative judgments of reasonableness as he had argued in *Gobitis*.

CONCLUSION

With the decision of the second flag-salute case, the free-exercise clause moved to the fringe of American constitutional politics for almost two decades. We shall not pick up the thread again until 1961. But in the course of disposing of the raft of business created by the fractious Witnesses in the 1930's and 1940's the Court skidded part way into a constitutional turn of the first importance, and in the 1960's it was forced to commit itself to the new road or back out. The secular regulation rule had been weakened, and it seemed quite possible by 1943 that the free-exercise clause would emerge as a far more important limitation on government's power to regulate behavior than would have been thought possible before *Cantwell.* Despite the efforts of Frankfurter and Jackson, their brethern Roberts, Douglas, Black, and Murphy *had written,* and their words remained for future advocates to weld into argumentative weapons.

Finally, it is worth reflecting why these innovating Justices, and the brief writers and commentators who supported them, chose to respond to problems posed by the Witnesses by tinkering with free-exercise doctrine rather than simple reliance on the free-speech clause. Speech was technically sufficient to the task, as Jackson proved in *Barnette;* why resort to a new version of the free-exercise clause?

Some of those involved probably did want more constitutional protection of non-conforming behavior—of action—than they saw possible under the speech clause. But for others the turn toward free-exercise seems accidental. It simply made their opinions and articles sound better to include references to freedom of religion. The Witnesses were, after all, very unpopular people. The only thing about them with which conventional Americans could identify was their use of the language of Christianity. Further, the speech clause was associated in the minds of many with the protection of political radicals who, as a class, were even less loved than the Witnesses. Liberal, humane judges and lawyers saw this small sect, set upon by party officialdom, and wished to protect it. Applying the free-exercise clause to the handing out of leaflets, the ringing of doorbells, the refusal to perform a certain school ritual seemed very different from applying it to polygamy. It had been a long time since any really bizarre or troubling religious claim had come before the Court. Against the background of events in Europe in the late '30's and '40's, religious freedom was a popular thing; why not get a bit of mileage out of it by linking it with speech in protecting the embattled Witnesses. By this partly calculated, partly accidental process, secular regulation rule was badly bent.

NOTES

1. *Selective Draft Law Cases,* 245 U.S. 366 (1918).
2. *Schwimmer* v. *United States,* 279 U.S. 644 (1929).
3. *United States* v. *MacIntosh,* 283 U.S. 605, 625 (1931).
4. 293 U.S. 245 (1934).
5. Manwaring, *op. cit.,* p. 27.
6. *Ibid.,* p. 121.
7. 303 U.S. 444 (1938).
8. 303 U.S. 147 (1939).
9. 310 U.S. 296 (1940).
10. See Chief Justice John Marshall's opinion for the Court in *Barron* v. *Baltimore,* 7 Peters 243 (1833). With special reference to the religion clauses see *Permoli* v. *New Orleans,* 3 Howard 589 (1845).
11. *Gitlow* v. *New York,* 268 U.S. 652 (1925). In *Palko* v. *Connecticut,* 302 U.S. 319, 324 (1937), Justice Cardozo refers to Hamilton as rendering the free-exercise clause operative against the states. This is a hard argument to support from the text of *Hamilton,* and few besides Cardozo have been attracted to it.
12. 310 U.S. 296, 303 (1940).
13. *Ibid.,* pp. 303–304 (italics mine).
14. 319 U.S. 103 (1943).
15. 319 U.S. 105 (1943).
16. 319 U.S. 157 (1943).
17. 319 U.S. 105, 109 (1943).
18. *Ibid.,* p. 114.
19. *Ibid.,* p. 117.
20. 319 U.S. 141 (1943).
21. The term derives from the name of the town from which one of the principal test cases involving prohibition of door-to-door solicitation arose: *Green River* v. *Fuller Brush Co.,* 65 F. 2d 112 (1933). The history

of how "commercial speech" became accepted as a lesser form of speech, without title to full First Amendment protection, is too complicated and murky to be explored here. The distinction is, however, well established in American constitutional law.

22. 319 U.S. 141, 146–147 (1943).
23. 319 U.S. 105, 136 (1943).
24. *Ibid.*, p. 140.
25. 319 U.S. 157, 179 (1943).
26. *Ibid.*
27. 341 U.S. 622 (1951).
28. Manwaring, *op. cit.*
29. 310 U.S. 586 (1940). For an early treatment of the flag-salute problem, revealing the understood limits on the meaning of the free-exercise clause before *Cantwell,* see Note, "Compulsory Flag Salutes and Religious Freedom," 51 *Harvard Law Review* 1418 (1938).
30. *Ibid.*, p. 594.
31. Manwaring, *op. cit.*, pp. 150–151.
32. 319 U.S. 624 (1943).
33. Manwaring, *op. cit.*, p. 226.
34. 319 U.S. 624, 644 (1943).

4

The Coming of Age of the Establishment Clause

It is another indication of the untidiness of history—even constitutional history—that the initial exposition of the establishment clause by the Supreme Court came in 1947—seventy years after the initial exposition of the free-exercise clause. The time lag was not, however, an indication of the relative importance of the clauses or of their difficulty for the Court. If anything, more controversy has swirled around "establishment" than around "free-exercise." Under the establishment rubric, two sorts of problems arise: first, to what extent may church-related institutions (principally, but not exclusively, schools) be supported in their activities with public monies, and second, to what extent may religious rituals and references be authorized or undertaken by the government. This Chapter will deal with the first sort of problem, Chapter V with the second. But before turning to the premier case of *Everson* v. *New Jersey* a few loose legal ends should be tied up, and a last jigsaw piece of background supplied.

THE CONSTITUTIONAL STATUS OF PRIVATE SCHOOLS

The due process clause of the Fourteenth Amendment has been authoritatively interpreted by the Supreme Court to prohibit states from requiring all children to attend public schools. School attendance is, with minor variations, universally mandated by law, but parents enjoy the constitutionally protected option of meeting their legal obligation by sending their children to a private school. States may require that these schools meet reasonable standards and subject them to inspection, but the government may not preempt the educational field altogether.

The test of this point came in the 1920's as a result of an upsurge of anti-German feeling triggered by World War I. In the mid-West, a few state governments moved to suppress the teaching of the German language and force students out of Catholic parochial schools, many of which had a German cultural coloration. Two cases finally reached the Court. The first, *Meyer* v. *Nebraska,*[1] saw that state attempting to forbid the teaching of modern foreign languages in any schools, public or private. The second case, *Pierce* v. *Society of Sisters,*[2] saw the state of Oregon attempting to require all children to attend its public schools.

Justice John McReynolds, no famous civil libertarian, wrote for a unanimous Court in both instances. What is important is that McReynolds did not attack what the states had done on First Amendment grounds. It was neither speech nor religion which was being unconstitutionally interfered with, he suggested, but the freedom to contract. His two opinions bristle with references to cases such as *Lochner* v. *New York*[3] and *Adkins* v. *Children's Hospital*[4] in which state and federal attempts to regulate economic life had been found to violate the due process clauses of the Fourteenth and Fifth Amendments. Property was the value which McReynolds saw at stake; in *Meyer* the teacher-plaintiff had a property interest in his capacity to teach German, and in *Pierce* the school was seen as the established livelihood of those who ran it. To interfere with the right of educators to sell their services and parents to buy them was an unacceptable restriction on economic activity.

Today, the intellectual underpinnings of *Meyer* and *Pierce* appear somewhat shaky. In the years since the so-called "Constitutional Revolution of 1937" the Supreme Court has repudiated many of the old property-contract decisions of the *Lochner* vintage. It might well be that were the Court required to redecide *Pierce* today, it would speak in First Amendment language. The point, however, is that it has not done so, and that the opinions in *Meyer* and *Pierce* do not bear directly on the question which will occupy us in the coming pages—whether public monies may be used to support church-related schools. The argument has been made from time to time that persons have a "constitutional right" to establish church-related schools, and that if the economics of running such schools become so difficult that survival is in doubt, then governmental support must be forthcoming or government is operationally depriving persons of the right. There is a certain engaging ingenuity in the argument, but using *Meyer* and *Pierce* to support it, as is often done, radically mistakes their meaning. These decisions are prime examples of what Philip Kurland has called the "apocrypha" of church-state law—they are quite widely believed to be what they are not.[5]

ACCOMMODATIONIST PRECEDENTS

It was suggested in Chapter 2 that something like a national policy of strict separation had been developed during the nineteenth century. While this is quite true, and while that policy continued to be generally adhered to up to 1947 when, as we shall see, it was adopted by the Supreme Court, there were a few long-standing arrangements and legal precedents at which the accommodationist lawyers of the 1940's could grasp. We have already examined one such example, Justice Story's utterances on the relation of religion to the public order, and there were others.

In 1899 the Supreme Court decided *Bradfield* v. *Roberts*,[6] a complicated action involving a congressional appropriation of $30,000 to pay for an addition to Providence Hospital, in the District of Columbia. Providence was chartered by Congress to care for the sick of the District without regard to creed, but the members of its board of directors were all Catholic nuns of the order which supplied the non-professional personnel for the hospital. Mr. Justice Peckham wrote for the Court, and "took" the case as raising an ordinary point of corporation law. As long as the board ran the hospital in a non-exclusive fashion in accordance with the purposes specified in the charter it did not matter whether its members were all Catholics or all Methodists or all spiritualists. The nuns might be members of a religious order, but the board on which they sat was the secular artifact of Congress. The new buildings went up.

In 1908 came *Quick Bear* v. *Leupp*.[7] Here certain funds were held by the federal government in trust for Indian owners, and the question was whether these monies could be disbursed to pay for the education of Indians at schools run by the Bureau of Catholic Indian Missions. The answer was an easy yes, since the money was, in law and fact, private.

What seems, at first glance, a clear precedent for accommodation in the matter of aid to church-related schools came out of Huey Long's Louisiana in the late 1920's. That state adopted the practice (one of the "Kingfish's" public welfare schemes) of providing textbooks, in secular subjects, for use in church-related schools; in 1930, when a challenge to the practice reached the Supreme Court (as *Cochran* v. *Louisiana*[8]) the Court sustained Louisiana. But the first glance is not enough. The Louisiana program had not been challenged on grounds that it violated the establishment clause. This was for the very good reason that *Cantwell* had yet to be decided, and it was not generally assumed that the religion clauses applied to acts of the states.[9] The suit before the Court attacked the textbook grants on the grounds that the expenditure was without a public purpose. The doctrine that public monies may not be spent without public purpose is an important thread in the weave of American constitutional law but it is quite distinct from the establishment clause. All the Court said in *Cochran* was that to provide textbooks was in aid of public purpose; it did not speak in any way to the question of whether Louisiana's arrangement constituted an establishment of religion.

Thus, while all three of these decisions were "citable" by accommodationist lawyers at the time *Everson* was being briefed and argued (1946–1947), none was quite on point. Two further "precedents" had greater value for accommodationists and were resorted to frequently.

The first involved the provision of military chaplains at government expense. This certainly was public support of an establishment of religion, and it had gone without serious opposition throughout our history. Separationists were always quick to point out the exceptional circumstances (uprooted young men, far from home) which, they suggested, justified the anomaly. Accommodationists, on the other hand, argued that what "exceptional circumstances" justified in one context they could justify in others, and that a severe economic hardship could be considered an exceptional circumstance.

The second involved transportation of pupils to church-related schools at public expense. This was the only area of governmental support for their schools in which Catholics had made any headway, and that had come late—in the 1930's and 1940's—and only in a few states. Nonetheless, these school bus victories had considerable symbolic importance. Here, finally, some state legislatures seemed to be recognizing, in however small a way, that Catholic parochial schools were performing a public service. Almost invariably these busing statutes were hard-won for Catholics. In New York, for instance, several bills were introduced in the early 1930's; one was vetoed by Governor Lehman: finally, in 1936, one was passed and signed. The Court of Appeals struck it down two years later as violating the state constitution's "Blaine Amendment" and this launched another year's struggle to amend that portion of the charter to specifically allow for transportation.[10] Finally, in 1939, the job was done, and a statute enacted which required school districts to pay the costs of transportation to non-profit private schools where the private school was "remote" from the student's home or where such transportation would be in the "best interests" of the students. Over the years this provision has been strengthened to require districts to transport students to private schools on the same terms students are transported to public schools. Among the states which have adopted some form of transportation support, programs have varied from simple authorizing resolutions—allowing school districts to do as they wished—to the present strict New York model. In the immediate postwar period Catholics were making bus transportation moves in some new states, and they were beginning to urge their transportation victories as precedents for aid of other sorts.

Neither the separationist nor the accommodationist precedents, of course, were perfectly conclusive of the meaning of the establishment clause. They were simply the tools with which the advocates had to work on the eve of *Everson.*

THE CHURCH-STATE MOOD OF 1947

It has already been suggested that intergroup tensions in America (at least those between Protestants and Catholics), have a fluctuating character, intensifying and declining in cycles. *Everson* was both a result and an accelerator of the increase in these inter-creedal tensions which immediately followed World War II.

If the election of John F. Kennedy to the Presidency in 1960 represented the coming of age of the American Catholic community, the Second World War represented the next-to-last step in the process of maturation. Somewhere along the way from the Depression through North Africa and Normandy to the deck of the *Missouri* in Tokyo Bay, Roman Catholic consciousness of itself as a minority, set apart from the mainstream of American culture and community life, evaporated. Laity and hierarchy alike, the Catholic community emerged from the Second World

War newly confident, and eager to exert its influence on a culture which it now perceived as its own, rather than the preserve of the Protestant middle class. Catholic utterances, typified by the annual statements of the bishops of the Administrative Board of the National Catholic Welfare Conference (the national secretariat of the American hierarchy—NCWC), took on a new tone which many Protestants considered profoundly disturbing and aggressive.

The statement issued by the Administrative Board in November 1946, for instance, was a broad-gauge treatment of the problems of rebuilding war-torn Europe, and it carried an implied criticism of the United States Government for not perceiving with sufficient clarity the nature of the Communist threat. The peacemakers were exhorted to come to an agreement on the basic "question of man as man" (which appeared to translate as protect Catholic freedom of worship in Eastern Europe), and that if this were done, secondary "defects in the peace may be tolerated in the hope of their eventual correction."[11] There was nothing really incendiary about the substance of the statement, but its cold-war edge and the tone of its prescription seemed to indicate a new posture on the part of Catholic leaders toward the conduct of American foreign policy. A decade and a half later, Methodist Bishop G. Bromley Oxnam specifically recalled the 1946 statement as a cause of alarm to him and his friends.[12]

Evidence of increasing Protestant unease in the face of what Oxnam described as a "cultural offensive" appeared in the spring of 1947 with the statements of various Protestant groupings at their annual conventions. On May 7, the Council of Bishops of the Methodist Church (at that time the largest Protestant denomination in the United States), met in Riverside, California, and "accused the Roman Catholic Church of political activities in this country and abroad, which the council said amounted to bigotry and denial of religious liberty."[13] Roman Catholic leaders in the United States, the Council's report concluded, condoned anti-libertarian practices "at the very moment that protestations of belief in democracy are made . . . and demands for the public support of parochial education are advocated as a contribution to the morality essential to freedom."[14] At the opening session of the meeting of the Southern Baptist Convention in St. Louis, the Reverend Louie D. Newton, President of the Convention, and later to be President of Americans United, declared that Protestants were "confronted by the most determined and adroit campaign" to alter the traditional American understanding of the proper relationship of church and state.[15] "The Baptist witness in behalf of the principle of separation of church and state," Newton declared, "should not be weakened upon any pretext whatever."[16] The Presbyterian Church in the United States (Southern) met in Atlanta, and its Committee on Christian Relations announced that it would ask the denomination to reemphasize Presbyterian commitment to the separation of church and state. The Committee spoke ominously about tax money going to "Roman Catholic activities whenever its political power permits."[17]

The foreboding with which many Protestants viewed this Roman Catholic sense of itself as having "arrived" is reflected by a widely discussed sermon delivered from one of the most prestigious Protestant pulpits in New York City on Sunday, August 18, 1947. The Reverend Theodore Cuyler Speers, of the Central Presbyterian Church at Park Avenue and Sixty-fourth Street, told his parishioners that "the pressure we feel from the aggressive action of the Roman Catholic Church" must not disarm Protestants, but cause them to "rethink and rediscover our historic faith."[18]

Perhaps the best illustration of the new Catholic style which prompted these expressions of concern came with the NCWC bishops' statement of November 1947. Its subject was the threat of "secularism" to the American way of life:

> The vague consciousness of God which they [many Americans] may retain is impotent as a motive in daily conduct. The moral re-generation which is recognized as absolutely necessary for the building of a better world must begin by bringing the individual back to God and to an awareness of his responsibility to God. This secularism, of its very nature, cannot do.[19]

And the meaning of this is clarified somewhat a few paragraphs later in this reference to birth control practices:

> A secularized pseudo-science has popularized practices which violate nature itself and rob human procreation of its dignity and nobility. Thus, selfish pursuit of pleasure is substituted for the salutary self discipline of family life.[20]

Of course, the "Catholic threat" was not perceived wholly in terms of mood and idiom.[21] There were three specific issue areas in which the concern was focused: American representation at the Vatican; Catholic anti-communism; and public support for parochial schools.

American Representation at the Vatican

On December 23, 1939, President Roosevelt named Myron Taylor, an Episcopalian layman and past chairman of the Board of the United States Steel Corporation, as his personal representative to Pope Pius XII. The appointment was roundly criticized in Protestant circles, but graver events of the spring of 1940 quickly overshadowed the "Taylor Mission." During the war it was difficult to argue against what was billed as a valuable "listening post."

With the coming of peace, however, Mr. Taylor was not recalled. Many Protestants began to fear that a permanent United States tie to the Vatican had been created *sub rosa.* Protestant restiveness was evidenced in late 1945 and early 1946, and the long simmering dispute again came to a boil in June 1946 when a delegation headed by Bishop Oxnam, then President of the Federal Council of Churches, called on President Truman to request clarification of Taylor's role, and register objection to his continuance in Rome.[22]

At the Biltmore Hotel in New York City, on June 11, 1946, Oxnam reported to his followers on the interview with the President. He suggested that Truman understood the Protestant point of view, regarded the mission to the Holy See as "temporary," and felt himself that it might be a violation of the separation of church and state.[23] The reaction of the Roman Catholic Archdiocese of New York to this announcement was swift. Cardinal Spellman, "fighting bigotry, untruth and distortions," suggested that only "the absence of goodwill can misrepresent Mr. Taylor's presence at the Vatican or charge our last two Presidents with violating the letter and spirit of the American Constitution by keeping him there."[24] Oxnam snapped back that "Cardinal Spellman knows the Roman Catholic Church does not believe in the separation of church and state,"[25] and the rhetorical battle was on. For months the "Letters" column of the *Times* bristled with the offerings of outraged clerics.[26]

The dispute simmered and boiled for four years through President Truman's nomination of General Mark Clark as Ambassador to the Vatican to replace Taylor (1950), the failure of the Senate (under heavy Protestant pressure) to consent (1951), and Truman's eventual decision to let the matter lie and not resubmit the nomination.[27] Throughout this time it was a serious source of tension which spilled over into other areas of Protestant-Catholic relations and lent force to arguments which were being made increasingly in courts over the meaning of the establishment clause.

Catholic Anti-Communism

Just as the anti-Catholicism of the late 1940's was non-nativist, so also it was diverse. It involved all sorts of Protestants, Jews, and secularists—those politically and doctrinally conservative, and those of extremely liberal persuasions. On the "Catholic threat" they could make common cause. Liberal, conservative, and fundamentalist leaders were all involved, for instance, in the founding of Americans United. An aspect of Catholic behavior which particularly stirred liberal Protestants was the hard line anti-communism which we have noted as appearing in the 1946 statement from the bishop of the NCWC.

In World War II, while the Soviet Union was America's ally and bearing the brunt of the German onslaughts on the

Eastern Front, anti-communism had rather gone out of fashion. With the coming of peace there were great expectations, especially within liberal Protestantism, of a new world order founded on great power cooperation as institutionalized in the Security Council of the United Nations. During 1946 and 1947, however, as the four-power accords governing Berlin broke down, and as the take-over in Eastern Europe progressed, many Americans were forced to a painful reappraisal of the Soviet Union and of Marxist-Leninism as a political persuasion. But on the part of the Catholic hierarchy there had never been any "softening," and in 1946 Catholic spokesmen could lay claim to having been right all along; with each piece of bad news from Moscow or Lake Success, they could say "we told you so," and this is never endearing.[28]

On April 26, 1947, Louis F. Budenz, a former editor of the *Daily Worker* and a convert to Roman Catholicism, shared a platform with Cardinal Spellman at the Astor Hotel in New York. Budenz declared that "the Catholic Church was the only agency able to challenge the slave state of Marxist-Leninist theory," and that "the deliverance of the United States will be marked by the day it demands the expulsion of the hypocritical (Russian) regime from the United Nations."[29] A few months later the Reverend Guy Emery Shipler, a liberal Episcopalian and editor of *The Churchman,* led a tour of Protestant clerics through Yugoslavia. On its return the group issued a statement supporting the actions taken by Tito against Archbishop Aloysius Stepinac, who was accused of collaboration with the former Nazi regime in Croatia. On August 19, Archbishop Richard J. Cushing, speaking before the 65th International Convention of the Knights of Columbus, in Boston, declared that "poison" was being spread in America "not by wily political agents, but by men who, may God forgive them, are introduced as Reverend and who ask to be heard as representatives of Christ."[30] As Oxnam put it at the time, "it would appear that the Roman Catholic Church has declared war on Russia by announcing a world wide war on Communism."[31] Both he and Shipler later turned up among the founders of Americans United.

Aid to Parochial Schools

The third, and by far the most troublesome issue which served to focus anti-Catholicism during this period was that of public aid to Catholic schools. As in previous instances in which this question had "heated up," Catholics initiated the action by a push for funding. In 1945 Monsignor Frederick G. Hochwalt, director of the education department of the NCWC, announced a change in the hierarchy's position on federal aid to education. Previously opposed to federal aid on the grounds that it would bring federal control, the organization of bishops would now accept federal aid programs *if* provisions were made for the participation of church-related schools.[32] And in other respects the line taken by the Administrative Board of the NCWC represented a new approach. Pointing to the absences of religious teaching in the public schools (for which Catholics had fought in the nineteenth century), it was argued that parents who did not wish their children to attend such "Godless" institutions should certainly be supported with public funds when they established their own schools in which, in accordance with the American tradition, religion was taught. Thus the bishops in November of 1947:

> Secularists have been quick to exploit for their own purposes the public policy adopted a century ago of banning the formal teaching of religion from the curriculum of our common schools. With a growing number of thoughtful Americans, we see in this policy a hasty and short-sighted solution . . . secularism breaks with our historical American tradition.
>
> When parents build and maintain schools in which their children are trained in the religion of their fathers, they are acting in the full spirit of that tradition.[33]

Such criticism of the common school was most alarming to wide sectors of the Protestant community, and especially to Protestant educators. The public school brought the children of a neighborhood together around a secular curriculum and presumed that worship and religious instruction could be accomplished privately according to the lights of the parents. To remedy the alleged Godlessness it would be necessary for the state to become involved in the subsidizing of religious exercises. Religious privatism would be replaced by state sponsorship of religious activity, and the argument against public financing of parochial schools would be weakened. Here Jewish and many purely secular organizations joined with Protestants.

Three events, coming close together in late 1946 and early 1947, brought the controversy to a high emotional pitch. The first of these was a seemingly innocuous speech delivered on November 22, 1946, by Dr. James Bryant Conant, President of Harvard University, on the subject of education and democracy. The second, on January 31, 1947, was the introduction in the Senate by Robert A. Taft (R., Ohio) of a bill which would have provided federal grants to the states to aid public education only.[34] The third was the decision by the United States Supreme Court, on February 10, 1947, in *Everson.*

There was nothing more remarkable about Dr. Conant's speech than the firm insistence that federal money should go only to public schools, and that the public schools constituted a "unique structure" of prime importance to "the free society we Americans have evolved."[35] Yet it drew heavy Catholic fire and seems to have had the effect of a pebble dropped into a brook. At the 1947 annual convention of the Association of School Administrators, Dr. John L. Childs, of Teachers College, Columbia University, seconded the Conant argument, and remarked of the recently introduced Taft Bill that:

> There are many now convinced that we shall never get a Federal aid bill passed unless it provides that the funds appropriated by the Government be made available to these private, religious schools, as well as to the public schools . . . I know that many devout Catholics are profoundly disturbed about this present tendency. I also know that many of them . . . would be happy were their church to put its strength behind the public movement. They fear, as do many others, that if these sectarian pres-

sures continue, serious religious cleavages may come to divide and embitter the American people.[36]

During the course of the spring, other educational leaders also followed Conant's lead and spoke out on the issue of federal aid and the importance of the public schools. On April 9, a counter-attack was launched. Speaking before the convention of the National Catholic Educational Association, Archbishop Cushing declared that:

> Whether it be in questions of school buses or emergency school subsidies or any other democratic aids to education, no phony plea of conflict between church and state, or any like smoke screen for secularism or bigotry, must be allowed to obscure the sovereign right of the parent to choose the teacher of his children . . . totalitarianism is a disease, the tendency toward which is present in some degree or other in all purely secular states.[37]

And in another address before the same gathering, the Reverend William McManus, second-in-command of the educational department of the National Catholic Welfare Conference, attacked Dr. Conant directly. Referring to testimony given by Conant at a hearing on the Taft Bill, McManus noted that the bill provided for aid only to public schools. Conant was scored for agreeing with this approach, which Father McManus labeled "discrimination against private education."[38]

With a night's rest, McManus was on the platform again, and on April 10, before another session of the convention, he pointed to the National Education Association (NEA) as being the villain of the piece:

> The N.E.A. wants all the funds [for the public schools] or nothing . . . beware of the anti-social and anti-democratic policies expressed by the leadership of the N.E.A. . . . Catholic schools ask for a reasonable and limited amount of public funds, just enough tax funds to make the Catholic school an integral part of American education, just enough money for our schools to disabuse the public school professional groups of any anti-democratic notions they have a monopoly on American education.[39]

This, of course, was just what many Protestants feared most—the token aid which would be "just enough" to establish a precedent.

Against this background *Everson* was decided, and the contemporary constitutional conflict concerning the meaning of the establishment clause was begun.

JUSTICE BLACK AND THE BUS

The facts of the case were quite simple. A 1941 New Jersey statute authorized school districts to subsidized the transportation of pupils to school and the districts were left to decide for themselves whether they wished to underwrite the cost of transportation of children to church-related schools. The board of education of Ewing resolved that it would reimburse parents for the money "expended by them for bus transportation of their children" to any school "on regular buses operated by the public transportation system."[40] A Ewing taxpayer sued in a state court (a proceeding countenanced by New Jersey law), contending that both the statute and the school board resolution constituted laws "respecting an establishment of religion," contrary to the First Amendment made applicable to the states by the Fourteenth Amendment, per *Cantwell.* The trial court sustained the objection on state constitutional grounds, but the New Jersey Court of Errors reversed, and the case came to the Supreme Court on the federal constitutional question. When the Justices accepted jurisdiction the establishment clause was at last squarely before them.

Everson brought out a bumper crop of briefs. The appellant, Arch Everson, was represented by Edward R. Burke, and there were three *amicus curiae* briefs. Ancient American nativism appeared in the form of the durable Order of United American Mechanics, and the American Civil Liberties Union offering bore the prestigious legal names of Henry V. Osborne, Whitney North Seymour, and Kenneth W. Greenawalt—the latter continues on the Union's Church-State Committee as of this writing, and had been involved with a number of important establishment cases over the years. The General Conference of Seventh Day Adventists' submission was written by E. Hilton Jackson, of the Religious Liberty Association and later of Americans United. Mr. Jackson was also allocated part of appellant's time for oral argument.

The Ewing board was represented by William Speer, of the state Attorney General's office, but Mr. Speer had some big-league help. With him on the appellee's brief was Porter R. Chandler, partner in the famous Wall Street firm of Davis, Polk, whose appearance backing up a small town New Jersey board of education in defense of an obscure state statute would have been curious indeed except for the special relationship of Mr. Chandler to the Chancery of the Roman Catholic Archdiocese of New York. For twenty-five years, in cases involving establishment questions in which Cardinal Spellman had an interest, Mr. Chandler would turn up, with the impressive resources of Davis, Polk, to assist whomever was arguing the accommodationist position. In addition, six states, through their attorneys general, filed briefs supporting New Jersey and Ewing.[41] These states had bus transportation arrangements of their own to protect. Finally, there was an *amicus* brief from the National Council of Catholic Men, endorsed by a number of other Catholic lay organizations.

Mr. Justice Black delivered the opinion of a Court divided 5–4. He began with a lengthy consideration of the background and meaning of the no-establishment clause, and concluded that the clause

> means at least this; neither a state nor the federal government can set up a church. Neither can pass laws which aid one religion, aid all religions or prefer one religion over another. . . . no tax in any amount, large or small, can be levied to support any religious activities of institutions, whatever they may be called, or whatever form they may adopt to teach and practice religion . . . in the words of Jefferson, the clause against the establishment of religion by law was intended to erect "a wall of separation between church and state."[42]

After so broad an interpretation of the prohibition of the First Amendment many observers who sat in the courtroom on that Monday afternoon of February 10, and listened to Black read the first portion of his opinion, felt that the New Jersey statute would be disallowed. Such was not the case. Black, while standing four-square against aid to religion, decided that money for bus transportation did not in fact constitute an aid to religious schools. The subsidy was seen as a legitimate public safety measure, undertaken by the local government under its police power, to keep children off dangerous streets.

Mr. Justice Jackson, who dissented, likened Black to Byron's Julia, who "whispering I will ne'er consent, consented."[43] Jackson saw the parochial school as an integral part of the Catholic Church in America. Anything which helped the school had the obvious effect of helping the establishment of religion, and nothing could help the school more than bringing children to it. Though Justice Black had said that the New Jersey statute went just to "the verge" of the permissible, Jackson saw it as a dangerous precedent.

Mr. Justice Rutledge opened his dissent by asserting that Madison would never have joined in Black's opinion, and pursued this theme through thirty-four pages of dissent, with the *Memorial and Remonstrance* reproduced as an appendix.[44] Justice Frankfurter agreed with both the Jackson and Rutledge productions, and Justices Jackson and Burton also associated themselves with Rutledge's opinion.

The decision pleased no one. Protestant leaders saw it as ominous that the Court was willing to allow any public money in aid of what they considered a private religious purpose, and Catholic spokesmen, while happy that the constitutionality of state aid for parochial school transportation had been established, saw in the early part of Black's opinion and in the dissents what they regarded as a very extreme reading of the establishment clause.

Cardinal Spellman noted the Protestant grumbling and defended the decision itself, while taking exception to the Court's reasoning. Speaking at the Fordham University Commencement, the Cardinal decried "bigotry" which was once again "eating its way into the vital organs of the greatest nation on the face of the earth."

> The Supreme Court has settled the question which never should have been raised. To me, an American citizen, it is embarrassing that this issue was raised in our nation which prides itself before the whole world as an example of fair play and tolerance.[45]

Singled out for special criticism by the Cardinal was the *Christian Century* and its editor, Charles Clayton Morrison, who within a year was to write the manifesto stating the objectives of the new formed Americans United (AU).

On June 14 the *Times* carried a response signed by the Reverend Stanley Stuber, Director of Public Relations of the Northern Baptist Convention, Clyde R. Miller, Associate Professor of Education, Teachers College, Columbia University, and the Reverend Guy Emery Shipler, (all future founders of AU).

> The point is that Protestant groups are alarmed as were four Justices of the Supreme Court. Would Cardinal Spellman characterize these dissenting Justices as "bigots?"[46]

And the excitement generated by *Everson* flowed directly into the second round of the federal aid to education fight. Taft's Bill had died with the 80th Congress. In the new, Democratic 81st Congress, which met in January of 1949, the effort to secure federal aid was led, for the Truman Administration, by Representative Graham Barden, Chairman of the House Education and Labor Committee. The "Barden Bill" provided federal aid only for public elementary and secondary schools.

Catholic spokesmen were quick to suggest that the recent decision in *Everson* made parochial schools eligible for at least some sorts of federal aid, and that their exclusion under the Barden formula was unwarranted. Separation spokesmen just as quickly pointed out that only transportation had been approved in *Everson,* and that the five-man majority in that case had seemed quite clear that nothing beyond transportation was allowable. On June 23, Mrs. Eleanor Roosevelt, in her syndicated column, "My Day," took the separationist line on federal aid, and followed this up with an even stronger piece on July 8. In an utterly graceless response, Cardinal Spellman denounced these columns as "unworthy of an American mother."[47] The public reaction was withering, and the Cardinal hastened to soften his his position, even making a trip to Hyde Park in penance. Barden's Bill was caught in the legislative logjam which trapped most of Truman's Fair Deal initiatives, and the controversy wound down as the country went first into a war and then into a decade of Eisenhower Republicanism. Since there was little prospect of new funding for education, federal or otherwise, there was nothing to fight about. But issues of aid to church-related schools lay through the 1950's like a log submerged below the surface of American politics. It took only the innovative efforts of John F. Kennedy to bring it to the top once more. When the Kennedy "Task Force on Education" submitted its report to the new President in the spring of 1961, excluding church-related schools from its recommended package of federal aid, Americans United was there to applaud and Cardinal Spellman bitterly to condemn.

This is not the place to detail the struggle over federal aid to education in the three years of the Kennedy Administration,[48] or the eventual passage under Lyndon Johnson of the Elementary and Secondary Education Act of 1965 (ESEA).[49] Suffice it that Title I of this statute provided for certain programs of compensatory education to be federally financed in poor school districts; that Title II provided for the enrichment of school libraries; and that Congress allowed for the participation of non-profit, private schools, church-related or not, in some of these programs. This initiative made it inevitable that the Supreme Court would be forced to provide further gloss on the establishment clause.

The years between 1947 and 1968 had seen a number of efforts by separationist interest groups to secure Supreme Court consideration of cases involving supposedly unconstitutional public support of religious schools and other institutions. Americans United, for example, challenged (1) federal grants for construction of hospitals affiliated with religious groups made under the

Hill-Burton Act of 1946 (one case involved the same Providence Hospital which had been involved in *Bradfield*), (2) grants by Vermont school districts without high schools to pay the tuition of their students at neighboring Catholic high schools, and (3) numerous instances in which financially straited small towns had taken the easy way out and simply chipped in to a parochial school and called it a public school.[50] The "captive school" cases were all won, the Vermont tuition case was won, the hospital cases were lost, and the Supreme Court agreed to review none of them. In the mid-1960's the Horace Mann League, with the backing of a number of separationist groups including Americans United and the American Jewish Congress, challenged grants by the State of Maryland to colleges within that state which were affiliated with religious denominations. The Maryland Supreme Court disallowed the grants to all but one of the institutions involved on federal constitutional grounds, but still the Supreme Court did not choose to intervene.[51] Up to the spring of 1968 the Court managed not to return to the question of what payments of public money violated the establishment clause.

THE PROBLEM OF STANDING TO SUE

One reason for this lapse in Supreme Court consideration of a problem which was certainly agitating the society was the difficulty separationist groups encountered in getting into courts to test church-state accommodations which they felt violative of the First Amendment.

In 1923 the Justices had decided *Frothingham* v. *Mellon*.[52] The case was far removed from the area of church and state, involving the federal Maternity Act of 1921, which provided grants to the states to reduce maternal and infant mortality. Mrs. Frothingham, a federal taxpayer, objected to this use of federal monies as unconstitutional (for archaic reasons which need not concern us). With an opinion by Justice Sutherland, the Court announced that a federal taxpayer, as such, did not possess a sufficiently substantial personal interest in the national treasury to have standing to sue to enjoin the disbursement of funds. Thus no matter how good one's constitutional case against a particular federal expenditure, one could not proceed against it unless it affected one adversely and in some more individual aspect than the broadly shared status as taxpayer. Until this barrier could be broken it was obvious to separationists that there was simply no way to challenge certain sorts of federal programs which they regarded as offensive.

Most states and municipalities, of course, did allow taxpayer suits, and where a federal question was decided by a state court in the course of such a challenge the Supreme Court could review —that, after all, was how *Everson* had come before the Court.[53] But it was a very chancy business;[54] even when separationist groups got clear federal constitutional rulings from state high courts the Justices in Washington could practice the "passive virtues,"[55] and simply not take the case—as happened with the Vermont tuition grants and the Maryland college grants. If a challenge could be mounted against an important federal program it would be much more difficult for the Court to sidestep. The separationists wanted further authoritative gloss on the establishment clause, and it was difficult, expensive, and in the final analysis futile to try to tease it out of state courts. Either a really dramatic state case had to be gotten up, one which the Supreme Court could be tempted into taking, or the *Frothingham* ban on federal taxpayer suits had to be overcome.[56] Separationist groups labored on both fronts and, as luck and the politics of the Court would have it, breakthroughs came, both in the same year—1968.

FLAST v. *COHEN*

This case was brought by a coalition of separationist groups in New York City challenging the constitutionality on Titles I and II of ESEA, and on their implementation in the city where Catholic parochial schools were participating in programs under both titles. The chief strategist was the experienced separationist lawyer Leo Pfeffer, by 1965 a professor at Long Island University, but for years a lawyer on the staff of the American Jewish Congress,[57] and veteran of many establishment and free-exercise campaigns. In order to get the constitutionality of Titles I and II before the Federal District Court for the Second District of New York, however, it was necessary to overcome *Frothingham,* and it was the question of standing, therefore, that most concerned Pfeffer. His original complaint did argue the merits of the case, but Pfeffer realized that if he were successful at all the case would go up to the Supreme Court the first time on the standing question, and if his taxpayer clients (members of the groups associated in supporting the case) were granted standing by the Justices, the matter would have to go back to the district court for decision on its merits. Of immediate interest was the standing question, not the constitutionality of ESEA.

Pfeffer first asked, and was granted, a special three-judge district court (a procedure reserved for suits challenging statutes on grounds that they are *prima facie* unconstitutional). He then asked that the *Frothingham* rule be overturned, or at least that an exception to it be recognized for taxpayers seeking to raise establishment objections to federal spending programs. After all, Pfeffer pointed out, Congress had passed a bold new Education Act, which over the years might involve the expenditure of billions of dollars; a number of American citizens thought parts of this law unconstitutional, but unless *Frothingham* were relaxed, their questions would go unanswered. Such an incapacity to revolve questions of basic law was incompatible with the theory of a written constitution and with American assumptions concerning the role of the courts. Only one of the three judges found this argument persuasive, but this one, Marvin Frankel, a prestigious former professor at the Columbia Law School, wrote a powerful opinion.[58] Pfeffer appealed directly to the Supreme Court (a procedure allowed after the decision of a three-judge court). The Justices took this one, and the decision came down on June 10, 1968, with Chief Justices Earl Warren writing for the Court.[59]

Warren first noted an ambiguity in Sutherland's *Frothingham* opinion which, over the years, had been the subject of much comment and speculation among commentators. Article 3 of the Constitution authorizes the Supreme Court to hear "Cases" and "Controversies," and the Court has, on that ground, refused to entertain "friendly" suits[60] or to render advisory opinions. It is a fixed principle of American constitutional law that the Justices decide only actual matters of contest, among parties who are actually injured or injuring. It is also part of American judicial practice (but not constitutional law) that the Supreme Court exercises a supervisory power over the entire federal court system. This includes setting rules of procedure. Now it was unclear whether Justice Sutherland had said that a taxpayer did not have standing because that individual was not hurt at all—in which case *Frothingham* enunciated a constitutional rule—or whether Sutherland had said that, as a matter of administrative tidiness a case where the hurt was small should not take up federal judicial time. While this may seem a nice distinction, as a matter of judicial politics it was crucial. If *Frothingham* had announced a constitutional rule, its reversal was certainly possible, but it was, in theory at least, a serious matter which the Justices would have to rationalize carefully. A constitutional amendment might even be thought in order. But if *Frothingham* had announced a rule of administrative convenience, changing it was a casual matter. Concluding at length that the constitutional and non-constitutional aspects of Sutherland's opinion could not be disentangled, Warren held that the question of taxpayer standing needed to be reexamined from scratch. Thus, ponderously but surely, the Chief Justice disposed of *Frothingham* as a precedent.

Turning to the advisability of taxpayer suits, Warren first suggested that many of the practical difficulties which, in 1923, had been seen to attend federal taxpayer suits, were no longer to be feared. For instance, class actions (in which one plaintiff sues for all similarly situated) were now possible under the Federal Rules of Civil Procedure, and would partially obviate the danger of the federal courts being swamped with individual challenges to federal statutes. Furthermore, the Supreme Court, and indeed all federal judges, had learned from a decade of civil rights battles how to deal with dilatory relitigation of a point once authoritatively settled by the Supreme Court.

Second, and even more important, Warren made clear he was approving only one sort of taxpayer action: (1) where the challenge was to a spending and not a regulatory program,[61] and (2) where the challenge was on grounds that a specific constitutional limitation on the spending power had been violated rather than that the federal government was simply without power under the Constitution to do what the statute purported to do. *Frothingham* was not over-ruled, because the attack there had been on grounds of lack of congressional power to act and no transgression of a specific constitutional prohibition had been alleged. Both spending and a specific prohibition (Congress shall make no law respecting an establishment of religion) were present in the *Flast* challenge, and to accept it would prevent a yawning gap developing in constitutional law, without making every taxpayer a private attorney general able to attack every action of the federal government.[62]

Four Justices simply associated themselves with Warren's opinion, and three concurred in the result with separate opinions. Of these latter, Mr. Justice Douglas would have done away with *Frothingham* completely, and allowed taxpayers to challenge everything—the more checks on the federal government being, for him, the better. Justices Stewart and Fortas, on the other hand, wished a narrower ruling allowing taxpayer suits only when the challenge was on establishment grounds. The history of the establishment clause, they suggested, made clear its special character. It was a protector of taxpayers specifically, guaranteeing their right not to have their forced contributions spent in aid of religious purposes of which they disapproved. As establishment is the problem area, Stewart and Fortas maintained, let us take care of it specifically, and not admit any wider exception to *Frothingham* than absolutely necessary.

Justice Harlan dissented, arguing that *Frothingham* should remain undisturbed and that the interest of the taxpayers was so small that to talk of a "right" not to have "their" contributions used in a certain way was simple nonsense. Furthermore, Harlan concluded, too much had been made of the difficulty of getting establishment questions answered. These questions could as well be put in state as in federal cases, and most states allowed taxpayer suits. By way of illustration, Harlan pointed to the case of *Board* v. *Allen* which was being announced that same day.[63] And indeed *Allen* was worthy of note. For while *Flast* overcame *Frothingham* (at least for establishment clause purposes) its bright promise for separationists was dimmed by what the Justices proceeded to do in *Allen*.

ALLEN

At the same time that Leo Pfeffer and the coalition of separationist groups were working up the *Flast* case in New York City, an even more important judicial battle was developing a hundred miles up the Hudson in a quiet suburb of Albany.

In 1965, the New York Legislature passed, and Governor Nelson Rockefeller eagerly signed, a bill requiring local school districts to furnish textbooks, from the state-approved lists, to non-profit private schools within their jurisdictions. Technically the school districts retained title to the books, which were on loan to the private school students. In fact, the books would remain in the repositories of the private schools until written off for wear and tear, and would never be under the physical control of the public authority. This was an arrangement separationists could not let pass. Many felt the "violation" by New York to be more serious than the federal "violation" under ESEA, and the Governor had made it painfully clear to them that if the textbook scheme got past the courts he would press on to further accommodationist arrangements with private schools. In addition, the New York plan appeared to offer an excellent chance of getting another establishment question before the Supreme Court. Here, after all, was a very visible spending program in a major state, not an obscure program in Vermont or Maryland. It could not easily be ducked by the Justices. There was, however, one serious difficulty—unlike most other States, but like the federal courts, New York does not allow taxpayer suits challenging state expenditures. The Supreme Court might bite if the New York courts took the case, but how to get New York to do so?

The New York Civil Liberties Union (NYCLU) took the lead in attempting to secure a challenge to the textbook program. The NYCLU director, Aryeh Neier, came up with an idea for overcoming the state standing problem and it worked. Neier persuaded a local board of education, in the town of East Greenbush, to sue the state Commissioner of Education, at that time Dr. James E. Allen, to enjoin him from requiring it (the Board) to spend funds in what a majority of its members regarded as an unconstitutional fashion. Standing was not based on taxpayer status, but upon the relation of one governmental unit to another. Later, other school boards joined East Greenbush, and some interesting support developed for Commissioner Allen and the textboook program. Six parents, with children in East Greenbush parochial schools, intervened in the case on the grounds that they had a financial stake in the outcome—whether or not the textbooks would continue to be purchased. The counsel for the Catholic intervenors, as with *Everson* twenty years before, was Porter R. Chandler of Davis, Polk.

The challenge to the textbook program was, of course, two-pronged: it was alleged that the arrangement violated the establishment clause of the federal Constitution and the "Blaine Amendment" of the New York Constitution. The trial court (called the Supreme Court in New York) agreed with the plaintiffs on both grounds, but the Appellate Division (the intermediate appellate court) reversed.[64] In the spring of 1967 the Court of Appeals (the state's highest) announced its decision sustaining the Appellate Division. By a vote of 4–3 the Judges of New York held that the textbook plan violated neither the establishment clause, nor the more pointed language of New York's Constitution (Article II, sec. 3).[65] In the fall, the Supreme Court docketed the case for argument on the federal establishment clause point.

Associate Justice Byron White wrote for the Court when *Allen* came down in the spring of 1968. In approving the New York practice he relied heavily on a proposed interpretation of the establishment clause which had gained great favor among accommodationists in the years between 1947 and 1968—the so-called "individual benefit theory." Purporting to be based on Black's *Everson* opinion, this argument held that if the primary beneficiaries of a governmental program were individuals (such as school children) rather than religious institutions (such as parochial schools) no violation of the First Amendment had taken place. Some versions of the theory stressed legislative intent (did the designers of the challenged program mean to help individuals or to help institutions?), and some versions stressed the practical effect of the program (were institutions, in fact, being aided substantially?). This "individual benefit theory" had been given a further boost in 1963 by Mr. Justice Clark in the case of *Abingdon School District* v. *Schempp*.[66] This case had to do with a religious exercise rather than governmental aid to a religious institution, and we shall examine it in Chapter V. Suffice it here that while disallowing the particular religious exercise in question, Clark had attempted to sum up the Court's previous establishment decisions in a single rule. His wording bore considerable resemblance to the "individual benefit" language.

Clark had spoken of the "purpose and primary effect" of governmental action as determinative of establishment clause violation, and in *Allen* Justice White seized eagerly on this phrase. Whether, in 1963, this Clark "test" constituted any advance beyond or alteration of what Justice Black and the majority of the Court had been saying in establishment cases (both religious practice and institutional aid cases) before 1963 is doubtful. I shall presently argue that in the context of its announcement in *Schempp* it was not. But the use White made of Clark's words in 1968 did seem, in 1968, to indicate a change in the collective posture of the Court on the problem of aid to religious institutions. All White asked of a governmental aid program for it to pass establishment clause muster was that there be a valid public purpose, and that there be no "primary" effect of advancing or inhibiting religion. A "primary" effect appeared to White as one prior in time to all other effects—not an important effect, or even a major effect, but simply the *first* effect. The first effect of the New York law was to give children books. Children were not churches, and in any case, White concluded, the record in *Allen* did not disclose any particular instances in which churches were assisted by the program. Taken in this fashion, Clark's language certainly could be used to open the way to approving public support for religious institutions which would have seemed certainly excluded before White wrote. If school buses had been the "verge" of the older approach, the Court appeared now to have plunged into the void.

Five other members of the Court, including the Chief Justice, associated themselves with White's remarkable if somewhat laconic opinion. Mr. Justice Harlan concurred with three paragraphs which would have allowed governmental aid to individuals or to institutions if there was a public purpose and no potential divisiveness or denial of anyone's free exercise of religion involved. Mr. Justice Black, whose *Everson* opinion was supposedly being adhered to, thought it was not, and that the New York arrangement represented precisely the sort of development he had been seeking to foreclose in 1947. Justice Douglas agreed with Black in a lengthy dissent which argued the centrality of books in education, and the essentially sectarian nature of the parochial school enterprise.[67]

Clearly Justice Black was right; the decision in *Allen* represented a step beyond *Everson* toward more accommodation between church and state. And yet there was an opacity about White's opinion which would allow for a quick, unembarrassing turn back in a separationist direction. White did not indicate how far he was prepared to go with his versions of the "individual benefit" and "purpose and effect" approaches. The answer was not long in coming, but before turning to the most recent cases, a mention must be made of the problem of tax exemptions of church property.

TAX EXEMPTIONS

Having examined some of the problems raised by governmental aid to church-related institutions, it remains to note the perplexing fact that no one has yet convincingly distinguished for constitutional purposes a governmental subsidy from a tax exemption.[68] And while we have seen a fascinating and hotly contested constitutional battle develop over the sorts of governmental subsidies allowable under the establishment clause, extensive tax exemptions for church and church-related institutions have been allowed throughout our history, and have gone virtually unchallenged until recent years. On reflection it seems passing strange that American opinion should assume, at one and the same time, that government may not contribute to the maintenance of religious institutions and that exemption of such institutions from the normal taxes paid by individuals, businesses, and so on, is perfectly permissible.[69] This is, in the words of one commentator, "one of the most pervasive and firmly established anomalies in American law."[70]

Religious institutions enjoy numerous tax breaks at all levels of government. All states, either by constitution, statute, or custom exempt actual church buildings from real property taxes. A few exempt all property owned by churches—even that employed for commercial purposes. Thus a church leasing a parcel of land to be operated as a golf driving range might, in some jurisdictions, bank the rent and pay no property tax.[71] In addition, contributions made by individuals to religious institutions are deductible for federal income tax purposes, and religious institutions often pay no tax on income earned through commercial enterprises (such as breadmaking and the rental of apartments). While many non-religious charitable and educational institutions enjoy certain similar advantages, none is treated quite so well as the churches. Of all non-profit corporations, for instance, the religious are the only sort exempt from filing with the Internal Revenue Service Form 990 indicating income received.

In the late 1960's, as combat over the meaning of the establishment clause increased and as *Flast* and *Allen* worked their way toward the Supreme Court, there was a quickening of interest in tax exemptions for churches and especially property tax exemptions. With so many municipalities straining their shrunken tax bases, a number of prestigious commentators, lay and clerical, political and legal, began to suggest that the property tax exemption, at least, should be reexamined.[72] While it would be possible, of course, to repeal or reduce religious tax exemptions by legislative action or by amending state constitutions, this procedure is unattractive to elective politicians. The better axis of attack for the opponents of exemption seems to run through the courts, and this they have followed.

In 1962 the Supreme Court sidestepped a tax exemption case coming on appeal from Rhode Island. In 1965, Mrs. Madalyn Murray, a militant free thinker and litigant of First Amendment questions, challenged the practice of the City of Baltimore in exempting church property from real property taxation on grounds that the practice violated the federal establishment clause and a parallel provision of the Maryland constitution. Her's was a taxpayer action, allowed by Maryland law, but when the Supreme Court of Maryland ruled against Mrs. Murray's claim the United States Supreme Court refused a petition for certiorari (a request that the Court exercise its discretionary power to hear a case). There, for several years, the matter rested.[73]

But in the wake of *Allen,* a tax exemption case was finally docketed for argument before the Supreme Court. It was a case springing from most unlikely beginnings. On May 20, 1967, one Frederick Walz purchased a small parcel of land in New York City for $25. The property was assessed by the City at $100, and Walz was taxed at $5.24 per year. In June of 1967 Walz brought suit in a New York court arguing that the exemption of church-owned property in the City had the effect of raising his taxes and forcing him to contribute to an establishment of religion.[74] The lower courts and the New York Court of Appeals made short work of this contention,[75] and with this shabby past, *Walz* v. *Tax Commission*[76] arrived in Washington.

The decision sustaining the New York courts was announced on May 4, 1970 with an opinion of the Court from the new Chief Justice Warren Burger. In a somewhat apologetic tone, Burger explained that while property tax exemption undoubtedly carried indirect economic benefits for religious institutions, and thus "involved" government with religion, the governmental "involvement" in the life of the churches would be far greater if the church properties were valued and taxed. (How, for instance, would the assessor "value" a stained glass window? What was the relevant market?) Presumably, although Burger did not say so, the same argument would also hold for federal taxation of church incomes as well as local exemption from real property taxes. To require disclosure and payment would require undesirable governmental intrusion, an "entanglement" toward which the establishment clause was implacably hostile. Of the two involvements—taxing or benefiting by exempting—the latter, for Burger, was by far the lesser constitutional and practical evil.

Justice Brennan, concurring, took a somewhat different tack. He began by pointing out that tax exemptions had been accorded churches for a long time in America, and while this ancient acceptance was not altogether sufficient to establish constitutionality, it certainly created a presumption in favor of the challenged practice. In addition, Brennan suggested, tax exemption for religious institutions in no way represented governmental favoring of church over secular societies. Tax exemptions are routinely granted by governments to all manner of voluntary associations which are supposed by legislatures to serve beneficent purposes. If government could constitutionally refrain from taxing the American Cancer Society or the Temperance Union, why not churches?[77] Churches contribute to the pluralism of American society, and their social service functions are legendary. What more, Brennan asked, was needed by way of justification?

In a final concurrence, Justice Harlan found that the particular tax exemption afforded by New York City and challenged in *Walz* neither encouraged nor discouraged participation in religious life. But Harlan left open the possibility that some sorts of exemptions might involve government so deeply with religious institutions as to contravene the establishment clause. Justice Douglas was the lone dissenter. The author of the famous "religious people" dictum began by assuming the establishment to command at least equality of treatment by government of religion and irreligion. Douglas went on to confess that his examination of New York practice revealed no provision for tax exemption of property used for atheistic or anti-religious purposes.

The militant believer and the militant unbeliever are not on equal footing as far as real property taxation goes in New York City. In short, the exemption suffered from the fatal fault of underinclusion. If government was to speak at all, it must speak to atheist, agnostic, and believer alike.

In the spring of 1970 it was difficult to assess the importance of *Walz* for the development of the establishment clause. The easy conclusion, to which a few jumped,[78] was that *Walz* moved the Court further away from *Everson* in the direction indicated by *Allen*—that it was an harbinger of still more accommodationist decisions to come in the Burger era. Yet this was far from obvious from the Chief's opinion. On reflection, it is hard to see how tax exemptions for churches could have lost. In their supportive effect they might be indistinguishable from grants, but psychologically and politically there was a great deal of difference. Very few prestigious scholars or interest groups were urging the Justices to find against tax exemptions. Furthermore, tax exemption was an ongoing, low-visibility governmental practice, lacking the divisive potential of new grant programs which must be visibly and controversially legislated, funded, and administered. What was obscure at the time was that Chief Justice Burger's opinion in *Walz,* while sustaining exemptions, laid the foundation for a new rationale for invalidating grants to religious institutions.

This disposition of the Burger Court on establishment problems became clear only in two critically important cases decided in the spring of 1971. The first involved federal aid to higher education; the second involved a so-called "purchase of service" arrangement in the State of Pennsylvania.

AID TO HIGHER EDUCATION—TILTON

Little attention has been paid, thus far, to the establishment clause challenges to programs of governmental aid to higher education.[79] Aside from the *Horace Mann League* case in Maryland, noted earlier in this chapter, there has been no mention of the rather special problems involved in deciding whether governmental aid to a church-related college or university violates First Amendment proscriptions.

In the early 1960's several states (notably New York) began experimenting with programs of aid to private institutions of higher learning within their borders in the form of tuition grants. After the passage, in 1963, of the federal Higher Education Facilities Construction Act, several states (notably Maryland) followed this federal model and began providing "brick and mortar" support to their private colleges and universities.

In 1966 the Maryland Court of Appeals took a fairly tough separationist line in response to arguments by counsel for the Horace Mann League of federal unconstitutionality.[80] There could be no support to sectarian (meaning identifiably religious) institutions. Considering such factors as the stated purpose of the institution, the composition of the faculty, and the financial relationships with denominational bodies, the Maryland Court found that of the four institutions involved, only one, Hood College, with its nominal attachment to the United Church of Christ, was "non-sectarian" and eligible. As has been seen, the United States Supreme Court declined to consider the case, and so the matter of grants to colleges and universities rested until 1971.

Tilton v. *Richardson,*[81] in 1971, was the culmination of a separationist challenge to the 1963 federal Act as implemented in Connecticut. The arguments made concerning the federal grants to four Connecticut colleges (all with Catholic affiliations) were substantially the same as those made eight years earlier concerning the four Maryland grants. This time, however, the U.S. Supreme Court was faced with a decision of a three-judge federal district Court disallowing all the grants as violative of the establishment clause, and the Justices did not duck.

Rather than proceeding as had the Court of Appeals of Maryland, by examining each institution involved for signs of fatal sectarianism, Chief Justice Burger (speaking only for a plurality of the Court including Harlan, Stewart, and Blackmun), relied on the doctrinal instrument he had fashioned the year before in *Walz*—the concept of "no-entanglement."

The crucial point for Burger was not the formal relationship of the institutions to religious bodies, but the distinction between institutions of higher learning and parochial elementary and secondary schools. College students were less "impressionable" than younger persons, and institutions of higher learning (even though they might have ties to religious organizations) were not characteristically so devoted as parochial primary and secondary schools to propagating the faith. Furthermore, the Chief argued, the sort of aid given (i.e., buildings) was not likely to involve governmental agents in close and continued monitoring of the work of the recipient institutions. The degree of entanglement was not sufficient to require disallowal on establishment clause grounds.

Burger did admit that it might be possible for a particular college or university to be so extensively engaged in the propagation of doctrine as to disqualify it from participation altogether. This was not the case, however, with any of the Connecticut institutions at bar, and it seemed clear Burger's idea of what was "too sectarian to take" was a great deal narrower than that of the Maryland Court of Appeals in the *Horace Mann League* case. Colleges, in short, were hard to become "entangled" in—especially when government was giving bricks and mortar, and not contributing directly to pay anyone's salary or support any particular program, which could require continuing review. Certainly some policing would be necessary to make sure that the federally granted buildings were not used for specifically religious activities, but this was a tolerable level of involvement.[82]

There were four dissenters in *Tilton*. Douglas, joined by Black and Marshall, found the distinction between elementary and secondary education and higher education unpersuasive. The grants conferred a substantial benefit on church-affiliated institutions (the four Connecticut campuses) and it was the end of the matter. To twist the knife, Douglas went on to speak of the "entanglement" which would result from the governmental "surveillance" of federally assisted facilities which would be necessary to insure that they were not converted to religious purposes. That the surveillance might be any easier when the issue was college buildings opposed to primary school teachers' salaries was roughly labelled "sophistry." Dissenting separately, Justice Brennan also refused to accept the distinction between higher and "lower" education, and argued further that the suggestion that policing a simple grant program presented problems similar to the entanglement which would result from taxation of church properties was overwrought.

The swing vote between Burger's four-vote plurality opinion and the four dissenters, was, of course, Justice White's. Once assured by the record that the federally assisted facilities of the Connecticut institutions were not used for actual propagation of religion, he sustained the Act on his *Allen* grounds—a combination of "individual-benefit" and "purpose-and-primary effect."

The significant point concerning *Tilton* is that, while failing to carry a majority of the Justices, Burger drew them all (with the exception of White) to argue the matter in terms of his preferred category of entanglement.

PURCHASE OF SERVICE PLANS—LEMON—DI CENSO

Decided together on the same day as *Tilton* were two cases (one from Pennsylvania, one from Rhode Island) in which state legislators had attempted to aid church-related schools on a "purchase of service" rationale. These programs, following the lead of White's opinion in *Allen,* provided support to the "secular teaching" done in parochial schools on grounds of contribution to the welfare of the community. In Rhode Island the support was for teachers' salaries alone; in Pennsylvania aid was available for textbooks and instructional materials as well as salaries. But where Burger had found no entanglement when the issue was bricks and mortar for church-affiliated colleges and universities, he did conclude (this time for the Court) that impermissible entanglement was likely when the state aid was flowing to elementary and secondary schools which were church-related.

The supervision necessary to insure that the subsidized teachers were not involved in religious activities would so involve government with religious institutions as to violate the non-entanglement standard which the new Chief Justice had developed in *Walz* and polished in *Tilton.* Thus the distinction between higher education and elementary and secondary education, which Burger had been so much at pains to establish in *Tilton,* was dispositive in *Lemon* v. *Kurtzman* (Pennsylvania) and *Earley* and *Robinson* v. *Di Censo* (Rhode Island).[83]

Only Mr. Justice White (the lonely author of *Allen* and the swing man in *Tilton*) had doubts. He would have distinguished between the Rhode Island program, which had been tested in a trial, and which was (by his lights) wholly unexceptional, and the Pennsylvania program, which, while constitutional on its face, might, in its administration, be managed in such a way as to render it unconstitutional. Since the original challenge there had been dismissed by the District Court for failure to state a cause of action, White would have remanded for trial.[84] In the Pennsylvania case, the plaintiffs, in short, must be allowed to make their case that, in fact, religion was furthered by the purchase of service arrangement. Nothing, White asserted, could be assumed in cases of this sort where the statute was not unconstitutional on its face. Everything must be argued and established by the weight of evidence. He was clear that this had been done in the federal and Rhode Island cases, but not in the Pennsylvania situation.

The only other opinion in *Lemon* was a concurrence from Mr. Justice Douglas, in which Justice Black joined. Douglas, who had dissented in *Tilton,* simply reiterated his view that any intermingling of religious outlook and teaching was an establishment of religion which could not constitutionally be aided with public funds. "One can imagine," he remarked, "what a religious zealot, as contrasted to a civil libertarian, can do with the Reformation or with the Inquisition."[85] Only civil libertarians, apparently, are fit teachers to be paid from the common treasury.

Thus, *Lemon* was the strict separationist prohibition against aid to church-related schools which accommodationists had long feared. It has been promised by *Everson;* yet it had not come through the fifties and early sixties; *Allen* had seemed a reprieve —an indication that the Court was turning from the direction pointed by *Everson.* But *Lemon* was the result. Certainly there was still some play in the joints of the establishment clause. *Tilton* indicated that, and immediately in the wake of *Lemon* there were excited speculations as to what possible programs might be approved. But there was a fevered quality to these speculations. The blow had fallen just when Catholic parochial schools, subjected to agonizing financial pressure, had had some reason to believe relief was at hand. The disappointment was grievous, and the remaining possibilities for support, while real, seemed very narrow.

EDUCATIONAL VOUCHERS—THE WAVE OF THE FUTURE?

In the reaction to *Lemon* there were distinct echoes of the reaction, almost a quarter-century before, to *Everson.* While the editorial board of the New York *Times* trumpeted the decision,[86] the leaders of the Catholic community gathered themselves for a counterattack.

On the evening of August 17, President Nixon addressed the annual meeting of the Supreme Council of the Knights of Columbus at the Waldorf-Astoria in New York. On the same platform, and speaking before the President, was Cardinal Spellman's successor to the Archbishopric of New York, Terrance Cardinal Cooke. Cooke attacked the Supreme Court's *Lemon* decision in general and the Chief Justice (Nixon's friend and first appointee) in particular. "As Catholic citizens of these United States, we call upon our fellow Americans for justice," he declared. "We call upon them not only for our constitutional rights but also for the governmental support which will enable our parents to exercise those rights."[87] The President, in his turn, spoke sympathetically, if unspecifically, of the Cardinal's complaint. The next morning, President Nixon breakfasted at the Waldorf with Governor Rockefeller and Attorney General Mitchell, and one of the topics on the agenda was the Governor's experience, in New York, in attempting to aid church-related schools in the face of stiff opposition.[88] Throughout these speeches, conversations, and the press handouts which followed them, there were allusions to "possible ways" of aiding parochial schools within the new constitutional confines set by *Lemon*. On reflection, however, these seem only two in number.

The first, which has attracted lesser attention, is tax relief. The President's Panel on Non-Public Education has reported favorably on a federal income tax credit scheme,[89] and Minnesota has already provided a deduction from its state income tax.[90] The tax relief approach has obvious attraction from the viewpoint of constitutional politics. Those responsible for the legal defense of a tax credit scheme could credibly seek some foothold in *Walz*. It is hard to see that any forbidden entanglement would result from scanning tax returns (at least not the sort of entanglement involved in valuing baptismal founts, which was at the nub of Burger's opinion), and it might be suggested, with only a little blush, that the underlying principle recognized by the Court in that case was that exemptions are simply less serious than grants, even though this conclusion was never expressly reached by Burger.

A second possible way of aiding church-related schools, which has become the focus of considerable attention, is the so-called "educational voucher" scheme. Urged by spokesmen as diverse as Milton Friedman and Christopher Jencks, the voucher idea is simple. Parents would receive a chit for each school-age child, approximately equal to the cost of educating that child in the local public school. This chit could then be taken to any school participating in the program, public or private, and accepted as full or partial payment. Variations on the basic notion are complicated and numerous. Restriction on parental supplements, agreements by participating schools to particular racial and economic mixes, and hedges against educational quackery are among the accessories being suggested and tried out.

The breakthrough for the voucher idea came in the spring of 1970, when the federal Office of Economic Opportunity decided to launch several pilot voucher programs.[91] While the results of these experiments are not yet in, the Court's decision in

Lemon propelled the voucher idea into prominence. There were exchanges of letters in the *Times,* and journals of opinion gave over considerable space to debating its merits.[92] To public school traditionalists it appeared a Devil's invention, to parochial school partisans a life-line to public support, and to many social critics, restive and unsatisfied with the recent performance of American public schools, it appeared both tempting and dangerous.

In these two approaches, however, tax relief and education vouchers, lie the hopes of the church-related schools for skirting *Lemon* and securing that governmental arm to lean on which may support them through the present financial buffeting. The outlook, for the accommodationist is bleak, but not altogether without hope.

In the wake of the *Lemon* decision, the legislature of Pennsylvania hastened to replace the purchase of service arrangement with one which provided simple tuition grants to the parents of children attending non-public schools. Other states (Ohio and New Jersey) started to follow suit. The argument relied on was simple, and fixed precisely on Chief Justice Burger's entanglement language. If the vice of the schemes struck down in *Lemon* and *Di Censo* was the degree of government supervision of religious institutions necessary to see that the monies were not used to propagate the faith, then simply giving all parents the money obviated the need for governmental supervision, and thus there would be no entanglement under a grant scheme.

There is a certain insouciant appeal to this argument, but it does not survive reflection. To accept it would be to acknowledge that as long as no supervision was involved, Governments could funnel support to religious schools without restriction. It is necessary to remember that there was, for Burger, a *reason* underlying the "no-entanglement"—government was not to aid religion. The secondary evil of entanglement resulted when government had to police against primary evil of public monies being put to religious purposes. Merely to say that no policing will take place does not, presumably, satisfy the establishment clause requirement completely.

This, in any case, was the view of the Third Circuit Court

of Appeals, which struck down the Pennsylvania improvisation on April 6, 1972.[93] President Nixon, however, remained committed. Speaking that same evening in Philadelphia to the convention of the National Catholic Educational Association, he declared that some way would be found to meet the needs of non-public schools, but that, "extra time" would be required to develop a program which would survive in the courts. White House Press Secretary Ronald Ziegler began to refer to tax relief as an "open option," and Msgr. William N. Novichy, Superintendent of the Ohio Catholic school system, discussed with the press a possible resort to civil disobedience by Catholics in an effort to achieve "justice." (The Ohio tuition-grant program was struck down by a three-judge Federal District Court two weeks after the Third Circuit's action in Pennsylvania.)[94]

CONCLUSION

While the Supreme Court certainly has tended to view public supports to religious institutions with disfavor, the line of decision from *Everson* to *Lemon* cannot be said to be altogether straight. *Allen* was something of a bend, and it is certainly not incredible that the Burger Court might veer back toward *Allen* when confronted with tuition grants, or tax credits, or educational vouchers.

What creates high political pressure around the issue, of course, is that "new money" for education is now coming in large amounts from both the state and federal governments. In the 1950's, the debate over funds for church-related schools was contained by its abstract character—dons and clerics might dispute, but *in fact* there was no government proposing to spend "extra" funds for education from which a share for church-related schools could be taken. Nothing was really at stake. But since 1965 we have witnessed a minor revolution in educational finance. With streams of "special" funding welling up, the question of whether the sectarian schools should be supported is anything but abstract. The old arguments are newly animated, the conflict has been widened, and larger numbers of people have found their emotions (and occasionally their intellects) engaged. Elementary and secondary education are now "in things"; after years of bare subsistence educators now look forward to a period of relative affluence and religious educators are determined not to be left out.

The Roman Catholic school system services about four million elementary and secondary students, and accounts for the vast majority of church-related schools in the nation. This system is desperate for funds. Enrollments have doubled in the last twenty-five years; the costs of plant and materials have skyrocketed; there has been a decline in religious vocations which means fewer teaching nuns are available and expensive secular faculty must be hired to fill the places. A declining percentage of Catholic children—and this is a rapidly growing population—can be accommodated in present facilities. At the same time the quality of these facilities is declining in comparison to public schools. Catholic educators are haunted by a vision of the future in which only public schools receive the new forms of financial aid, and only public schools are able to afford the expensive hardware (teaching machines, closed circuit TV, computers) which the "education industry" is presently tooling up to produce. There are more and more frequent predictions that unless public aid is forthcoming, the Catholic system must contract (e.g., into the first 6 grades) or be cut back piecemeal. All this is acutely painful to the Catholic parents and educators involved, and may yet evoke considerable sympathy beyond the Catholic community.

And while Catholic school enrollments are declining, there is an increasing middle-class demand for private schooling which has nothing to do with religion. In the South, court-ordered integration of the public schools spurred efforts, backed by substantial state aid, to provide private, lily-white alternatives. As de facto school segregation has been reduced in Northern cities middle-class demand for private schools has also risen. It is common knowledge around New York City that the most marginal and struggling private schools of ten years ago now have multiple applicants for each student opening.[95] And while we lack up-to-date national figures on private school starts, rates of growth, and admission pressures, there is every impressionistic indication that when we get the data they will be dramatic. All these are potential allies of Catholic educators in the matters of grants, tax credits, and vouchers.

NOTES

1. 262 U.S. 390 (1923).
2. 268 U.S. 510 (1925).
3. 198 U.S. 45 (1905).
4. 261 U.S. 525 (1923).
5. Philip B. Kurland, *Religion and the Law* (Chicago: Aldine, 1961), pp. 26–31.
6. 175 U.S. 291 (1899).
7. 210 U.S. 50 (1908).
8. 281 U.S. 370 (1930).
9. My friend Arthur Sutherland argues that this conclusion is too abrupt. *Gitlow* had been decided by the time of *Cochran,* and in *Gitlow* Justice Sanford had "assumed" that the speech and press guarantees operated against the states. Nothing was said about the religion clauses, however, and I can find no evidence that *Cochran* contemporaries felt all the First Amendment applied in the wake of *Gitlow.*
10. *Judd* v. *Board of Education,* 278 N.Y. 200 (1938).
11. New York *Times,* November 17, 1946.
12. Interview with G. Bromley Oxnam, April 23, 1962. See also *Time,* August 18, 1947, p. 74, where Reinhold Niebuhr is quoted on the "uneasiness" within the Protestant community with regard to the Catholic Church.
13. New York *Times,* May 8, 1947. See also *Time,* May 19, 1947, pp. 70–73, and *Christian Century,* May 28, 1947, pp. 648 and 664.
14. *Ibid.*
15. *Ibid.*
16. *Ibid.*
17. New York *Times,* May 21, 1947.
18. New York *Times,* August 18, 1947. See also *Time,* June 23, 1947.
19. New York *Times,* November 16, 1947.
20. *Ibid.*
21. Interview with Oxnam, April 23, 1962.
22. New York *Times,* June 12, 1946.
23. *Ibid.*
24. New York *Times,* June 13, 1946.
25. *Ibid.*
26. An indication of what was happening in denominational publica-

tions during this period can be found in John J. Kane, *Catholic-Protestant Conflicts in America* (Chicago: Regnery, 1955).

27. For a careful analysis of this entire episode see Alan F. Westin, "U.S.–Vatican Relations" (unpublished doctoral dissertation, Harvard, 1965).

28. On this phenomenon see Vincent P. DeSantis, "American Catholics and McCarthyism," 51 *Catholic Historical Review* 1 (1965).

29. New York *Times,* April 27, 1947.

30. *Ibid.,* August 20, 1947.

31. *Ibid.,* October 28, 1946.

32. See Philip Meranto, *The Politics of Federal Aid to Education in 1965: A Study in Political Motivation* (Syracuse: Syracuse University Press, 1967), p. 53.

33. New York *Times,* November 16, 1947.

34. *Ibid.,* February 1, 1947. The Taft approach was to return a portion of federal income tax revenues to the states for use in education according to the provisions of the state constitutions. Since many states have church-state provisions stricter than the federal, the effect of the bill was to cut out parochial schools. This was recognized by Catholic spokesmen and the approach has been consistently opposed by NCWC.

35. *Ibid.,* November 22, 1946.

36. *Ibid.,* March 6, 1947.

37. *Ibid.,* April 10, 1947.

38. *Ibid.*

39. *Ibid.,* April 11, 1947.

40. 330 U.S. 1, 3 (1947).

41. Illinois, Indiana, Louisiana, Massachusetts, Michigan, and New York.

42. 330 U.S. 1, 15–16 (1947).

43. *Ibid.,* p. 19.

44. *Ibid.,* p. 63.

45. New York *Times,* June 12, 1947.

46. *Ibid.,* June 14, 1947.

47. See Stokes, *op. cit.,* Vol. I, pp. 746–758. For an historical treatment of the issue see Seymour Paul Lochman, "The Church-State Issue as Reflected in Federal Aid to Education Bills, 1937–1950" (unpublished doctoral dissertation, New York University, 1963).

48. The best brief treatment is Hugh D. Price, "Race, Religion, and the Rules Committee," in Alan F. Westin, ed., *The Uses of Power* (New York: Harcourt, Brace and World, 1961), updated as "Schools, Scholarships, and Congressmen: The Kennedy Aid-to-Education Program," in Westin, *The Centers of Power* (New York: Harcourt, Brace and World, 1964).

49. On the politics of ESEA passage, administration, and amendment, see Dean M. Kelley and George R. LaNoue, "The Church-State Settlement in the Federal Aid to Education Act: A Legislative History," in Donald A. Gianella, *Religion and the Public Order, 1965* (Chicago: University of Chicago Press, 1966); Stephen K. Bailey and Edith K. Mosher, *ESEA: The Office of Education Administers a Law* (Syracuse:

Syracuse University Press, 1968); Morgan, *op. cit.;* Meranto, *op. cit.;* and Eugene Eidenberg and Roy D. Morey, *An Act of Congress* (New York: W. W. Norton, 1969).

50. There were also several efforts to challenge bus transportation arrangements in the hope that the Court, with its changing personnel, might be prepared to reverse *Everson* or at least to hold that elaborate transportation arrangements—e.g., separately maintained fleets of buses servicing church-related schools—went over the "verge" of which Black had spoken.

51. *Horace Mann League* v. *Board of Public Works,* 242 Md. 645, op. dis. and cert. don., 385 U.S. 97 (1966).

52. 262 U.S. 447 (1923).

53. See Morgan, *op. cit.,* pp. 81–84. See also Kenneth Culp Davis, "Standing to Challenge Governmental Action," 39 *Minnesota Law Review* 353 (1955); Louis L. Jaffe, "Standing to Secure Judicial Review: Public Actions," 74 *Harvard Law Review* 1265 (1961). A great deal of interesting material on standing is compiled in *Judicial Review;* Hearings before the Subcommittee on Constitutional Rights of the Senate Committee on the Judiciary, 89th Cong., 2nd sess., Parts I and II. See also "Taxpayer Suits: A Survey and Summary," 69 *Yale Law Journal* (1960); and the Arthur Garfield Hay Civil Liberties Conference, "Public Aid to Parochial Schools and Standing to Bring Suit," 12 *Buffalo Law Review* 34 (1962). And most recently see Boris Bittker, "The Case of the Fictitious Taxpayer: The Federal Taxpayer's Suit Twenty Years After *Flast* v. *Cohen,*" 36 *Chicago Law Review* 364 (1969); and Kenneth Culp Davis, "The Case of the Real Taxpayer: A Reply to Professor Bittker," 36 *Chicago Law Review* 375 (1969). On possible limitation of the significance of *Flast* see Note, "Taxpayer Suits and the Aggregation of Claims: The Vitiation of *Flast* by *Snyder,*" 79 *Yale Law Journal* 1577 (1970).

54. And even with state taxpayer actions, which have been accepted and decided by state courts, the Supreme Court established a limitation. The challenge must be to an appropriation of funds and not to a governmental practice which only incidentally or marginally involves expenditures. See *Doremus* v. *Board,* 342 U.S. 429 (1952), in which the Justices refused a New Jersey taxpayer challenge to Bible reading in the schools. Originally the plaintiff had had a child in New Jersey schools, but by the time the case reached the Supreme Court the child had graduated, having only taxpayer status as a basis for standing; the expenditure involved in the Bible reading was held insufficient.

55. On the question of when the Court must, or should, take a case which comes to it on appeal or on petition for cetiorari, see the opposing views of: Alexander M. Bickel, *The Least Dangerous Branch* (Indianapolis: Bobbs-Merrill, 1962); and Gerald Gunther, "The Subtle Vices of the 'Passive Virtues'—A Comment on Principle and Expediency in Judicial Review," 64 *Columbia Law Review* 1 (1964).

56. Separationists regarded the matter as so serious that several efforts were made in Congress to provide exemption from the *Frothingham* standing rule. See Hearings on S 2097 before the Subcommittee on Constitutional Rights of the Senate Judiciary Committee, 89th Cong., 2nd sess. (1966).

57. Involved were the New York Civil Liberties Union, the American Jewish Congress, the United Federation of Teachers (the AFL-CIO local of New York City public school teachers), and the United Parents Association (a city-wide organization of parents active in local PTA's). For a brief history of the litigation, see Morgan, *op. cit.*, pp. 98–109.

58. *Flast* v. *Gardner,* 271 F. Supp. 1 (1967).

59. 392 U.S. 83 (1968).

60. There is some misunderstanding surrounding this term. What is meant is an action where there is nothing *at issue* between the parties. It does not apply to suits which are arranged as matters of convenience to clarify points for cooperating parties who *do* have something at issue between them. What is important is not that the parties are "friends," but that the issue exists in fact and is not a hypothetical construct. The litigants must actually stand in a certain relationship to one another, and not just stipulate that they do. It is a formal or objective distinction, not a psychological one having to do with the "feelings" of the parties. Two professors of constitutional law cannot make up an action between themselves to satisfy their professional curiosity on a particular point. But if one happens to be an officer of a corporation and one a stockholder there might be a number of perfectly acceptable suits which they could organize around these statuses. The stockholder, for instance, might seek to enjoin the officers from obeying a federal statute, the effect of which was to reduce the profits of the corporation (and thus its dividends). The fact that the officer agrees with his friend the stockholder plaintiff that the federal statute is unconstitutional does not make the issue between them any less real.

61. The same notion applied to state suits in *Doremus.* See fn. 54, *supra.*

62. The distinctions Warren drew between "spending" and "regulatory" programs, and between violations of specific constitutional commands and violations, involved absence of power and are not altogether satisfactory. See Louis Henkin, "On Drawing Lines," 82 *Harvard Law Review* 63 (1968).

63. 382 U.S. 236 (1962).

64. See 273 N.Y.S. 2d 239 (1966); and 27 A. 2d 69 (1966).

65. 20 N.Y. 2d 109 (1967).

66. 374 U.S. 203 (1963).

67. The best analysis of the opinions in *Allen* is Paul Freund, "Aid to Parochial Schools," 82 *Harvard Law Review* 1687 (1969).

68. The most recent attempt is Boris Bittker, "Churches, Taxes, and the Constitution," 78 *Yale Law Journal* 1285 (1969).

69. It is interesting that President Grant's address to the veterans of the Army of the Tennessee (discussed in the preceding chapter) did include a call for eliminating tax exemptions. That item was not, however, included in Representative Blaine's Amendment.

70. Avro Van Alstyne, "Tax Exemption of Church Property," 20 *Ohio State Law Journal* 461 (1959). This is still the best survey of the problem. For a brief in favor of exemption see Paul Kauper, "The Con-

stitutionality of Tax Exemptions for Religious Activities," in Dallin Oaks, ed., *The Wall Between Church and State* (Chicago: University of Chicago Press, 1963).

71. See Van Alstyne, *op. cit.,* fn. 5.

72. Morgan, *op. cit.,* pp. 42–44.

73. *General Finance Corp.* v. *Archette,* 93 R.I. 392, ap. dis. 369 U.S. 423 (1962); and *Murray* v. *Comptroller,* 241 Md. 383 (1966); cert. den. 385 U.S. 816 (1966).

74. Brief of the United States Catholic Conference, Amicus Curiae, in *Walz* v. *New York,* 397 U.S. 664 (1970), p. 22.

75. 24 N.Y. 2d 30 (1969).

76. 397 U.S. 664 (1970).

77. This agreement presumed equality of treatment of voluntary associations. In the federal income tax context, at least, this condition does not obtain, but Brennan was not forced by the facts of *Walz,* a property tax case, to account for such a situation.

78. See, for instance, Wilbur G. Katz, "Radiations from Church Tax Exemptions," 1970 *Supreme Court Review* 93. Professor Katz sees *Walz* as a clear retreat from *Everson,* but overlooks a number of awkward facts. *Inter alia,* that Black went along with the majority in *Walz* without a murmur. That this is not Justice Black's habit when he thinks he is being "over-ruled" is well known. Recall his reaction in *Allen* where *Everson* was, in fact, being diluted. Black may just have been fooled or lazy, of course, but his silence should put one on one's guard against over-reading Burger's opinion.

79. An excellent article summarizing the law on the subject as of mid-1970 is Walter Gellhorn and R. Kent Greenawalt, "Public Support and the Sectarian University," 28 *Fordham Law Review* 395 (1970). An expanded version of this article appeared as *The Sectarian College and the Public Purse* (Dobbs Ferry, N.Y.: Oceana, 1970).

80. In fact, the *Horace Mann League* served as a spokesman for a coalition of separationist groups which contributed to the costs of the litigation.

81. No. 153. Decided June 28, 1971.

82. Burger did find that the provision of the Act which lifted the ban on religious activities in federally assisted buildings twenty years after their completion was unconstitutional. Once federal dollars had been spent, the "period of federal interest" was the life of the facility.

83. No. 153.

84. No. 89. Decided June 28, 1971.

85. *Ibid.,* dissent, Douglas, J., p. 11.

86. New York *Times,* June 29, 1971.

87. *Ibid.,* August 18, 1971.

88. *Ibid.,* August 19, 1971.

89. *Ibid.,* August 26, 1971; and April 21, 1972.

90. ACLU and AU court challenges are presently being organized.

91. For further developments see New York *Times,* April 25, 1972.

92. For instance, the *New Leader,* Robert Lekachman, "Vouchers and

Public Education," July 12, 1971; and comments by Christopher Jencks and Judith Areen, Aaron S. Carton, Don Davies, Leonard Gardner, Milton J. Gold, Daniel E. Griffiths, Richard E. Morgan, Sister Mary Ramona, John Oliver Wilson, plus a reply by Robert Lekachman, September 6, 1971. See also George R. La Noue, ed., *Educational Vouchers: Concepts and Controversies* (N.Y.: Teachers College Press, 1972).

93. New York *Times,* April 7, 1972. For an excellent analysis of the implications of Burger's "entanglement test," see Donald A. Gianella, "Lemon and Tilton: The Bitter and the Sweet of Church-State Entanglement," 1971 *Supreme Court Review* 147.

94. New York *Times,* April 21, 1972.

95. It is important to distinguish here between private *boarding* schools, which are having a very rough go indeed, and private day schools located within upper-middle class "compounds."

5

Prayer in Public Places

On the whole, the Supreme Court has dealt more crisply and coherently with the problem of governmentally sponsored religious exercises than it has with the problem of governmental support to religious institutions. But while the line of decisions is relatively clear, the public and professional reaction to the Court's work has been divided and intense. There has been considerable resistance to and defense of the Court's decisions. Only in the areas of race relations and criminal defendant's rights have the Justices exposed themselves to a similar mixture of praise and calumny.[1] Even more than the use of public funds to support religious institutions, the question of government's relationship to the great symbols of religion has the capacity to stir men's feelings. In the spring of 1962, I recall, in the wake of the Court's decision in *Engel* v. *Vitale*,[2] bemused New Yorkers boarding their subway trains found KEEP GOD IN SCHOOL! scrawled in lipstick across the sides of many cars. By the 1970's, of course, Manhattan's subterranean vandals had become thoroughly politicized, but in the innocence of 1962, their reflexive piety was an indication of the remarkably wide awareness in American society of what the Justices in Washington were saying about certain governmental practices which most people had taken for granted for a long time.[3]

The Court's work in the area of religious practices began the year after the opening up of the establishment clause in *Everson;* the case was *McCollum* v. *Board of Education,*[4] which involved a "released time" arrangement by which sectarian religious instruction was offered during the school day.

ACCOMMODATION—PROTESTANT STYLE

While nineteenth century Americans talked and generally practiced a tough separationism where specific expenditures of public funds were involved, they tended to accept a sort of low-key, watered-down Protestantism as a public religion. Prayers opened legislative days in the House and Senate and state legislatures; the national motto (In God We Trust), suggested at least monotheism; Sunday closing laws proliferated on the books of states and municipalities; and, most importantly, public schools built "non-sectarian" prayers, Bible readings (King James version), and Christian holiday observances into their programs. Many legislators who supported state "Blaine amendments" advocated, apparently without sense of contradiction, the perpetuation of this public religion. At the same time that they were voting that no public funds go to any private school under any form of sectarian control, they were presiding over the development of public school systems in which it was thought proper for the teachers to inculcate what was often referred to as "basic piety." On the occasions when such residually Protestant practices in the public schools were challenged, usually by a Catholic parent as in the *Donahue* case in Maine, mentioned in Chapter 2, the courts were unsympathetic. Lower court judges stated again and again in the late nineteenth and early twentieth centuries that publicly sponsored invocations of the Deity, and even of "our Lord Jesus Christ," did not violate state or federal establishment clauses. The "God" in question was held to be a non-denominational one, and hence legally benign. The Supreme Court simply did not confront the question.

There were, to be fair, occasional political reversals for this public religion, as when, in the late 1820's, Congress rejected petitions from Protestant groups urging that mail deliveries, which were then being made on Sundays, be halted out of respect for the majority-Christian observance. But the Post Offices were eventually closed on Sundays for reasons of "convenience and economy," and the pious succeeded in closing down numerous other Sunday activities at the state and municipal levels. By 1900, Stokes tells us, the statute books around the country were heavy with such restrictions.[5]

During the 1930's and 1940's, furthermore, this easy-going public religion was bolstered by a change in the posture of the American Catholic community. Where before Catholics had taken the lead in challenging Protestant-tinged religious practices in public schools, now Catholic leaders and educators were coming around to a better-something-than-nothing view. In part this was because of increased clerical confidence that Catholic children in public schools were not being lost to the fold or converted to Protestantism. In part it was because of modifications of school practices (and other public religious practices) which reduced or eliminated their specifically Protestant content. In contrast with the nineteenth century public religion, that of the mid-1940's was increasingly referred to as a distillation of "Three Great Faiths."

The difficulty was that while Catholics were prepared to settle for, and even vigorously support, such modified practices, the third great faith was not. Jews, generally, were not comforted by passing references to Hanukkah at Christmas time, and they entered the battle against religious practices vigorously at about the time the Catholics were withdrawing.

It is worth remarking that Jewish groups have not, thus far, figured prominently in this account. We have noted the activity of the American Jewish Congress and Leo Pfeffer in connection with support for church-related schools, and it is true that other Jewish groups have been active on that front. But by far the most important Jewish effort in regard to the religion clauses of the First Amendment has been on the issue of governmentally sponsored religious exercises. In this area not only has the American Jewish Congress been active, but the older, more prestigious American Jewish Committee, and the large, well-financed Anti-Defamation League of B'nai B'rith have been continually involved. School prayers, Bible reading, Easter pageants (with catsup-stained twelve-year-olds playing Christ), and Christmas creches erected on public land have all been attacked. Christological observances sponsored by government have, of course, an especially sinister significance for Jews.[6] Whatever emphasizes Jewish separateness in public is regarded as threatening, and considerable resources have been made available from within the Jewish community to combat programs perceived as having that effect.[7] Allies have most often been secular separationist groups such as the ACLU, and radical Protestants, such as the Unitarians. Protestant separationist groups with a fundamentalist coloration, such as American United, have tended to express disapproval of state sponsored religious practices, but leave the legal challenging of such accommodations to the Jews and others.

McCOLLUM

The *McCollum* case came to the Supreme Court against this backdrop of casually accepted "Judeo-Christian" public religion. Government could, in fact was rather expected to, make gestures and expressions of support toward the "God of our Fathers" as long as no money changed hands. Dissenters were in a tiny minority.

Nor, from a strict separationist viewpoint, were the legal precedents very encouraging. Before 1948, as already observed, courts had disallowed very few religious practices in public schools. The Jehovah's Witnesses had prevailed on the flag salute, but that had been a combination of *free exercise* and *free speech* grounds. In addition, several state high courts had ended arrangements in which garbed Roman Catholic nuns were teaching in public schools.[8] The habits had to come off for the nuns to remain. If they wore them, it might appear to children that the state was endorsing a distinctly sectarian practice. *Everson,* the year before, had produced some rousing separationist rhetoric, but the decision had sustained the challenged governmental practice. Thus, *McCollum* represents the first unambiguous disallowal of a governmentally sponsored religious practice on establishment grounds, but the Court's reasoning, unhappily, was less than clear.

Illinois, by a 1943 statute, provided for district school boards to control the use of all school buildings within their districts, and the Champaign board undertook a program whereby local clergy came into the school for thirty-five and forty-five minute periods a week to give religious instruction to those children whose parents had given written consent for participation. The instruction took place during the regular school day, and in regular classrooms. Children not participating in the program were forced to leave their classrooms and were taken somewhere else in the school building for study halls. Attendance was taken in the religious classes and in the study halls.

A faculty wife at the University of Illinois, Mrs. Vashti McCollum, a militant "rationalist" and mother of one Terry McCollum, who attended a Champaign public school, brought suit as parent and taxpayer raising the establishment question.[9] By the time the case was heard by the Supreme Court, it was accompanied by separationist *amicus* briefs bearing familiar names—among them Leo Pfeffer for the Synagogue Council of America and a number of other Jewish groups, and Kenneth W. Greenawalt for the ACLU. Aside from the Attorney General of Illinois, the only *amicus* supporting the Champaign board was Charles H. Tuttle for the Protestant Council of New York City —an organization which had cooperated vigorously with New York's Catholic hierarchy in establishing that City's released time program.

Writing for a six-man Court, Justice Black began by affirming the broad version of the establishment clause set forth in his

Everson opinion. It had been, of course, under heavy fire, with accommodationist spokesmen suggesting that the estabishment clause should be read to require only simple equality of treatment by government of religions. This, Black repeated, was quite wrong. The narrow interpretation was neither historically justified nor desirable as policy. What had been said in *Everson* had been meant. Only Justice Reed (who had been silent the year before) now dissented from this view, embracing the narrow version and arguing that the American acceptance of a public religion was precedent for the sort of non-discrimination arrangement Champaign had evolved.[10]

The Champaign arrangement could not stand, Black announced: first, because of the use of tax-supported property for a religious purpose; second, because the operation of the state's compulsory attendance law assisted in a fundamental way the program of religious instruction.[11] What Black did not make clear was whether the element of compulsory school attendance was sufficient to invalidate the arrangement, or whether the element of facilities use also was necessary.

Mr. Justice Frankfurter wrote a lengthy separate opinion which is the best statement of his views on the establishment clause generally, and governmentally sponsored religious exercises in particular. Maintaining that *Everson* had not gone far enough, Frankfurter attacked religious exercises in public schools as incongruous vestiges of a past in which the schools had been creatures of the churches. This was precisely what the American public school movement had been meant to end. Far from the least-common-denominator religion in the schools being a precedent for anything such as released time, it was a troubling anomaly to be eliminated as quickly as possible. The public schools, for Frankfurter, performed a crucial integrating function in the polyglot American society, and to allow those schools to be involved with religious exercises, no matter how minimally, was to create the potential for bitter conflict which could undermine them and subvert their high mission.

It is interesting that while a moderate on the use of the Court's constitutional power in most areas, Frankfurter was quite an "activist" on establishment questions. In *McCollum,* Justice Jackson filed a grudging concurring opinion which, if addressed to most other subjects, would have sounded decidedly "Frankfurterian." Jackson pointed out that no one in *McCollum* had been *forced* to do anything (as had been true in the *Flag Salute* cases), and that no substantial tax revenues were at stake (at most, wear and tear, and a share of janitorial costs). This being so, Jackson argued, it would have been better for the Court not to have decided the case. If the Justices got themselves into the business of deciding such marginal establishment cases as this, he suggested, there will be no end to work as a national school board. But Frankfurter remained unmoved by these arguments for judicial self-restraint which he himself had so often urged on his brethren.

ZORACH

When the *McCollum* case came down, it was acclaimed by separationists as fulfilling the promise of *Everson,* and attacked by accommodationists as flying in the face of American tradition. The Court, however, was not finished with the problem of released time. New York City, as witness the concern of the Protestant Council with the fate of the Champaign program, had an extensive program of released time instruction operating in middle-class districts. The New York arrangement differed from that in Champaign in that instruction was given off the school premises. Participating clerics waited in church buildings while volunteer parents went to the schools, during regular school hours, and brought students out for the sectarian instruction. Non-participating students were grouped together in study halls until their fellows were returned from religious instruction and the regular public school activities recommenced.

The major separationist groups were not anxious to test the New York program. Standing alone, *McCollum* was a strong separationist precedent, and to challenge the off-premises New York arrangement was to risk the weakening of *McCollum.* There was, in short, the danger that the Supreme Court might distinguish the two situations on the matter of facilities use and legitimatize one sort of released time program which was at least arguably unconstitutional under *McCollum*. This view of the tactical situation was not shared, however, by militant atheists. They let it be known that they were going to press New York whether anyone joined them or not. Faced with this demarche, lawyers of the major groups decided that they had better bring the action themselves rather than run what seemed the greater risk of having the unpopular, and many thought inexpert, atheists do it.

Thus when *Zorach* v. *Clauson*[12] reached the Supreme Court, the appellants' brief bore the names (but not the group identifications) of Kenneth Greenawalt (from the ACLU), Leo Pfeffer (American Jewish Congress), and Edwin Lukas (American Jewish Committee). Defending the New York program, along with City attorneys, were Charles H. Tuttle and Porter R. Chandler. In addition, the attorneys general of eight states submitted *amicus* briefs seeking to protect similar programs in their jurisdictions.[13]

The initial fear of the separationists was realized. Justice Douglas wrote for a six-man majority, distinguished *Zorach* from *McCollum* on facilities use, and concluded that the underwriting of religious instruction by compulsory school attendance law does not sufficiently involve the state with an establishment of religion to render the arrangement unconstitutional. New York, through its schools, had exercised no coercive power, said Douglas. As if this were not sufficient punishment for the separationists, Douglas went on to one of the most famous bits of dicta[14] in modern constitutional law. "We are," he remarked in passing, "a religious people whose institutions presume a Supreme Being,"[15] and went on to ask sarcastically whether anyone was seriously suggesting that there might be something unconstitutional about the national motto.

Black, Frankfurter, and Jackson (who had, apparently, gotten over his *McCollum* qualms), each dissented. Black argued that his *McCollum* opinion made it "categorically clear" that the operation of a compulsory attendance law was sufficient to condemn under the establishment clause, and that the only constitutional arrangement would be one where school was closed early and the children allowed to use their time as they and their parents wished, with no required attendance for anyone.[16] In their dissents both Frankfurter and Jackson savaged Douglas' contention that no state coercion was present in the New York program, and hinted that perhaps the majority Justices had been influenced by sentiment to overlook the obvious and extensive governmental involvement when public schools dispatched children to churches and then retrieved them—all within the normal school day.

Zorach boosted the spirits of accommodationists who had been uneasy after *Everson* and positively depressed after *McCollum*. Now it seemed that the Supreme Court might not take a tough, consistently separationist line. The outlook for extensive public support for religious institutions might be bleak, but at least there seemed hope for preserving the public religion in the schools and elsewhere.

It was not to be. In the spring of 1961, after nine years of silence on the establishment clause, the Court, through Justice Black, struck down a provision of the Maryland Constitution which required prospective state officials to affirm the existence of God as a condition of assuming office. (This practice, it will be recalled, was a vestige of Maryland's ancient colonial establishment, discussed in Chapter 1. Neither the federal government nor a state, Black emphasized, could enact a law which discriminated between conventional believers and non-believers or between theists and non-theists.[17] This set the stage for further consideration of the public religion in the schools.

"*ESTABLISHMENT ACCORDING TO* ENGEL"

The sub-head belongs to Arthur Sutherland,[18] and it aptly describes the importance of the New York prayer case for the development of constitutional law on governmentally sponsored religious practices. It dashed accommodationist hopes, nurtured for a decade, that the Justices would allow traditionally sanctioned governmental sponsorship of religious exercises to continue.

Engel v. *Vitale,* decided in the spring of 1962, brought the Court face-to-face with a typical manifestion of the public religion —a non-denominational school prayer. The Regents, a body exercising general supervisory power over education in the State of New York, had authored a short prayer for recitation in classrooms:

> Almighty God we acknowledge our dependence upon Thee, and beg Thy blessings upon us, our teachers, and our Country.

Schools did not have to use this prayer, and if they did use it no child was required to repeat it. But if any prayer was used in the opening exercises in New York classrooms it had to be this one —there was to be no innovating in the field; the schoolroom praying in the Empire State was standardized.

The test came from the village of New Hyde Park, on Long Island. The plaintiffs were Unitarian and Jewish parents, and by the time it was docketed by the Supreme Court in Washington, after the anticipated defeat in the New York Court of Appeals, the case had acquired the normal political following: Herbert A. Wolff (American Ethical Union), Pfeffer, and Lukas were among those submitting *amicus* briefs in support of appellants. Twenty-one state attorneys general came to New York's (and their own) defense. And for a group of New Hyde Park parents, intervening in the action to keep the Regents' Prayer for their children, there was, inevitably, Porter R. Chandler.

Much nonsense has been written about the principal opinion in *Engel.* Justice Black spoke for a six-man Court as if *Zorach* had never happened. Continuing the separationist line of *Everson* and *McCollum,* Black concluded that a state simply had no business involving itself with prayers. Much fevered post-decision comment asked whether the case had turned on the actual writing of the prayer by officers of the state, or whether it had turned on the degree of informal coercion exerted on reluctant students to participate.[19] These inquiries missed Black's point—"that by using its public school system to encourage recitation of the Regents' Prayer, the State of New York has adopted a practice wholly inconsistent with the Establishment Clause."[20]

The most interesting opinion in *Engel* was Douglas' concurrence. Here the author of *Zorach* returned to his "religious people" dictum. For a decade students had wondered what he had meant by it, and finally they were told—nothing! The fact that Americans were a religious people did not mean that the state could be involved in supporting a Three-Faiths public religion. In the New York case public employees were leading prayers in public buildings, and the Establishment Clause, Douglas concluded, was rightly invoked against it. The hope which had been afforded defenders of the public religion was abruptly withdrawn. Where ten years before Douglas had asked rhetorically whether anyone was suggesting that there might be a constitutional problem about the national motto, he himself now suggested that there was.[21] *Zorach,* thus, was left high and dry. With Douglas committed to such a separationist course, it was clear that a solid Supreme Court majority had set its constitutional face against governmentally sponsored religious exercises and references to the Deity.

The lone dissenting voice in *Engel* was Justice Potter Stewart's. "With all respect," he began, "I think the Court has misapplied a great constitutional principle."[22] Tending toward the old Reed view that the establishment clause forbade only an official state church, Stewart went on to suggest that the Court should be guided by American tradition and practice unless some free-exercise problem were involved. If no one was being forced into anything, he concluded, why worry? There was, in short, no establishment value separate from the free-exercise value. While unsuccessful within the Court, this view has its defenders among accommodationist groups, and, as we shall see in Chapter 8, within the academic community.

If any doubts about the direction of Supreme Court action on the religious exercise issue remained after *Engel,* they were altogether dispelled a year later by the decisions in the *Lord's Prayer* and *Bible-reading* cases. The public reaction to *Engel* had hardly begun to subside when the Justices drove home the point that devotionals in public schools were out! While only a strained reading of *Engel* could have made it appear that any exercises could be preserved against constitutional challenge, many school systems continued to use the Lord's Prayer and Bible-reading, and hoped that these could be somehow distinguished from the Regents' Prayer situation. A Bible-reading case came to the Court from Pennsylvania and a Lord's Prayer case came from Maryland.[23] The plaintiff in the Maryland case was Mrs. Madalyn Murray, the enthusiastic atheist whom we encountered in Chapter 4, challenging church property tax exemptions in Baltimore.

As these cases represented a mop-up operation after *Engel*, some students have been puzzled by the 115 pages of opinions which the Justices spent on them. It has been suggested that certain Justices, at least, must have been seeking to modify or add to Black's *Engel* opinion.[24] A more likely explanation is that these cases were perceived by some Justices as the last involving school devotionals which would require Supreme Court consideration for some time. In light of the furor following *Engel*, several Justices who had not spoken concerning religious exercises wanted to say an extended word by way of conclusion.

As we noted in Chapter 4, *Schempp* was the occasion on which Justice Tom Clark set forth a test for unconstitutionality under the establishment clause which had not appeared in any of the previous opinions often quoted:

> What are the purpose and primary effect of the enactment? If either is the advancement or the inhibition of religion then the enactment exceeds the scope of the legislative power as circumscribed by the Constitution. That is to say that to withstand the strictures of the Establishment Clause there must be a secular purpose and a primary effect that neither advances nor inhibits religion.[25]

Clearly this was an attempt to state the sense of the Court's earlier pronouncements both on religious exercises and on aid to religious institutions—an attempt, that is, to forge a single clear establishment clause test. To have a single "test" is to have something, perhaps, but it is difficult to see that, at the time it was offered, Clark's formulation added either a new idea or increased precision to the "official," majority theory of the establishment clause, set forth by Black in *Everson, McCollum,* and *Engel.*[26] For a brief season it seemed that, as used by Justice White in the *Allen* case, Clark's words might become a bridge to a new more permissive interpretation of the establishment clause as it bears on aid to religious institutions. But *Lemon* has made such development highly unlikely.

Justice Douglas concurred briefly in *Schempp* with remarks which seem more directed to the problem of aid to religious institutions than to religious exercises in the schools.[27] He ended on the note he had struck in *Engel;* if there was any expenditure of public funds, no matter how small, the establishment clause was violated. Justice Brennan, also concurring, shook Madison's *Memorial and Remonstrance* before the faces of Pennsylvania and Maryland council, and proceeded in a skillful essay to argue the disruptive potential of politicized religious issues in a heterogeneous society. The Madisonian theory of separation was designed precisely, Brennan suggested, to preclude the development of such religiously motivated political conflicts by getting government out of the business of encouraging or cooperating with religion.[28] Justice Goldberg, joined by Justice Harlan, concurred briefly but cautioned against a governmental policy of hostility to religion (which, Goldberg pointed out, was certainly not commanded by the establishment clause). Again, Justice Stewart dissented, expanding on and sharpening his *Engel* grounds—the records before the Court did not show free-exercise type coercion, and without such coercion, Stewart would not find an establishment violation.

In the years since *Schempp,* compliance by local school boards with the Supreme Court mandate has been spotty to say the least.[29] This non-compliance means business for the lower courts for decades to come. In addition, there are certain school practices—Christological Christmas pageants, for instance—which, arguably, are not excluded by *Engel–Schempp.*[30] School devotionals will be back to the courts, but, along with the Justices at the time of *Schempp,* one suspects later rather than sooner.

BLUE LAWS (ESTABLISHMENT CLAUSE)

Another facet of the religious exercise problem are the myriad state laws which close businesses and prohibit other sorts of secular activities on Sunday—the majority-Christian day of religious observance. These laws, as remarked earlier, represent one of the great collective victories of the American public religion. Protestants wrote the law; and, with a few minor exceptions, such as Sunday bingo games, Catholics could comfortably abide by them. The rub came with Jews, Seventh-Day Adventists, and secular entrepreneurs. Furthermore, the Sunday laws were enacted in fits and starts, were incontinently amended, and took on a crazy-quilt quality which became more pronounced with each passing year. Aside from prohibiting open saloons during the hours of Sunday morning, there is little uniformity among jurisdictions, or within jurisdictions as between permitted and forbidden activities. Thus baseball may be played but not hockey, fish sold but not red meat, Martinis drunk at tables but not at bars, and so on *ad absurdum.*

Occasionally, challenges to local or state blue laws succeeded where it could be argued that the distinctions drawn in a particular statute were so abritrary as to leave the regulation without rational or substantial relation to any legitimate object of legislation. The argument was also made, from time to time, that the object of such legislation was not a legitimate one—that for the state to seek to protect the peace of the majority-Christian Sabbath by closing down work-a-day activities was for the state to legislate respecting an establishment of religion, no matter how rational and ordered the distinctions. In addition, it was suggested, the closing laws deprived sabbatarian businessmen of free-exercise by forcing them by law to close on Sunday after they had closed on Saturday out of religious conscience. Their Saturday observance was burdened by a state-imposed financial loss. We shall deal with the establishment claim here, and the free-exercise claim in the following chapter.

The Court decided four blue law cases in the spring of 1961; two were principally concerned with the establishment point, two with the free-exercise point.[31] The proximate reason for the Court's finally involving itself with the issues presented by Sunday closing laws was the development, during the 1950's, of the shopping center and the highway discount store as powerful competitors to Main Street merchants for the dollars of suburban Americans. Everyone along Main Street happily closed on Sunday because few shoppers were available. But with affluent suburbanites available on weekends, the out-of-town stores, to which suburbanites had easy access, strained to stay open. Their managers were quite willing to accept an occasional small fine as a cost of doing business. Main Street merchants, not surprisingly, sought means of retaliation. They could not meet the competition by opening themselves—the station wagons simply would not come into town on Sunday—but they could lobby prosecutors and police chiefs to crack down on blue law violators, and they could urge state legislatures and town councils to tighten such laws. This tactical use of blue laws in commercial warfare superheated the issues and made it imperative that there be some answers to the constitutional questions. Thus came the four cases, each reflecting a somewhat different variant of the Sunday closing problem.

Chief Justice Earl Warren wrote for the Court in *McGowan,* the leading establishment case. After a brief survey of the development of Sunday closing laws in America, Warren concluded that while initially religious in purpose, these statutes had come over the years to perform the valid secular purpose of providing a day of rest for members of the community—a social welfare measure. The fact that the chosen day was Sunday was not constitutionally significant. If one day a week were to be devoted effectively to family and community rest and recreation, then the day had to be the same for everyone in the community; the fact that Sunday had religious significance for majority-Christians did not make the day unavailable for choice by legislatures.

Justice Frankfurter could not pass the matter off so lightly. Referring to the Chief Justice's history as a "partial recital of isolated instances and events,"[32] he proceeded to a long separate opinion in which Justice Harlan joined. Citing authorities from Gilbert Murray to *The King's Book of Sports,* Frankfurter ended one of the most elegantly researched essays ever to grace the *United States Reports* by agreeing with Warren—Sunday closing laws were reasonable measures toward a legitimate secular purpose.[33] Only Justice Douglas, he of the "religious people," could not accept this secular rationale for blue laws. Certainly the state may mandate one day's rest a week; it may even mandate the same day for everyone. But choosing Sunday is simply too suspicious. The question was not whether states *could* conceivably pick Sunday for a secular purpose, but whether it was credible that they had done so.

The fact that the Justices labored so long and hard over the question is indicative of how very seriously they had come to take the separation of church and state. The establishment clause argument against blue laws had been around for a hundred years without anyone thinking it had much force, but by the time the pressure of events put it before the Supreme Court, eight Justices were sorely put in rejecting it and one was apparently persuaded.

DE MINIMUS

And what of the problems raised by Douglas in his puckish opinion in *Engel?* The Justices managed to check their separationism short of cutting down the Sunday closing laws, but will they be likewise able to stop short of scraping "In God We Trust" off the pennies? Several different approaches have been suggested to this problem.[34]

One might, for instance, agree with Douglas that consistency requires that the last vestiges of the public religion be uprooted, but argue that the motto, the Supreme Court crier ("God save the United States and this Honorable Court"), unscheduled

Bible-readings from outer space, and the use of an occasional religious symbol in the design of a postage stamp are simply not religious exercises in the sense, for instance, of the Regents' Prayer. As Black put it, "such patriotic or ceremonial occasions bear no true resemblance to the unquestioned religious exercise New York has sponsored. . . ."[35]

Or, one might fall back on Clark's "purpose and primary effect" formulation in *Schempp,* and suggest that as it is neither the intention nor the direct effect of these invocations of the Deity to foster belief or emotional reliance, they are not really governmental involvements with religion.

Finally, one might take the more realistic approach of arguing that while some of these ceremonial references do have a residually religious character, they are simply not important enough to be bothered with—*de minimus non curat lex.* The law does not concern itself with trifles, and anyone who asks it to is either a buffoon or a fanatic. The sensibilities of serious men will not be offended if the pennies continue to carry their ritual assertion of confidence.

There are, however, some practices which cannot be disposed of in any such cavalier way. No one who has sat through the lengthy praying that opens the legislative days of the United States Senate can think that there is not some purpose to inspire belief (misshapen though it may be) underlying these outpourings. One need not be a fanatic to feel a contradiction between forbidding school children in Wichita to be led in classroom prayers, and then holding them captive in the Senate gallery for ten minutes on their Washington trip.[36]

An even better illustration is the Oregon cross case. In a city park, overlooking the City of Eugene, a citizens group had erected a fifty-one foot pre-stressed concrete Latin cross. Inset neon tubing provided lighting for the cross at Christmas and Easter. No public money went into the building, but there the cross stood, on city-owned Skinner Butte, equally unavoidable to those who regard it as sacred and those who regard it as a profanation. The Oregon Supreme Court ruled the placement of the cross violated both the federal and Oregon constitutional provisions concerning establishment of religion, and the Justices in Washington refused two requests to review the matter.[37]

Or another example. On Friday, December 12, 1969, the ACLU and the American Jewish Congress announced that they were bringing suit to enjoin the erection of a life-size nativity scene at the official federal Christmas exercise, the Pageant of Peace, which President Nixon was to open the following Tuesday.[38] Efforts to obtain a temporary restraining order failed, and before the case could go further, Christmas was over. But there is always a next time.

CONCLUSION

Thus, despite the generally forthright fashion in which the Justices have dealt with the issue of religious exercises, there are fringe problems that will continue to trouble. What is teaching about religion and what is worship? How perfunctory need an invocation of "God" be, to be considered a secular ceremony?

An indication of the staying power of public prayer as an issue of emotional consequence was the brief revival enjoyed, as this was being written in the autumn of 1971, of the movement to alter the language of the First Amendment to permit specifically prayer in public schools. The most familiar such First Amendment tinkering was proposed by the late Senate minority leader, Everett McKinley Dirksen of Illinois. His initiative was in reaction to the *Engel-Schempp* decisions,[39] and although it failed of passage in either house, Senator Dirksen revived it from time to time until his death in 1970. The 1971 effort was led by Republican Representative Chalmers Wylie, of Ohio. It also failed.

The treatment of prayer proposals by Congress seems, as much as anything, a reflection of the state of the level of morale within the institution. If congressional morale is high and much is going on, little attention is paid to such hardy perennials. When, however, Congress begins to feel excluded and ineffectual, the bad penny of a prayer amendment seems to turn up and begins commanding interest again.[40]

It might even be argued that the occasional surges of interest in the Dirksen Amendment are really a sort of "referred" congressional pain—that restiveness over the intractability of some other social problem (e.g., crime in the streets) which legislators would like to "solve" but cannot, manifests itself in enthusiasm for school prayers. However that may be, prayer in public places may continue to nag American society for a while.

NOTES

1. Murphy and Tannenhaus, "Public Opinion and the Supreme Court," and Walter F. Murphy and Joseph Tannenhaus, "Public Opinion and the Supreme Court: The Goldwater Campaign," 32 *Public Opinion Quarterly* 31 (1968).
2. 370 U.S. 421 (1962).
3. For an overview of this excitement see William E. Beaney and Edward Beiser, "Prayer and Politics," 13 *Journal of Public Law* 475 (1964).
4. 333 U.S. 203 (1948).
5. Stokes, *op. cit.,* p. 8.
6. See Morgan, *op. cit.,* pp. 23–24.
7. Of course there is not unanimity within the American Jewish community on establishment questions. Over the past few years the Jewish day school movement has gained momentum, and a few small Jewish organizations are now actively working for public aid to church-related schools; see Morgan, *op. cit.,* pp. 66–67. In addition, a few Jewish intellectuals, such as Will Herberg, have argued that Jews should support the "Three Great Faiths" public religion as a check against secularism. Finally, there have been instances in which local Jewish groups have opposed a national group's making an issue of some local practice on grounds that such action will stir up anti-semitism which the local Jews, not the lawyers in New York, would have to live with.
8. For instance, *Zellers* v. *Huff,* 55 New Mexico 501 (1951). For a review of the case law see Note, "Religious Garb in the Public Schools—A Study in Conflicting Liberties," 22 *University of Chicago Law Review* 888 (1955).
9. The Court assumed that having a child in a school conferred standing beyond simple taxpayer standing (cf. *Doremus*). But absent a claim of personal coercion—a free-exercise claim—it is difficult to see why this should be so. See Ernest J. Brown, "Quis Custodiet Ipsos Custodes?—The School-Prayer Cases," 1963 *Supreme Court Review,* 23. With the relaxation of the Court's hostility to taxpayer actions in *Flast,* however, this question has become irrelevant.
10. Since Reed's retirement in 1957, only Associate Justice Potter

Stewart has been attracted to the narrow theory. Reed's championing of it won him considerable acclaim among accommodationists. See William O'Brien, *Justice Reed and the First Amendment* (Washington, D.C.: Georgetown University Press, 1948).

11. 333 U.S. 203, 209 (1948).

12. 343 U.S. 306 (1952).

13. The New York courts had loyally sustained the City's program.

14. Lawyers refer to language in a judicial opinion, which is unnecessary to the actual decision of the issue before the Court, as *obiter dicta*. *Dicta* for short.

15. 343 U.S. 306, 313 (1952).

16. The crucial sentences in Black's *McCollum* opinion read "Here not only are the State's tax-supported buildings used. . . . The State also affords sectarian groups an invaluable aid . . . through use of the State's compulsory school machinery." Unhappily for Justice Black, the meaning of these words is not "categorically clear." They are open to the interpretation Douglas chose to put on them. We shall probably never know why Black wrote as he did, but it is pardonable to guess that he joined the two arguments as he did to lend force and appeal to his opinion, without noting the ambiguity that was thereby introduced. It is also possible that the internal politics of the group of Justices supporting Black's opinion required him to waffle. If this was the case, we may discover it as the papers of the Justices become available.

17. *Torcaso* v. *Watkins*, 367 U.S. 488 (1961).

18. Arthur E. Sutherland, "Establishment According to *Engel*," 76 *Harvard Law Review* 25 (1962).

19. At about this point in the constitutional dialogue over governmentally religious practices, a terrible confusion developed around the term "coercion." The Justices have clearly used it in two senses: an "establishment" sense and a "free-exercise" sense. The establishment sense refers generally to the law-making and tax-gathering powers of government which are not to be employed in aid of religious institutions or purposes (*McCollum*). The free-exercise sense refers to individuals being required to undergo experiences distasteful to them on religious grounds (*Flag Salute* cases). Some commentators, despite repeated instruction from the Court in the matter, doggedly continue to assume that a governmentally sponsored religious exercise does not controvert the establishment clause unless *free-exercise* coercion is present. Whether or not the Court should decide this way will be discussed in the Conclusion; the point here is that the Court *has not* done so.

20. 370 U.S. 421, 424 (1962).

21. *Ibid.*, p. 441.

22. *Ibid.*, p. 445.

23. 374 U.S. 203 (1963), both the Pennsylvania Bible-reading and the Maryland Lord's Prayer cases were reported *sub. Nom. School District of Abington Township* v. *Schempp*.

24. For instance, Brown, *op. cit.*, p. 5.

25. 374 U.S. 203, 222 (1963).

26. *Per contra* see Robert G. McCloskey, "Principles, Powers and Values: The Establishment Clause and the Supreme Court," 1964 *Religion and the Public Order* 3.

27. 374 U.S. 203, 229 (1963).

28. It is worth noting that Brennan's opinion contains the best available short review of case law and literature on the establishment clause up to 1963.

29. Rampant non-compliance with *Engel-Schempp* has afforded a field day to political scientists interested in the political dynamics of compliance with Supreme Court decisions. See Richard M. Johnson, *The Dynamics of Compliance* (Evanston: Northwestern University Press, 1967); William K. Muir, Jr., *Prayer in the Public Schools* (Chicago: University of Chicago Press, 1967); Gordon Patric, "The Impact of a Court Decision: Aftermath of the *McCollum* Case," 6 *Journal of Public Law* 455 (1952); Frank J. Sorauf, "*Zorach* v. *Clauson:* The Impact of a Supreme Court Decision." 53 *American Political Science Review* 785 (1959); Ellis Katz, "Patterns of Compliance with Schempp," 14 *Journal of Public Law* 396 (1965). For a summary of these works, and of the "impact" literature generally, see Stephen L. Wasby, *The Impact of Supreme Court Decisions* (Homewood, Ill.: Dorsey Press, 1970).

30. See, for example, *Paul* v. *Dade County,* 202 S.2d 833 (1967).

31. While establishment and free-exercise argument ran through all four, two were principally on the establishment point—*McGowan* v. *Maryland,* 366 U.S. 420 and *Two Guys* v. *McGinley,* 366 U.S. 582—and two were principally on the free-exercise point—*Braunfeld* v. *Brown,* 366 U.S. 599 and *Gallagher* v. *Crown Kosher Market* 366 U.S. 617. For convenience I will refer to the establishment pair as *McGowan,* and to the free-exercise pair as *Braunfeld.*

32. 366 U.S. 420, 460 (1961).

33. The Court did not, of course, foreclose the possibility that a *particular* Sunday law might be federally unconstitutional if a showing could be made that it was, in fact, religiously motivated.

34. McCloskey, *op. cit.,* p. 10.

35. 370 U.S. 421, 435 (1962).

36. Military chaplains have drawn relatively little separationist fire because of the free-exercise argument for their maintenance: if the government impresses into service, and orders one of its servants away from his home and home church, the spirit, if not the letter, of the free-exercise clause obliges government to provide a spiritual surrogate.

37. Eugene *Register-Guard,* March 1, 1969.

38. New York *Times,* December 13, 1969.

39. Morgan, *op. cit.,* pp. 75–77.

40. For particulars of the 1971 resurgence, see New York *Times,* November 8, 1971.

6

The Decline of the Secular Regulation Rule

At this point we should return to the development of the free-exercise clause. As detailed in Chapter 3, the 1940's had seen a partial turning away from the nineteenth century notion that if governmental regulation served a valid secular purpose it could be enforced against a free-exercise claim. In the early 1960's, a new set of free-exercise problems began to come before the Justices, and commentators wondered whether a majority of the Warren Court would move further away from the old secular regulation line or return to it as representing the basic meaning of the First Amendment provision. Was the free-exercise clause to be accorded constitutional stature as one of those crucial limitations on government, such as the free-speech clause, around which public officials must very carefully tread and which may not be prejudiced except for the gravest of reasons after the clearest of showings? Or was it to remain confined approximately within the limits of *U.S.* v. *Reynolds*—a bar against governmentally imposed orthodoxy of belief, but affording little protection of otherwise proscribable action?[1]

BLUE LAWS (*FREE-EXERCISE*)

Where *McGowan* and *Two Guys* had posed the establishment question (whether the state could prescribe Sunday as the community day of rest), the *Braunfeld* and *Crown Kosher* cases posed the free-exercise question (whether sabbatarians could be punished if their religious conviction required them to observe another day, and they then worked or shopped on the forbidden Sunday). On the establishment question only Douglas had dissented, but on free-exercise this relative unity was shattered.

There were no "opinions of the Court" in *Braunfeld* and *Crown Kosher*. Chief Justice Warren, joined by Black, Clark, and Whittaker, announced the judgments, sustaining the convictions in both instances. Warren's two opinions stressed the indirect character of the burdens imposed on the non-conformists. The states, the Chief pointed out, were not forcing anyone to work on Saturday; if a person closed his business or refrained from shopping on that day for religious reasons, well and good. All the state was saying was that the loss of custom or time could not be made up on Sunday.

Justice Frankfurter, whose single opinion in *McGowan* applied to all four Sunday closing cases, also dwelt on the indirect character of the state-imposed burden. Counsel for the sabbatarian plaintiffs had urged that to escape the reach of the free-exercise clause a state must provide *at least* that those who show they observe a weekly day of rest other than Sunday be exempted from the requirement of ceasing business on that day. To this Frankfurter responded that:

> A legislature might in reason find that the alternative of exempting Sabbatarians would impede the effective operation of the Sunday statutes, produce harmful collateral effects, and entail, itself, a not inconsiderable intrusion into matters of religious faith. However preferable, personally, one might deem such an exception, I cannot find that the Constitution compels it.[2]

Thus nothing commanded by plaintiffs' faith had been forbidden, and the fact that they suffered inconvenience or competitive disadvantage as opposed to the majority of Sunday observers was not an imposition of sufficient magnitude to raise a free-exercise question. The Constitution, it was suggested, does not promise that it shall be equally convenient or costless to exercise all religions.

While neither the Warren nor the Frankfurter opinions contained a clear reaffirmation of the secular regulation approach, both reflected its spirit and relied on precedents in the *Reynolds* line. In their invocation of the direct-indirect dichotomy, the Warren and Frankfurter efforts may even be viewed as attempting to reconcile and conjoin the old, hard-boiled version of secular regulation (only beliefs are protected), and Justice Roberts' suggestion in *Cantwell* that both belief and action were protected by the free-exercise clause. Following Warren and Frankfurter, one sub-set of the set of otherwise valid secular regulations (those which bear *directly* on acts in exercise of religion) would be invalid, but the sub-set imposing indirect burdens (always presuming a valid secular purpose) would pass First Amendment muster.[3]

Justice William Brennan dissented in *Braunfeld* and *Crown Kosher,* and was joined by Justice Potter Stewart. While subscribing to the secular purpose argument developed by the Chief to get the Sunday closing laws around the establishment clause, Brennan balked at enforcing these otherwise valid laws against the sabbatarians who would suffer commercial disadvantage. A state may not confront an individual with a "choice between his business and his religion."[4] With glowing confidence Brennan translated Roberts' innovation of 1940 into an historical truth: "Religious freedom—the freedom to believe *and to practice* strange and, it may be, foreign creeds—has *classically* been one of the highest values of our society."[5] (This was followed by citation of the Jehovah's Witnesses cases discussed in Chapter 3.) While evincing a becoming sensitivity to the plight of the small Orthodox Jewish merchant, Brennan's opinion neither suggested limiting cases for exercises of religion (snake handling?),[6] nor did it address at all satisfactorily the direct-indirect distinction —which was, after all, the basis of the majority opinions Brennan was supposedly refuting.

SHERBERT v. *VERNER*

However, any thoughts that the Court might take refuge in the Warren-Frankfurter approach[7] as a half-way house between the unvarnished nineteenth century secular regulation and reading of the free-exercise clause as a new constitutional protector of otherwise punishable action was exploded with the reading on June 17, 1963 of Brennan's opinion for the Court in *Sherbert* v. *Verner.*[8]

Mrs. Sherbert, a Seventh-Day Adventist, lived and sometimes worked in Spartanburg, South Carolina. When discharged by her employer because of her refusal to work on Saturday, she found herself unable to accept other employment because of required Saturday work and applied for unemployment compensation benefits under the ongoing South Carolina program. The State Employment Service Commission refused on the grounds that a person who "refuses suitable work when offered . . . by the employment office or by the employer . . ." was disqualified from receiving benefits. The South Carolina Courts agreed but seven members of the U.S. Supreme Court did not.

The conclusion seems inescapable that *Sherbert* and *Braunfeld* cannot be reconciled. The burden imposed on Mrs. Sherbert was of precisely the same indirect sort as that imposed on the Orthodox Jewish merchants. They were all forced to choose between religious observance and economic disadvantage. No one was told by government he had to do anything on Saturday. It is, indeed, hard to imagine situations which are, in lawyers' jargon, so clearly "on all fours." Of the old *Braunfeld* majority Frankfurter had been replaced by Arthur Goldberg, and Warren, Black and Clark switched sides *sub silentio.* In an expanded, more sophisticated form, Brennan's dissent in *Braunfeld* now became the controlling constitutional law.

Reiterating that governmentally imposed choice was a cruel one, Brennan now relied heavily on an explicit analogy to free-speech cases, arguing that state imposed burdens on free-exercise, whether indirect or incidental, could only be justified if the state could show a "compelling interest" in the regulation at issue. (South Carolina, he concluded, could not.)

It should be quite clear that a "compelling interest" is very much more than the reasonable legislative purpose which is all that is needed for secular regulation to be enforceable under the old test. Brennan was holding that the special tests of necessity and the unavailability of alternative means (which are applied when governmental regulation touches upon free speech) must now be applied when a regulation touches upon religiously motivated action.[9] This translation of the free-exercise clause from the old secular regulation language into a new idiom drawn from the speech area increased potential importance of free-exercise as a protector of unorthodox behavior dramatically. Thus, Roberts' whispered promise in *Cantwell* was now fulfilled.

However, this increase in constitutional stature has brought with it three very knotty problems. One involves the apparent contradiction between the new theory of free-exercise and the Court's repeated declaration in establishment cases that government may not favor religious persons or motives as against irreligious persons and motives. A second involves the way in which a Court goes about saying what is "religion" and what is not—who should enjoy the new protection of actions which Brennan made available. The third involves the notion of "compelling interest" and the potential awkwardness of conditioning the existence of an individual constitutional right on the number of people who avail themselves of it.

THE ESTABLISHMENT DILEMMA

Clearly if Mrs. Sherbert had been addicted to two-day fishing weekends or to doing the family laundry every Saturday, neither activity would have protected her from being denied unemployment compensation after refusing jobs which entailed Saturday work. The Justices have left people with a religious reason for refusing to work markedly better off than those whose reasons are more mundane. Nor were those who concurred and dissented in *Sherbert* unaware of this problem. Mr. Justice Stewart drove the point home brutally in his concurrence. Recalling his oft-voiced dissent from the prevailing establishment theory, Stewart applauded the good sense of Brennan's innovation and ended by urging that the Court make a job of it and jettison the idea that government cannot over-aid religion or prefer it over irreligion on certain occasions. The now familiar Stewart theme was restated: if no one's freedom of worship is restricted, it does not matter what supports or advantages government makes available.

Justice Harlan (joined by White), on the other hand, not thinking that the establishment cases were wrongly decided, dissented from Brennan's result. Pointing out that the South Carolina requirement that an individual be available for work in order to qualify for benefits meant exactly what it said, and noting further that the prevailing pattern of work in the Spartanburg area involved a six-day week, he concluded that the state could by no stretch of the imagination be accused of discriminating against religion. Mrs. Sherbert was literally unavailable, and to prefer her reason to other reasons was to establish religion. While a legislative exemption of sabbatarians might pass establishment clause muster, no exemption could be required on free-exercise grounds.

The difficulty with treating the free-exercise clause as a protector of unorthodox expression, it appears, is that the speech clause is comprehensive—it applies to all persons. The free-exercise clause—at least presumably—applies to a narrower class of religious persons.

THE DEFINITIONAL MAZE

Even supposing Justice Stewart's view ultimately prevails, and the establishment clause is read to permit governmental discrimination in favor of religion, the problem of delimiting the category of eligibles will remain. How can the Court identify the religious claimant unless it has a definition of religion?

The difficulty of arriving at such a definition is dramatized by the case of *U.S.* v. *Ballard.*[10] Decided with an opinion for the Court by Justice Douglas in 1944, *Ballard* involved a federal prosecution for mail fraud of the organizers of the "I Am" movement—one of the more exotic minor enthusiasms of the late

1930's. By way of defense the Ballards (messengers from God according to their own teachings) asserted the religious character of their beliefs and of their appeals for funds. Though writing three years before *Everson,* Douglas (relying on cases such as *Watson* v. *Jones*) found the Court incompetent to inquire into the comprehensibility or tenability of asserted religious belief. The only question for judges, Douglas concluded, was whether the belief at issue was sincerely held.

The trouble with this was that the Ballards were charged with perpetrating a *fraud.* The common law theory of this crime involves a determination of whether a reasonable man could have believed that he could fulfill the promise on the basis of which funds were solicited. (The Ballards, for instance, had claimed to be able to effect miraculous cures.) But the reasonable man test cannot be applied to religious beliefs: to inquire in any way as to reasonableness would be an act of establishment. Douglas said that only sincerity can be tested. If the Ballards were found to have been sincere no crime could have been committed. And, as Justice Jackson eloquently and briefly pointed out in dissent, judging sincerity is no easier than judging the quality and tenability of beliefs. The temptation is for the ordinary juryman to conclude that what sounds unreasonable or unfamiliar cannot be sincerely believed.

Surely once the Court has abandoned the secular regulation rule, a "sincerity" definition for religion presents even greater awkwardness. More people will seek the increased protection, and Jackson's objection must somehow be met. What are the indicia of sincerity? Are judges to be guided by the length of time during which an individual has expressed particular beliefs? By this test anything that anyone has been talking about for long enough becomes religion, and behavior based on or motivated by the "belief" would have available the protection of the free-exercise clause. But if not time, then what? Perhaps the fervency with which the views are advanced might be the test? But how, in turn, is fervency to be gauged—timbre of voice and brightness of eye?

Nor can one throw up one's hands and retreat from the problem by saying "very well, we will simply take everyone at his word!" Were this approach taken, it would be possible, using the *Sherbert* situation as an example, for anyone to refuse work for any reason asserted to be religious and continue to receive unemployment compensation in South Carolina. Or, to use the *Ballard* example, it would be possible for any con man to escape punishment by claiming a sincere religious conviction in the miraculous validity of whatever offer he has made. In short, whatever protection of behavior came to be afforded by the free-exercise clause by this approach would be available to everyone for the asking on assertion of sincerity. This objection, as we shall see, also applies to an approach which would read the word "religion" in the First Amendment to mean individual conscience. Such a reading well might be a way of relieving the developing tensions between the establishment and free-exercise clauses, since the irreligious have consciences as well. But without a test for sincerity it leads to an absurd result: an otherwise valid law could be enforced only against those who accepted its enforcement—the reluctant others could claim conscientious immunity.

But for the purpose of argument, let us further assume away the inhibition against judicial scrutiny of religious beliefs which troubled Douglas in *Ballard*. This capacity to "test for religion" saves us from relying on a sincerity approach, but poses another problem. The Justices may now define religion but they must do the job coherently. Three ways of proceeding immediately present themselves: the Justices may examine the intrinsic quality of the beliefs asserted; they may examine forms of worship or practice associated with the asserted beliefs; or they may do both. (A possible fourth, "psychological" approach will be treated in the next chapter.)

To inquire into the quality of beliefs required that standards be set for determining what are assertions about the diety, about basic nature of man and about the human condition—standards which distinguish such assertions from trivial notions not worthy of the term religion. The mind boggles at the thought of judges hacking away, case by case, at this level of abstraction. Inchoate judicial subjectivism could be the only result.

But to examine practices is even worse. Must there be regular meetings? Must there be exercises of a liturgical sort? It is hard to see how judges could avoid taking the familiar forms of religious worship as covert norms; the orthodox would be advantaged over the believer practicing in strange ways—just the sort of person whose behavior the free-exercise is presumably being expanded to protect.

Nor does combining the first two approaches seem to improve prospects for coherence. Either the "standards" will let anybody qualify, or judges will be invited to discriminate against the unfamiliar. The dilemma is exquisite. If the Court is to extend the free-exercise clause to action, it must define religion, and to define religion is to arbitrarily impose an orthodoxy.

And the end is not in sight.

HOW MANY IS COMPELLING?

It was very silly, of course, for the Attorney-General of South Carolina to assert that his state had a great stake in keeping Mrs. Sherbert off its unemployment compensation rolls. It would even have been silly for South Carolina to assert this of all sabbatarians; surely they are a tiny part of the state's population, and the unemployment compensation machinery would not be wrecked if all such people were allowed to refuse Saturday work and draw benefits. South Carolina could, in short, have accommodated the petitioner, and all those similarly situated without sacrificing anything of its valid secular interest—making sure that the general run of able-bodied people who refuse work receive no benefits. This, indeed, is the basic, seemingly commonsensical consideration which moved the Court away from the old secular regulation rule. The government always seemed to be picking on a very small group that could be exempted without upsetting anything. The natural, humane response was to help out the little guy—especially so when the value he asserted was the emotionally powerful one of religious practice.

But what if a state has a substantial population of sabbatarians? One may attempt to dodge the difficulty by suggesting that if this were the case the political process would prevent the passage of unemployment compensation statutes which require Saturday work of anyone. Or, failing this, one might argue that it would be impolitic for a slender majority to pass a six-day statute against the deeply-felt opposition of a significant minority. Neither argument is to the point. It remains perfectly possible to conceive of a situation in which a solid majority insists on a six-day week, and a minority, large enough to frustrate the system, refuses work on Saturdays for reasons of religious conscience.

Does the right which existed for Mrs. Sherbert exist for the numbers now swamping the raft; or does the state now have the sort of "compelling interest" it previously lacked? If the latter is the case, how does one explain to someone now claiming the free-exercise "right" enjoyed by Mrs. Sherbert that he does not have it because too many others are attempting to exercise it?

Nor is it possible to escape by suggesting that, after all, there are other Bill-of-Rights guarantees which are similarly evanescent. It is not presumed, for instance, that one's Fourth Amendment protection against unreasonable searches and seizures is affected by the occurrence of crime waves. Nor is the privilege against self-incrimination of the Fifth Amendment to be diminished because of crowded court dockets. And even in the area of First Amendment protected expression (where the notion of "compelling state interest" is often employed by the Court), the right to speak is independent of numbers wishing to exercise it. The state does not have to let everyone who wants to express himself in a particular park do it *at the same time,* but it has to let him, and sooner rather than later. The "right" may be conditioned, but it does not *disappear* simply because of the number of claimants. There is only a superficial resemblance between the "numbers test" for compelling interest and the various "clear and present danger" approaches to deciding under what circumstances speech may be repressed. The "clarity" and "proximity" of danger contemplated by these approaches must arise from the character of the *particular* context and expression at issue—it must be "fighting words," or obscene, or advocacy of violent overthrow. It is hard to see how an intrinsically innocent expression could become proscribable (as opposed to regulatable) only because many others are expressing themselves similarly. But this is just what happens to the free-exercise of religion under a numbers test.

Of course, no difficulty is quite unique in constitutional law, and no doubt if we searched far enough we could discover some parallels to the numbers test (some invocations of "compelling interest" in equal protection cases have had a numerical ring). Finding them would not, however, make reliance on a numerically defined "compelling interest" any less treacherous.[11] Courts are not, generally, in a very good position to argue with legislatures over how much is too many.

THE PROMISE OF POT

The Justices can always, of course, back off—decide that the problems presented are too tricky and retreat toward the cover of a modified secular regulation rule. *Braunfeld* and *Sherbert* may be in tension, but *Braunfeld* has not been overruled. There is no evidence, however, of any such inclination. Indeed, all signs point in the *Sherbert* direction.[12] And let it be thought that the three problems we just discussed are remote or contrived, consider the California case of *People* v. *Woody,* decided in 1964.[13]

Jack Woody, a Navajo Indian, was a member of the Native American Church. An important part of the ritual of this body is the chewing of peyote cactus buttons—rich in mescaline. On Saturday night the faithful meet in a private house and the ceremony continues until dawn Sunday morning; adult males chew varying numbers of buttons, breakfast is served, and everyone goes home. Woody and others were followed, observed, arrested, and convicted under a California law making it a felony to ingest peyote. In defense, a free-exercise claim was raised.

The California Supreme Court to which the case eventually came was one of the most distinguished of American state benches. The opinion in *Woody* was written by Matthew O. Tobriner, and the unanimous Court included the highly regarded Chief Judge Roger Traynor.[14]

After a preface, in which he detailed the valid secular purpose underlying the legislature's proscription of peyote use, Tobriner turned to the question of an exemption on federal free-exercise grounds and found such an exemption constitutionally required. Tobriner's reasoning, however, was less clear than his final answer. The problem of a possible establishment objection to an exemption in favor of religious users was simply ignored. The problem of saying what is a religious exercise was leap-frogged with the assertion that the ritual of the Native American Church had been anciently so considered.[15] After pointing out that *Sherbert* required a compelling interest as opposed to mere validity of purpose and rationality of means, Tobriner stumbled into the final pit of suggesting so few people were involved that the state could exempt them and still secure the objective which underlay the legislation. In fact, Tobriner noted, other states (e.g., New Mexico) had specifically exempted the Native Americans from their anti-pot statutes. The opinion ended with a lyrical invocation of the ideal of cultural pluralism in America:

> The varying currents of subcultures that flow into the mainstream of our national life give it depth and beauty.[16]

But we are left with the curious result that if one gets high on mescaline in California for fun he may be subjected to criminal sanctions; if, however, he chews peyote as part of a religious observance he is immune—not as a matter of legislative grace but of federal constitutional law.[17]

The population which may attempt to avail itself of such an exception is potentially very large. With the use of hallucinogens spectacularly on the rise, a casual reading of the daily press indicates the frequency with which mystical and religious invocations and rituals are becoming associated with this use. As sales of books on astrology and the occult soar, and drug-using spiritualist "communes" mushroom, judges may be forgiven a shudder as they contemplate dealing with future free-exercise claims armed only with the *Ballard* sincerity test. Already a free-exercise claim for the sacerdotal use of pot has been made before the U.S. Supreme Court by attorneys for that dean of the drug-culture, Timothy Leary. The Justices managed to dispose of Leary's case on other grounds, but the next time they may not be so fortunate.[18]

SOME DIFFICULT MARGINAL ISSUES

Several other sorts of free-exercise questions, while not of as immediate importance as those just surveyed, are worthy of note.

The Crime of Blasphemy

It is unclear whether the status of the ancient crime of blasphemy should be discussed as an establishment question or a free-exercise question. Although there have been only two reported prosecutions in the last fifty years, a number of states still have statutes on their books which punish various forms of blasphemous address.[19] Nor has the Supreme Court ever had occasion to hold such regulations unconstitutional. But whether on establishment grounds (a discrimination in favor of religious sensibilities), or on free-exercise grounds (punishment of the expression of a belief which cannot be suppressed no matter how disagreeable it may be to some hearers), it should be clear that the crime of blasphemy is out.[20] Sooner or later, some jurisdiction will probably initiate a prosecution which will reach the Supreme Court. Indeed, Maryland did initiate an action two years ago, and the matter was sorted out in the state courts. However, it is hard to imagine a situation in which the Justices would allow resuscitation of the crime of blasphemy, and concern about blasphemy statutes remaining unrepealed seems a bit farfetched.

A more interesting case involving the establishment clause and the proscription of supposedly anti-religious views is *Epperson* v. *Arkansas*.[21] The facts of *Epperson* evoke the images of Clarence Darrow and William Jennings Bryan and the famous "Monkey Trial" of 1925. There the unhappy John Scopes, a Tennessee biology teacher, was accused of violating a state law which forbade presentation in a public school of the theory that man had evolved from lower orders of animals. Scopes had been convicted at trial and the constitutionality of the Tennessee act had been upheld by the Tennessee Supreme Court. During this same period of fundamentalist enthusiasm, Arkansas had adopted a statute similar to that of Tennessee. In 1965 another young biology teacher, Susan Epperson, teaching in the Little Rock Central High School, challenged the Arkansas prohibition.

As with Tennessee earlier, the Arkansas Supreme Court upheld the statute as a legitimate exercise of the power of the state to specify the curriculum of its public schools. This time, however, the case found its way to the U.S. Supreme Court. The principal arguments offered against the statute by Miss Epperson's counsel and by the American Civil Liberties Union and the National Education Association in *amicus* briefs, involved free speech and an asserted constitutional right to "academic freedom" teased out of the speech and association clauses.

It is interesting that the majority of the Justices steered well clear of endorsing a "right" of a public school teacher to teach what she liked. Instead Justice Fortas, speaking for himself and six others, anchored himself in that portion of the ACLU brief, written by ubiquitous Leo Pfeffer, which suggested that since the sole reason for the Arkansas ban on evolutionary theory was its contradiction of a Christian orthodoxy (i.e., the *Genesis* account of creation) the act was an impermissible establishment of religion. This was a very neat twist. Fortas was able to underscore the teaching of the school prayer cases that the state may not favor religious doctrine; he got rid of an obnoxious, if archaic, statute; and he avoided diminishing the general power of states to prescribe public school curricula which would have resulted from launching a constitutional theory of academic freedom.

Enforced Medical Care

Two sorts of cases trouble here: persons who refuse certain sorts of medical care for themselves or minor children when life is in danger (primarily Jehovah's Witnesses), and persons who fail to seek medical care for sick or injured children because of religious scruples (primarily Christian Scientists).

Is there a free-exercise right to refuse a needed transfusion if one's life, or that of one's child, is in danger on grounds of the Biblical injunction (interpreted literally by Witnesses) against eating blood? The "authorities" are by no means agreed. Where minors are involved, the tendency has been for the courts to remove children from parental authority and appoint guardians who then consent to the treatment.[22] With adults the outcomes have been mixed, unless the patients were incapable of understanding or communicating, in which case courts have tended to treat them in the same manner as children and appoint guardians. Typical of one persuasion is the opinion written by Judge J. Skelly Wright of the Circuit Court for the District of Columbia in a case involving the request of a hospital to administer blood to a conscious and nonconsenting Jehovah's Witness.[23]

> . . . I spoke to Mr. Jones, the husband of the patient. He advised me that, on religious grounds, he would not approve a blood transfusion for his wife. He said, however, that if the court ordered the transfusion, "the responsibility was not his." The patient herself said that the transfusion would be "against my will," but when asked "whether she would oppose the transfusion if the court allowed it," she indicated that "it would not be her responsibility." [24]

Thus Judge Wright reasoned that the order for the transfusion could issue: "Mrs. Jones had no wish to be a martyr. And her religion merely prevented her *consent* to the transfusion."[25] The free-exercise question did not arise.

While Wright's distinction between being given a transfusion and consenting to a transfusion might strike some students as a trifle sophistic, the result seems preferable to that in the Illinois case *In re Brooks,*[26] which typifies the other approach. Here the patient refused consent, the order was issued and the transfusion administered, but the Supreme Court of Illinois later held that a free-exercise violation had occurred. Thus the issuing judge was left with the knowledge that he had saved Brooks and violated the First Amendment which he had sworn to uphold.

Furthermore, one cannot fall back comfortably on the "common sense" view which holds that when human life is in danger it is unnecessary to worry about "legal technicalities." A principled working out of the enforced medical care problem must involve tackling issues such as the interest society properly has in a single life. Presumably this is a sufficient interest to proscribe suicide (although this is being subjected to increasing question). In the case of suicide, it might be argued, there is no colorable constitutional right involved; while the act of refusing a transfusion may be religiously motivated, the act of blowing one's brains out is not. Even here, however, a Shintoist might disagree. Happily (at least for judges), cases of enforced medical care tend to be quickly mooted (the patient either dies or is treated and gets well) so that higher appellate courts are rarely forced to consider the problem.

This is not true, however, of cases involving criminal prosecutions of parents for failing to seek medical help for children who later die. The limiting factor on the number of these cases is the tendency of prosecutorial authorities not to move against grief stricken and otherwise upstanding Christian Scientist parents. When the decision to prosecute is made, however, the result is an agonizing tension between compelling values.

In 1967, in Barnstable County, Massachusetts (Cape Cod), for example, a prosecutor secured a manslaughter conviction of a Christian Scientist mother whose five-year-old daughter had died, unattended, of pneumonia.[27] Sentence was suspended and there was no appeal, but the free-exercise question was raised, and it is quite possible that a case of this sort will reach the U.S. Supreme Court one day. Under the old secular regulation approach[28] the answer would have been clear, but in the post-*Sherbert* context, a coherent resolution of the matter will be a tricky business, to say the least.

The Plain People

For as long as compulsory school attendance has been the practice of American states (and that is almost a hundred years) there have been occasional parents who have refused, for religious reasons, to submit their children to the requirement. They have sometimes suffered criminal penalties, and, in rare instances, lost custody of their children. One major source of such resistance has been that hard-bitten, cohesive, German sect, the Amish (more precisely, several fundamentalist branches of the Mennonites). With their buggies and their beards and their determinedly pastoral way of life, the Amish seem almost too good to be true. Spread in a narrow belt across the country from eastern Pennsylvania to the far Midwest, it is the disposition of the Amish to reject formal schooling for their children beyond the eighth grade. Their agricultural communities, according to doctrine, should be "separate from the world," and advanced secular education is regarded as reducing the chances of salvation of those subjected to it. Over the years, various states worked out awkward accommodations with the Amish, and the free-exercise question was generally scrupulously avoided. In December, 1971, however, the Supreme Court heard oral argument of a case testing the conviction of an Amish parent against a free-exercise clause challenge.[29]

Wisconsin chose to force the issue of Amish children continuing past eighth grade until they reached the state's established school-leaving age of 16. The Wisconsin Supreme Court held this enforcement the normal rule against Amish children a violation of the federal free-exercise clause, and the U.S. Supreme Court, speaking through its Chief, agreed.

This was Warren Burger's first free-exercise opinion, and he firmly associated himself with the *Sherbert* line. He seemed quite untroubled that religious motives were being accorded better treatment than non-religious.

> . . . if the Amish had asserted their claims because of their subjective evaluation and rejection of contemporary secular values accepted by the majority, much as Thoreau rejected the social values of his time and isolated himself at Walden Pond, their claim would not rest on a religious base.[30]

As for the problem of determining who was religious, Burger dwelt on the long and respectable history of the Amish in America. It was almost as if the Chief Justice was concluding that durability should be the test—if you have been around for a long while, and everybody has regarded you as religious, you are entitled to free-exercise clause protection.[31]

Finally, *Yoder* is fascinating for what it implies concerning Burger's reading of the establishment, and concerning the direction in which his "no-entanglement" approach may be developing. It suggests that Burger may be in the process of persuading himself that "no-entanglement" is an altogether independent value; that there is no establishment clause violation absent of entanglement. Government may create favored classifications for the religious as long as it does not administratively intermeddle. We noted in Chapter 4 that in *Walz* and *Lemon* Burger's idea of impermissible entanglement seemed to depend on basic, anterior values such as no favoritism of religion over irreligion, and avoiding religious classifications; the suggestion that government could aid if it did not "entangle" received short shrift. After *Yoder,* it is almost incredible that "no-entanglement" is assuming a life on its own, and if this should prove to be so, it would constitute a departure of the first importance in American Constitutional law. It would no longer be understood that the establishment clause is set against forcing religious motives over irreligious.

CONCLUSION

It is fair to say of the majority of the Warren Court that in the free-exercise area a diffuse desire to protect unorthodox minorities led it, helter-skelter, into a major doctrinal innovation. The free-exercise clause has now grown far beyond the confines of *Reynolds,* and it is problematical whether the Burger Court, even if a majority wished to, could reduce free-exercise to its pre-*Sherbert* dimensions. This does not mean, of course, that the Burger Court is in some sense foreordained to continue straight down the trail which the Warren majority was taking. But the choices, unhappily, are *not* restricted to going back to *Reynolds* or confronting the problems outlined above in this Chapter and satisfactorily rationalizing future decisions in cases resembling *People* v. *Woody.* A third choice, unheroic but perhaps politic, is to waffle—to dispose of the appealing religious claims with ringing references to *Sherbert* and dispose of the obnoxious claims with equally convinced reliance on the *Reynolds* line of cases. The present confusion of precedents and turbulence in American manners, morals, and religious styles may make this expedient (or series of expedients) irresistible. For reasons which will be argued later, this sort of fudging will not, in the long run, produce adequate constitutional law, but it has powerful short run attraction.

On one free-exercise problem, however, the Burger Court has indicated how far it is (or is not) prepared to go. This is the specialized problem of conscientious objection to compelled military service, and it is to that we now turn.

NOTES

1. A warning is in order. It is not suggested that the old belief-action distinction was altogether without ambiguity. What about the actual ritual of the Mass? This was "action" but surely it should enjoy the protection of belief. Despite this fuzziness at the fringes, however, the distinction and the secular regulation rule which followed from it was a powerful and fairly precise instrument of discrimination. As is so often the case, its critics pointed to its irreducible ambiguity as an excuse for replacing it with something more ambiguous still. But this gets ahead of our story.

2. 366 U.S. 420, 521 (1961).

3. While differing somewhat in spirit, this reading is reconcilable with the letter of Waite's opinion in *Reynolds;* see J. Morris Clark, "Guidelines for the Free Exercise Clause," 83 *Harvard Law Review* 327 (1969).

4. 366 U.S. 420, 611 (1961).

5. *Ibid.,* p. 612 (italics mine).

6. *Lawson* v. *Commonwealth,* 164 S.W. 2d 972 (Ky. 1942).

7. For discussion of the advantages of that approach see Note, "A *Braunfeld* v. *Brown* Test for Indirect Burdens on the Free Exercise of Religion," 48 *Minnesota Law Review* 1165 (1964).

8. 374 U.S. 398 (1963).

9. This is especially clear at the end of Section I of the opinion on p. 403.

10. 322 U.S. 78 (1944).

11. This is not to suggest that "compelling interest" may not be defined in other ways than by reference to numbers. It happens that the phrase as used by Brennan in *Sherbert* has a numerical implication. An example of an equal protection case which seems to relate compelling interest to numbers is *Shapiro* v. *Thompson,* 394 U.S. 618 (1969). Brennan was also the author of *Shapiro.*

12. See *In re Jenison,* 375 U.S. 14 (1963). Here the court remanded for reconsideration in light of *Sherbert* the Minnesota conviction of a woman who had refused jury duty for religious reasons ("Judge not . . ."). Had she refused service on the grounds that judging others was a psychologically painful business for her, there would, presumably, have been no bar to conviction.

13. 40 Cal. Rptr. 69 (1964).

14. The Attorney General of California chose not to ask for U.S. Supreme Court review of the California Court's interpretation of the federal First Amendment. There the matter rested.

15. This was quite true. References to the use of peyote in rituals of worship occur in Spanish sources as early as 1560. See generally, James Slotkin, *The Peyote Religion* (Glencoe, Ill.: Free Press, 1956).

16. 40 Cal. Rptr. 69, 74 (1964).

17. Or consider the practice of Rutgers (the State University of New Jersey) which requires a certificate of vaccination of all entrants, but exempts Christian Scientists. See *Kolbeck* v. *Kramer,* 84 N.J. Super 569 (1964), and cf. *Jacobson* v. *Massachusetts.* If Rutgers stops exempting as an act of "grace" might Christian Science applicants have a free-exercise *right* to be exempted?

18. *Leary* v. *U.S.* 395 U.S. 6 (1969). The free-exercise claim was elaborately argued at trial. See 383 F. 2d 851 (1967).

19. An excellent review of the question, including a discussion of the one recent blasphemy prosecution (in Maryland), is Note, "Blasphemy," 70 *Columbia Law Review* 694 (1970).

20. The same argument applies to the related notion of "sacrilege" which figured in the famous free speech case of *Burstyn* v. *Wilson,* 343 U.S. 495 (1952).

21. 393 U.S. 97 (1968).

22. See generally, Note, "Compulsory Medical Treatment," 51 *Minnesota Law Review* 293 (1966), and W. K. Archibald, "Medical Aid for Children Without Parental Consent," 13 *Wyoming Law Journal* 83 (1958).

23. *Application of the President and Directors of Georgetown College, Inc.*, 331 F. 2d 1000 (D.C. cir. 1964).

24. *Ibid.,* p. 1007.

25. *Ibid.,* p. 1009 (italics mine).

26. 32 Ill. 2d 361 (1965).

27. *Commonwealth* v. *Sheridan,* No. 26307, Barnstable County Superior Court (1967).

28. As exemplified by *Prince* v. *Massachusetts,* 321 U.S. 158 (1944), which held it constitutional for the state to prohibit minor children distributing religious literature; or *Jacobson* v. *Massachusetts,* 197 U.S. 11 (1905), which vindicated compulsory vaccination against a free-exercise objection.

29. *Yoder* v. *Wisconsin.*—U.S.—(1972).

30. *Ibid.,* p. 10.

31. Cf. *Cassius Marsellus Clay, Jr., also known as Muhammad Ali* v. *U.S.,—U.S.*—(1971). In the spring of 1971, the Court announced, *per curium,* that the Black Muslim profession of the heavyweight champion was a religion for selective service act purposes. How does this square with *Yoder?* Will the Black Muslims be entitled to precisely the same free-exercise protection available to the established Amish? Or will the Muslims be entitled to any constitutional protection? Or will they be entitled to some lesser degree of protection corresponding to their *parvenue* status. Are there to be grades of religion for First Amendment purposes, or is it an all-or-nothing proposition? It seems clear that the Chief Justice has obligated himself to enlighten us.

7

The Conscience Explosion

The coincidence of an erosion of conventional patriotic assumptions among elite young people and an unpopular war, along with conscription, has resulted in suddenly increased concern over the terms on which persons may be exempted from required military service. Proposals to afford greater latitude for conscientious objection, rare a decade ago, are now commonplace. Yet the problem of specifying the terms of exemption is far from new. Each time the American Congress has felt itself forced to resort to conscription, there has been concern expressed that perhaps some men, because of the quality of their religious beliefs, should be exempted from the draft. In the twentieth century Congress has grappled with the problem of providing a religious exemption on four major occasions. In addition, the argument is heard increasingly of late that the free-exercise clause should be read as affording a *constitutional* right of religious or conscientious exemption. We shall consider the legislative and then the constitutional dimensions of the controversy. While the two are obviously related, confusing them is instantly fatal to understanding.

THE HISTORY OF RELIGIOUS EXEMPTION

Shortly after the Declaration of War in 1917, Congress enacted the Selective Service Draft Act.[1] While departing in various minor respects, successive American drafts have followed generally the 1917 model. Seeking to provide for what was generally perceived as a small population of religious objectors to participation in war, section 7(d) of the 1917 Act allowed for the exemption from combatant service of members of a "well-recognized sect or organization" that held strict pacificism a part of its essential doctrine. The exempted class was, clearly, composed of members of the historic peace churches. This approach had the advantage of objectivity. The historic peace churches were well known (Quakers, Brethren, Amish, Adventists, etc.), and it was easy to say who was exempted and who was not. The only possible ambiguity concerned what constituted membership, but even here there were some guidelines in the rules and practices of the churches themselves.

The trouble with the section 7(d) exemption was that recognized and respectable religious bodies other than the historic peace churches (e.g., the Methodists) had pacifist minorities, and these people received no relief. The Selective Service Administration dealt with this problem by issuing a regulation "interpreting" the statutory language to include members of *any* recognized church who objected on religious grounds to any participation in war.[2] With this modification, draft boards muddled through to the Armistice.

It was to incorporate the World War I administrative ruling into the statute that section 5(g) was written into the next Selective Service Act, that of 1940.[3] This section exempted those who "by reason of religious training and belief" were opposed to participation in war. Political, sociological, philosophical, and personal moral grounds were specifically disallowed as grounds for exemption. What then of those who were not members of recognized churches, whose religious training had been negligible, and whose beliefs were nontheistic? As cases came to the federal courts during World War II different answers were given.[4] In *U.S.* v. *Kauton*,[5] in 1943, the Court of Appeals for the Second Circuit suggested (through Augustus Hand) that the promptings of an "inward mentor" might in some circumstances be sufficient for a claimant to qualify under 5(g). Thus the judicial reading of "religious training and belief" in *Kauton* was quite broad (even though the defendant in that case was found ultimately not to qualify), and the Second Circuit held to this view in subsequent decisions.[6] In 1946, however, the Ninth Circuit decided *Berman* v. *U.S.*[7] In direct contradiction of the Second Circuit interpretation, the judges of the Ninth gave it as their opinion

> . . . that the expression "by reason of religious training and belief" . . . was written into the statute for the specific purpose of distinguishing between a conscientious social belief, of a sincere devotion to a high moralistic philosophy, and one based upon an individual's belief in his responsibility to an authority higher and beyond a worldly one.[8]

Against the background of these clashing interpretations of 5(g) Congress moved, in 1948, for the third time, to write a religious exemption clause. Section 6(j) of the Universal Military Training and Service Act of 1948 was described in the committee report which accompanied it to the Senate floor as follows:

> This section re-enacts substantially the same provisions as were found in subsection 5(g) of the 1940 act. Exemption extends to anyone, who, because of religious training and belief and belief in his relation to a Supreme Being, is conscientiously opposed to a combatant military service or to both combatant and non-combatant military service. (See *United States* v. *Berman*. . . .)[9]

The term "Supreme Being" had been employed as a term of art in *Berman*, and it is inconceivable (I choose my words) that the term and the parenthetical reference to *Berman* were included by the congressional authors for any other reason than to express approval of the Ninth Circuit reading, and to indicate that theistic religious belief was indeed to be required for exemption under 6(j). While it is always foolish to pronounce confidently concerning the "intent of Congress" on the evidence that a few members of a subcommittee approved one set of words as opposed to another, section 6(j) is as clear an example as we ever get of the Congress taking its pick between conflicting interpretations of what it had meant by a past enactment and giving fresh instruction to the courts.

THE SAGA OF SECTION 6(j)

The crucial test of 6(j) came in 1965 (as opposition to the draft mounted among elite youth) in the case of *Seeger* v. *U.S.*[10] Daniel Andrew Seeger had received a conventional religious upbringing but had ceased to practice by the time he registered for the draft at age 18. In a timely fashion he requested and returned to his local board Selective Service System Form No. 150 which was, in effect, an application for CO classification under 6(j). Question 1 of Series II on the Form 150 required the registrant to respond "yes" or "no" to the question "Do you believe in a Supreme Being?" Seeger indicated that he could not answer this question. Furthermore, in response to a question as to whether his objection was based on religious training and belief, Seeger found it necessary to cross out the words *training and;* he placed quotation marks around the word religion, and attached a statement of his personal views on the immorality of war and his incapacity to participate in it. Seeger's local board denied the claim, and the district court convicted.

On appeal Seeger's lawyers argued that 6(j) must be read either as exempting Seeger's sort of conscientious objection (basically the old *Kauton* theory) or that 6(j) was a congressional preferment of religion to irreligion proscribed by the establishment clause. The Second Circuit combined the two arguments and held 6(j) (insofar as theistic belief was required) unconstitutional,[11] but Seeger himself was excused on the grounds that a *Kauton* style exemption could be substituted.[12]

The disincentives to the Justices of the Supreme Court to follow the Second Circuit were, however, considerable. Not only was there the usual reluctance to declare an act of Congress unconstitutional—it is one thing for the Second Circuit to play the gadfly, it is another thing for the Supreme Court to act with final authority—but it was possible in early 1965 that if the Court struck down the Supreme Being requirement of 6(j), Congress would eliminate the exemption provision altogether while Seeger was before the Court. The monthly draft calls were increasing ominously, and thousands of respectable, appealing college boys were being faced with the choice of a step forward or years in prison. Section 6(j) was a valuable escape valve; without it incidents of resistance might have multiplied. The Justices were loath to let it go completely or explicitly substitute for it.

On the other hand, reading 6(j) to accommodate Daniel Seeger (without finding at least the Supreme Being clause unconstitutional) and thus to follow the Second Circuit was no easy task. While it is traditional procedure for the Court to read a problematical act in any possible way in order to preserve its constitutionality, it has never been suggested that there are no limits on the possible.[13] And while interpreting statutes is wild and woolly activity ("unstructured," in contemporary parlance), there are a few generally accepted guiding notions (if not rules):[14] it is simple obscurantism to argue that since Congress never speaks with a single or clear voice, anything goes in construing language which is finally voted and sent to the President. The awkward fact was that Seeger was precisely the sort of person which the *Kauton* court had tried to slip by under the old 5(g), and which 6(j), with its references to a Supreme Being and its citation of *Berman,* had been drawn to exclude.[15]

Nonetheless, the Court managed. In an opinion for himself and seven others, Mr. Justice Clark relied heavily on Seeger's own characterization of his views as "religious." In an attempt to evade the difficulties of defining religion, Clark suggested a new "test." Religion was

> A sincere and meaningful belief which occupies in the life of the possessor a place parallel to that filled by the God of those admittedly qualifying for the exemption. . . .[16]

Any judicial inquiry was to be restricted to whether the belief was "sincere and meaningful" and, whether in the registrant's "own scheme of things," was thought of as religious.[17]

Thus the establishment-clause challenge to 6(j) was, for the time being, avoided. But the nagging question remained: "How far could 6(j) be stretched?" Could it be infinitely elastic in the hands of resolute and resourceful Justices? What of the registrant who refused to characterize his beliefs as religious—even religious in quotation marks? And what, most particularly, of the "selective objector," who was not opposed to war in any form, but conscientiously opposed to participating in wars of which he disapproved?[18] An answer to the first question came in the *Welsh* case, decided in the spring of 1970.[19] The second was dealt with by the Court in the spring of 1971, in *Gillette* v. *U.S.* and *Negre* v. *Larsen.*

THE WELSH CASE

Elliott Ashton Welsh, II, enjoyed an upbringing similar to Seeger's, and he also felt compelled to edit his Form 150 extensively. Where Seeger had settled for quotation marks around religion, Welsh crossed the word out. His beliefs, he stated, had been formed "by reading in the fields of history and sociology." He was a considerably larger camel for the needle's eye of 6(j).

Not all the Justices were up to the stretching this time. Justice Black announced the judgment of a Court divided six to two, and read an opinion for himself, Douglas, Brennan, and Marshall. Taking note of Welsh's refusal to characterize himself as religious (as contrasted to Seeger), Black explained why this did not distinguish the two cases:

> The Court's statement in *Seeger* that a registrant's characterization of his own belief as "religious" should carry great weight.

> 380 U.S. at 184, does not imply that his declaration that his views are non-religious should be treated similarly.[20]

Put simply, if you say you are religious it counts for you; if you say you are not, the Court will overlook the indiscretion and proceed to an independent determination of the question for 6(j) purposes. Having freed himself from this *Seeger* entanglement, Black went on to find that Welsh's belief that taking life was morally wrong was held with a fervor equal to that of traditional religious convictions, and the 6(j) required no more.

Justice Harlan found himself able to concur in the result, but by a much different route. He was not able to follow Black's construction of 6(j); indeed, reading Black's opinion made him repent of subscribing to Clark's in *Seeger*. After reviewing the legislative history of 6(j), Harlan concluded:

> Against this legislative history it is a remarkable feat of judicial surgery to remove, as did *Seeger,* the theistic requirement of section 6(j). The Court today, however, in the name of interpreting the will of Congress, has performed a lobotomy and completely transformed the statute by reading out of it any distinction between religiously acquired beliefs and those deriving from "essentially political, sociological, or philosophical views or a merely personal code."[21]

Harlan concluded that the only coherent course was to find 6(j) unconstitutional as an establishment of religion. Having done this, however, he saw two further options available to the Court:

> Where a statute is defective because of underinclusion [non-religious objectors left out] there exists two remedial alternatives: a court may either declare it a nullity and order that its benefits not extend to the class that the legislature intended to benefit, or it may extend the coverage of the statute to include those who are aggrieved by exclusion.[22]

In other words, the Court could say no exemption existed, or it could return to a *Kauton* theory and leave it up to Congress whether it wished to let this stand as the meaning of 6(j) or eliminate the entire exemption itself. This was the result which the Second Circuit seems to have contemplated in its *Seeger* decision, and it had the virtue of saving the statutory exemption for conscientious objectors without necessitating verbal contortions concerning the intent of Congress. The fact that it found no supporter other than Harlan is surprising; it is hard to see why a Court prepared to read 6(j) so preposterously would not be prepared to tell the Congress that its obvious intent was unconstitutional and that a judicial substitute would be employed until the lawgivers could do better.

Mr. Justice White wrote the single dissenting opinion in *Welsh,* joined by Justice Stewart. Agreeing with Harlan as to the intent of Congress in section 6(j), he differed in the result as far as Mr. Welsh was concerned. Welsh was clearly not of that class for which Congress had provided exemption. That classification might indeed be unconstitutional (White forbore answer here), but if it was, then, contrary to Harlan, White thought there could be no exemption at all. Welsh was in violation either way.

Despite the stinging punches landed in the concurrence and the dissent, the majority position in *Welsh* appears one which those Justices will cling to tenaciously. After the stretching necessary to slip Mr. Welsh through 6(j), might not the majority hold their position against all comers until, perhaps, Congress changed the statute? Meanwhile, applications for CO classification soared, and one draft board in Chicago suspended operations, explaining that plain men, working on a part-time basis, could not deal with the post-*Welsh* crush, or distinguish those who felt strongly against killing from those who simply said they did.[23] And, as if this were not enough, there remained the question of selective objections and the argument for a constitutional exemption under the free-exercise clause.

THE SISSON *CASE*

On March 21, 1969, in the United States District Court in Boston, a jury returned a verdict that John Heffron Sisson, Jr., was guilty of refusing to submit for induction under the Military Selective Service Act of 1967. After this verdict, Sisson's lawyers made a motion for arrest of judgment, reminding Judge Charles Wyzanski of the argument raised during trial that section 6(j) as written was an unconstitutional establishment of religion, and asking for a *Kauton*-style reading which would exempt their client. Judge Wyzanski, a distinguished and innovative jurist and Chief Judge of the district, addressed his opinion granting the arrest of judgment to the constitutionality of 6(j) *and* to the further constitutional question of whether the free-exercise clause itself could be read as affording some exemption from required military service on grounds of conscientious objection.[24]

Sisson, in fact, posed the ultimate question for 6(j). He not only based his objection on political and philosophical grounds (he had not even returned his Form 150), and he objected only to combat service in Vietnam, not to participation in war *per se.* At least Seeger and Welsh had come to the courts as principled pacifists; for them, war itself was the evil in which they believed they could not take part. Sisson thought some wars might be justified, and if so he would participate. He reserved to himself the judgment of acceptability, and he felt he could not participate if the war in question (e.g., Vietnam) failed his test.

As with Seeger and Welsh, Sisson's attorneys had argued either that 6(j) must be read as sufficiently comprehensive to exempt their client (the *Kauton*-style reading) or it was an establishment in contravention of the First Amendment. Wyzanski, rather than engaging in wishful thinking concerning the intent of Congress, disposed of section 6(j) in terms resembling those of Harlan's *Welsh* concurrence. But then he simply swept past the question of whether 6(j) should be judicially rewritten in *Kauton* terms or considered a nullity. Instead, he seized the distinction of being the first Federal judge to assert the existence of a *constitutional* (free-exercise clause) exemption to which all conscientious objectors—even selective objectors—could appeal.

Wyzanski's argument for a free-exercise exemption had two prongs. First, while courts might be constrained by the intent of Congress in interpreting the word "religion" for section 6(j) purposes, no such restraint operated when the word "religion" in the First Amendment was being construed. Wyzanski simply elevated the *Seeger* "parallel role" test to constitutional status. (The Framers' intent, apparently, was more amenable to such a construction than that of Congress when it used "religion," but it was not made clear why.) Second, the free-exercise clause forbids conscripting conscientiously opposed individuals for service in a war so remote from the defense of the continental United States as that in Vietnam. Wyzanski conceded that in a situation in which the national soil was threatened with invasion, and in which Congress had declared war, it might be within the power of Congress to conscript without granting any exemptions. But, he suggested, when Congress conscripts in time of peace (with no declaration of war) it is constitutionally required to exempt conscientious objectors—always provided, following the *Seeger* formula, they could demonstrate that their beliefs were as important to them as religious beliefs to an orthodox, theistic pacifist.[25] And just here the perceptive reader might experience a sense of *deja vu*. The argument that Congress can conscript without exemption for big wars which it declares, but not for little wars which it merely funds, bears a family resemblance to the "compelling interest" test espoused in *Sherbert:* here it is a notion of the size of the conflict rather than the number of claimants which is determinative.

As for the selective character of Sisson's objection, Wyzanski passed over this point, noting that a person could feel just as strongly and sincerely about one war as another person could feel about all wars. The establishment clause problem of favoring religious reasons over non-religious did not exist for Wyzanski; after elevating the "parallel role" test to constitutional standing there was no longer any religious coloration to the classification and the problem ceased to exist (the First Amendment was read "law respecting an establishment of religion, or prohibiting the free exercise of conscience"). And on the final problem of how judges are to distinguish claims of conscience from claims, say, of convenience, Wyzanski responded charmingly:

> The suggestion that courts cannot tell a sincere from an insincere conscientious objector underestimates what the judicial process

performs every day. Ever since, in *Edginton* v. *Fitzmaurice* (1882) L.R. 29 Ch. Div. 359, Bowen, L.J., quipped that "the state of a man's mind is as much a fact as the state of his digestion," each day courts have applied laws, criminal and civil which make sincerity the test of liability.[26]

Now this is quite true. The embarrassment, of course, arises when it is remembered that in the common, garden variety legal situtaions in which judgments must be made as to states of mind, the question to be answered is *not* what the individual at bar actually believed, but what a *reasonable man* who behaved in the way the individual had behaved would believe. Defendants in criminal cases are usually held to have intended the natural and probable consequences of their actions, but what is natural and probable is not determined according to the subjective judgment of the defendant, but by references to what a reasonable man would have seen as natural and probable. Only if Wyzanski was willing to employ this "reasonable man" as the measure of conscience would his invocation of Lord Bowen be allowable. Now the reasonable man, as we noted in our discussion of *Ballard* in the preceding chapter, is a model rather than an exceptional man; he is, we are continually taught in law school, the ordinary, hard-working, middle-class fellow who mows his lawn every Saturday—in Britain he is "the man on the Clapham omnibus." This man's posited sensibilities would, then, discriminate between conscience and cowardice—between what sets of behaviors indicated sincerity and what indicated shirking. Again the potentials for favoring the glib over the bumbling and the conventional over the exotic is clear. And it is supposedly the inarticulate and the very unconventional whom Wyzanski was seeking to help.

But if the reasonable man is not to be the standard, then Wyzanski's confident assertion of the ability of the judicial process to deal with state of mind collapses.

And the difficulty is increased by the selective character of Sisson's objection. At least under the 6(j) exemption, local draft boards could look at a history of general objection to war in determining sincerity for *Seeger* or *Welsh* purposes. The Supreme Court, fully aware of the razor-sharp edges presented by *Sisson,* avoided the case by holding Wyzanski's action below to have been on acquittal (which is not appealable by the government) rather than arrest of judgement (which is appealable). Thus the matter was not properly before the Justices and need not be decided. But while the particular difficulties of the *Sisson* case were avoided, the general problem of selective conscientious objection to military service could not be kept long on ice. Two cases were docketed for the 1970 term.

GILLETTE

Gillette v. *U.S.* and *Negre* v. *Larsen* were decided together on March 8, 1971 and represent the limiting cases of the meaning of 6(j) which had begun in *Seeger*.[27] Here both petitioners made clear that they did not object to war in any form, but rather to the U.S. involvement in Vietnam. Their attorneys, following the *Seeger-Welsh-Sisson* pattern, argued that section 6(j) established religion, that it was unconstitutional as written, and unconstitutional even if read as exempting only objectors to all wars. In other words, they suggested, the Justices had not gone sufficiently far in sanitizing 6(j) in *Seeger* and *Welsh*—it was also necessary to extend its protection through judicial interpretation to selective objectors in order to preserve its constitutionality.

Associate Justice Thurgood Marshall wrote for himself and seven others. The overarching purpose of the establishment clause, he said, was to insure governmental neutrality both toward and between religions. Skirting, as always, around the apparent intent of Congress, Marshall reasoned that the Court's past reading of the statutory exemption rendered it secular in nature as to satisfy the requirement of neutrality. All sorts of sincere objectors to all wars were exempted, and it in no way discriminated in favor of or between religions to require that the objection be general as opposed to particular; that is, the secular quality of the Court version of the section 6(j) exemption was undisturbed by holding it to principled pacifists. After all, Marshall concluded,

> Neutrality in matters of religion is not inconsistent with "benevolence" by way of exemptions from onerous duties, so long as the

> exemption is tailored broadly enough that it reflects valid secular purposes.[28]

The key phrase, of course, is "tailored broadly enough." The point, it seems, is that government may not prefer religiously grounded reasons for non-service, but this does not mean that it may not prefer the quality of some objections over the quality of other objections. As long as religion is not the criterion of discrimination between objections, all is well, and since either general or particular objection could grow from either religious or irreligious reasons, the "Court-Congress" preference of general objectors was a legitimate secular classification.

Justice Douglas filed the lone dissent. In characteristic fashion, he rejected the judicial compromise of the statutory exemption, and would have raced ahead, like Wyzanski, to a "free-exercise of conscience" exemption. "It is true," he remarked,

> that the First Amendment speaks of the free exercise of religion, not of the free-exercise of conscience or belief. Yet conscience and belief are the main ingredients of the First Amendment rights. They are the bedrock of free speech as well as religion.[29]

THE LONG-RANGE PROSPECT FOR A CONSTITUTIONAL EXEMPTION

So notion of free-exercise exemption will not down. The Court may have avoided *Sisson* and settled on *Gillette* as the compromise statutory exemption, but the questing and dissatisfaction with the draft goes on. As a number of commentators have pointed out, the Supreme Court has never held, unambiguously, that Congress *has* the power to conscript for any soldiering which appeals to it.[30] The clearest suggestion of such a congressional power came to Sutherland's opinion in *Macintosh*. Here, it will be remembered, the Court upheld the denial of citizenship to an applicant who refused to pledge in advance to fight whenever called to by Congress. "Submission and obedience to the laws of the land," Sutherland had said, "are not inconsistent with the will of God."[31] But opponents of the decision have pointed to a brisk dissent from Chief Justice Charles Evans Hughes, who spoke as well for the prestigious trio of Holmes, Brandeis, and Stone. Hughes relied heavily on the consideration Americans generally and Congress in particular have shown historically for religious objectors.[32] (Remember Madison's suggestion that an exemption be written into the Second Amendment.)

More importantly, the specific holding of *Macintosh*—an unqualified willingness to fight as a requisite of citizenship—was overturned in 1956 by *Girouard* v. *U.S.*[33] "We conclude," said Justice Douglas in that case, "that the *Schwimmer, Macintosh* and *Blond* cases do not state the correct rule of law."[34] Note, however, that while Sutherland's *dicta* in *Macintosh* went to a matter of constitutional law (i.e., that there was no free-exercise exemption), the *holding* was a matter of statutory interpretation —that Congress had intended in the Naturalization Act to exclude from citizenship all aliens who refused an unqualified pledge to bear arms. The Hughes dissent had been to the point that Congress had *not* so intended, and *Girouard* overruled *Macintosh* on the statutory grounds. Chief Justice Stone, who had dissented in *Macintosh,* made this clear in his *Girouard* dissent. He felt that a statutory interpretation of fifteen years standing should be let alone—even though he had disagreed with it when made. Furthermore, Stone reminded Douglas that no one on the *Macintosh* Court had ever suggested that if Congress had wished to exclude non-pledging aliens it could not do so:

> No question of the Constitutional power of Congress to withhold citizenship on these grounds was involved. That power was not doubted. See *Selective Draft Law Cases* . . . [and] . . . *Hamilton* v. *Regents* . . . The only question was of construction of the statute which Congress at all times has been free to amend if dissatisfied with the construction adopted by the Court.[35]

The distinction is crucial: only when it is made does it become clear that to the extent the *Selective Draft Law Cases, Hamilton,* and the *dicta* from Macintosh, taken together come close to constituting a constitutional rule, and that "near-rule" is undisturbed by *Girouard*.[36]

But very little is impossible to a determined Supreme Court majority, and the tissue of precedent described here could be brushed aside anytime the Court is ready to assume the burdens and potential embarrassments of something like Wyzanski's *Sisson* approach. At the beginning of the American build-up in Vietnam in 1965, few constitutional lawyers would have thought the suggestion of a free-exercise exemption other than bizarre. Seven weary years later, as this is written, the suggestion is generally regarded as problematical but commonplace. Who can tell what a few more years of conscription for an unpopular war may bring?

FREE-EXERCISE AND THE SEPARATIONIST INTEREST GROUPS

One further aspect of the struggle over the meaning of the free-exercise clause needs noting. It is interesting that many of the same groups which urge no public funds for church schools and no Madonnas on postage stamps have been actively urging the extension of the free-exercise clause to protect otherwise regulatable action.

Perhaps it should not be surprising that the list of attorneys and *amici* in *Seeger* read like a Who's Who of separationists. Briefs came from the ACLU, the American Jewish Congress, the American Ethical Union, and even one from the American Humanist Association signed by Paul Blanshard. Seeger himself was represented by Kenneth Greenawalt. The attack here was on section 6(j) with its clear religious classification. It certainly is not surprising to find Jewish groups ranged in support of Mrs. Sherbert's argument for special treatment based on a religious classification. That Jewish groups were still sore from *Braunfeld* is understandable.

Beyond this, however, the alacrity with which separationists, especially politically liberal separationists, have welcomed the new directions in interpretation of the free-exercise clause suggests a fundamental ambiguity in the attitudes of these elites concerning the proper posture of government toward religion. To oppose religious classifications in two contexts (aid to religious institutions and publicly sponsored religious exercises) and to favor such classifications in another context (exemption from secular regulations of individual behavior) may be fashionable liberalism, but it is hardly good constitutional law.

With some groups, such as the ACLU, the problem of creating religious classifications is obviated by the expedient of defining religion in the First Amendment as meaning all conscience. There are still difficulties with such an approach as noted earlier, but it does eliminate the establishment embarrassment. Not all the groups which seek strict separation *and* expanded free-exercise protection are prepared to read "religion" so comprehensively, however, and for these the tension between the two clauses should be of as much concern to the group leaders as it is to the courts.

CONCLUSION

It is devoutly to be hoped that an early elimination of the draft (by winding down the Vietnam War, or moving toward a professional army, or both) will absolve the Courts of further labors in the dusty vineyard of section 6(j) and relieve the pressure for carving out a constitutional exemption from conscripted service. The *Gillette* reading of the congressional exemption—any sincere, deeply-felt objection to war in all forms—is terribly strained,[37] but Congress has shown no indication of producing a new exemption with which the Court can live more easily. And rationalizing the free-exercise exemption is, as we have seen, an awkward business, at best. When the Court is faced with the alternatives of substantially modifying an act of Congress or striking out on a new and dangerous constitutional path on which the Justices cannot see beyond the first bend of military service exemptions, the institution is at its weakest and is most vulnerable to criticism and congressional counterattack. That the attack has not yet come, or at least has not come very forcefully, is probably a function of the unpopularity of the war (and a resulting disinclination in Congress to slug the matter out with the Court) rather than a function of the craftsmanship of the Justices. Rather the best that can be said is that Marshall's opinion in *Gillette* provides some cushioning of the impact of the draft on elite young people, while assuming only marginally political risk for the Court.

NOTES

1. 40 Stat. 78 (1917). A number of reviews of these developments are available. A good short one is Robert L. Rabin, "When is a Religious Belief Religious: *United States* v. *Seeger* and the Scope of Free Exercise," 51 *Cornell Law Quarterly* 231 (1966).

2. See Rabin, *op. cit.*

3. 54 Stat. 889 (1940).

4. For an account of conscientious objection during World War II, see Mulfred Q. Sibley and Philip E. Jacob, *Conscription of Conscience: The American State and the Conscientious Objector* (Ithaca: Cornell University Press, 1952).

5. 133 F. 2d 703 (2d Cir. 1943).

6. *U.S. ex rel. Phillips* v. *Downer,* 135 F. 2d 521 (2d. Cir. 1943); *U.S. ex rel. Reel* v. *Badt,* 141 F. 2d 845 (2d Cir. 1944).

7. 156 F. 2d 377 (9th Cir. 1946).

8. *Ibid.,* p. 380. Nor was the distinction merely the easy one between the familiar theistic forms and the unfamiliar non-theistic. Much of the original justification of the 1917 section 7(d) exemption stressed the peculiar plight of the orthodox theistic pacifist who is forced to disobey his country's law *or suffer eternal damnation.* It was depriving men of the hope of eternal life which was perceived by many in Congress as distinctively and impermissibly cruel. Whatever one thinks of the persuasive quality of this rationale, it is clearly not available to non-theists.

9. S. Rep. No. 1268, 80th Cong., 2d Sess., p. 14.

10. 380 U.S. 163 (165).

11. *U.S.* v. *Seeger,* 326 F. 2d 846 (2d Cir. 1964).

12. All the briefs supporting Seeger, and Judge Kaufman who wrote for the Second Circuit, seemed to assume that the requirement of theistic belief could be found unconstitutional, but that a *Kauton*-style exemption would remain. It is less than obvious that this should be so. If Congress rejected *Kauton* and the Court rejected the congressional substitute, a strong case can be made that *no* exemption exists.

13. See the concurring opinion of Mr. Justice Brandeis in *Ashwander* v. *Tennessee Valley Authority,* 297 U.S. 288 (1936); and Note, "Supreme Court Interpretation of Statutes to Avoid Constitutional Decisions," 53 *Columbia Law Review* 633 (1953).

14. A good short review of the literature on statutory interpretation (specifically legislative purpose) is Note, "Legislative Purpose and Federal Constitutional Adjudication," 83 *Harvard Law Review* 1887 (1970).

15. No clearer indication of the general pre-*Seeger* understanding of 6(j) can be found than the 1965 *Handbook for Conscientious Objectors,* edited by Arlo Tatum for the Central Committee for Conscientious Objectors. The discussion on pp. 13–15 presumes a theistic intent in 6(j).

16. 380 U.S. 163, 176 (1965).

17. A final, almost surrealistic, touch was added to *Seeger* by Justice Douglas. He suggested in a concurring opinion that Congress had inserted the "Supreme Being" language in 1948 to broaden rather than narrow the scope of the exemption. *Adversa virtute repello.*

18. It was open to Congress, of course, to attempt to clarify further its intent. The issue had become so super heated, however, that when the question of "correcting" *Seeger* came up in the June 1967 debate over extension of the Selective Service Act, a confusing succession of maneuver and counter-maneuver resulted only in a deletion of the "Supreme Being" language added in 1948. The change cannot be "scored" for either side. The Military Selective Service Act of 1967 (81 Stat. 100), the draft law now in force, contains 6(j) unaltered except for the "Supreme Being" phrase. The requirement of "religious training and belief" and the exclusion of "political, sociological, or philosophical views" remain.

19. 398 U.S. 333 (1970).

20. *Ibid.,* p. 341.

21. *Ibid.,* p. 351.

22. *Ibid.,* p. 361.

23. New York *Times,* July 25, 1970.

24. *U.S.* v. *Sisson,* 297 F. Supp. 902 (D. Mass. 1969).

25. *Ibid.,* p. 909.

26. *Ibid.,* p. 909–910. An unsympathetic commentator might point out that we have learned more about the differences between bowel and brain in the years since 1882.

27. *Gillette* v. *U.S.* and *Negre* v. *Larsen,*—*U.S.*—(1971).

28. —U.S.—,—(1971).

29. —U.S.—,—(1971).

30. For an early argument to this effect see Thomas Reed Powell, "Conscience and the Constitution," in William T. Hutchinson, ed., *Democracy and National Unity* (Chicago: University of Chicago Press, 1941). An elegant recent attempt is John Mansfield, "Conscientious Objection—1964 Term," 1965 *Religion and the Public Order.*

31. 283 U.S. 605, 625 (1931).

32. Hughes' opinion drew heavily on the brief for *Macintosh* by the great conservative constitutional lawyer, John W. Davis. Davis presented some historical materials to suggest that it might have been part of the intention of the Framers of the First Amendment to exempt religious objectors from required military service. Hughes used the brief, but did not adopt its constitutional assertion.

33. 328 U.S. 61 (1946).

34. *Ibid.*, p. 69.

35. *Ibid.*, p. 72.

36. Professor Mansfield's otherwise well-carpentered argument for a free-exercise exemption (supra, n. 24) is marred by a failure to make this distinction clearly.

37. It has been suggested by people I respect that I am over-reading the *Welsh* and *Gillette* opinions, and that there are some conceivable sincere objections to war in all forms which could not qualify under 6(j): sincere hedonists, sincere cowards, and so on. This seems to play on words. The Court would simply find lack of sincerity. The best extended discussion of the implications of *Gillette* is Kent Greenawalt, "All or Nothing at All: The Defeat of Selective Conscientious Objection," 1971 *Supreme Court Review* 31.

8

Advice from Academe

Thus far we have concentrated on the efforts of judges, and particularly the Justices of the United States Supreme Court, to develop principled interpretations of the religion clauses of the First Amendment. While the judges have encountered many difficulties, these have not included a dearth of advice from non-judges. A very large literature exists in which professors of law, political science, religion, philosophy, and history presume to tell the Supreme Court how to read the words "establishment" and "free-exercise." In completing our survey of the development of the religion clauses this stream of proffered alternatives must be briefly traced. Not every nuance of every argument will be noted, and a certain ruthlessness in simplifying and classifying is also necessary if a wide range of arguments is to be reflected in a limited compass. However, the intellectual and critical context in which judges work is important to the process of constitutional decision and change, and any study of constitutional politics would be incomplete without it.[1]

THE APPEAL TO HISTORY

An important group of constitutional critics has argued that the Madisonian reading given the establishment clause by Black in *Everson* is simply incorrect on historical grounds. To assert that government may not aid religious institutions in a non-discriminatory fashon, they suggest, is to misread a clear, powerful American tradition to the contrary. Among those espousing this position was the dean of constitutional historians, Edward S. Corwin. It is superficially attractive advise for the Justices. If it could be taken there would be no need to grapple with doctrinal ambiguities nor to consider what is sound public policy. Unless government was found to be preferring some particular denomination (a rare development for political reasons), there would be no issue. As Corwin put it:

> What the "establishment of religion clause" of the First Amendment does, and all that it does, is to forbid Congress to give any religious faith, sect or denomination a preferred status; . . .[2]

This was, indeed, the position toward which Justice Reed was drawn in his *McCollum* dissent, and although it may be argued as a possible reading of the historical materials, to view the historical record as clear is seriously in error. It is one of the puzzles of this area of constitutional law that some otherwise sophisticated lawyers have been drawn to the position. Thus former Harvard Law School Dean (and present Solicitor-General) Edwin N. Griswold castigated Justice Black for simple-minded separationism in his *Everson* opinion and, by confidently asserting equally simplistic historical interpretation, convicted himself of the very crime he sought to prove against the Justice.[3]

A more subtle historical critique of the *Everson* approach to the establishment has come from the late Professor Mark DeWolfe Howe. In his last short book, *The Garden and the Wilderness,*[4] Howe recalled for his readers that there were two strands of separationist thought in the American weave: the secularist

(Madisonian-Jeffersonian) and the Protestant (which Howe, through the quotation which he took for his title, associates with Roger Williams). The Justices, he argued, have fixed on one strand or variety of separationism to the exclusion of the other.

In the Protestant version, of course, separation is for the protection of the church against the state, not, as was the case with secular separationism, the other way round. Williams was concerned to keep the wilderness of the secular state from encroaching upon and choking the delicate garden of the church. But to the extent that it was possible to accept state aid without state control or meddling, Howe suggests, Williams was prepared to countenance cooperation. There are, however, difficulties.

First, while Howe is correct in recalling that secular and Protestant separationism differed, his rendering of the Protestant variety is itself over-simple. Protestants, generally, did accept the diluted public religion in the schools which we examined in Chapter 2, but in some denominations (e.g., Williams' own Baptists) there remained an adamantine suspicion (only lately beginning to modify) that the state could aid churches impartially. Interference was seen to follow cooperation as the night the day. No doubt Howe was correct in his reading of Williams, but Protestant separation was a more various tradition than Williams, taken alone, suggests.

Second, even if we (or the Justices) accept Howe's rendering of the Protestant tradition at face value, it is not clear *why* that tradition should be elevated into constitutional law rather than the Madisonian theory which, at least in the past, the majority of the Justices who have sat in establishment clause cases have preferred. Howe did not deny the existence of the Madisonian stand, and he did not make clear why, when faced with several historical footholds, the Court should choose one rather than the other. A close reading of *The Garden and the Wilderness* does reveal Howe's own basis for choosing. He preferred to read the religion clauses as embodying the single purpose of protecting freedom of worship. He saw no independent purpose to the establishment clause, and so he advised the Justices to overlook the theory of separation which did. This, of course, is a perfectly legitimate argument. As we shall see in a moment, many have made it, and no one was better fitted than Mark Howe to give it superb expression. It is sad that it became overlaid in his book by the ultimately pointless hassle over historical materials.

The lesson here is, again, that the historical materials themselves will not settle anything.[5] The task of the judge is not the task of the academic historian—the judge is not concerned with the loving recreation of the past in all its diversity.[6] The job of a constitutional Court is precisely to choose *between* conflicting traditions. The Justices of the Supreme Court must decide whether *they* think the establishment clause should serve a peace-keeping purpose independent of freedom of free-exercise of religion. If they do so decide they should tell us why (as Justice Frankfurter so clearly did), then use the available historical materials to legitimatize the choice. Mr. Justice Black may be properly faulted for hiding behind history and for failing to explain the policy choice involved in adopting the Madisonian theory in *Everson,* but the fault is only compounded by critics who then urge their own historical interpretations as dispositive—whether crudely, as with Griswold, or elegantly, as with Howe.

CLAIMS FOR DISTRIBUTIVE JUSTICE

A number of commentators, many Catholic but some not,[7] have argued that it is fundamentally unjust for religious institutions, and particularly the church-related schools, which admittedly perform public functions, to be denied all governmental support. Such commentators, naturally, have been quite critical of the Court's establishment decisions.

A quite forceful version of this critique has come from Congressman Robert F. Drinan, S. J., former Dean of the Boston College Law School. In a number of occasional pieces, and in a book entitled *Religion, the Courts, and Public Policy,*[8] Drinan argued that the *Pierce* case, while not decided on First Amendment grounds, did recognize the right of church-related schools to exist and spoke of parental responsibility for the education of children. Working from there, Drinan urged that a parent's sending his child to a church-related school should properly be considered an exercise of religion. This being so, he concluded that for the state to put such a parent at a financial disadvantage by requiring him to pay taxes for the public school fund while denying his children benefit from this fund, is a contravention of the spirit, if not the letter, of the free-exercise clause.[9]

To the objection that the establishment clause prohibits payment of public money which would go into the coffers of church-related schools, Drinan relied on the now familiar individual-benefit notion—it would be the student, not the school, which would be helped by the support. Any incidental advantage rebounding to the school was of less than constitutional significance.

One trouble with this argument involves the nature of the holding in *Pierce*. It was not the religious schools which were guaranteed the right to exist, but all *private* schools. Drinan would certainly not argue that parents sending their children to Choate or Groton have any claim on their local school boards for reimbursement. But posh prep schools also perform a public function, as, indeed, do a variety of charitable organizations concerned with everything from heart disease to the preservation of the bald eagle. Unless the free-exercise argument is taken seriously, there is no basis for support of church-related schools unless all the rest are supported.

And the trouble with the free-exercise argument is that if parents have a right to support for one sort of exercise of religion, it is hard to see why they should not enjoy public support for certain other important exercises (e.g., pilgrimages) which they find expensive. Nor can the argument be salvaged by contending that taxes are collected specifically for the public schools, and that if monies are coercively collected to provide a public service, which is for some citizens a religious exercise, then the First Amendment requires a rebate. Taxes are not collected specifically to pay for the public education. The property tax, for instance, falls equally on the childless and the fecund, the resident and the absentee owner. No suggestion has been quite so productive of confusion in the discussion of church-state relations in America than the notion that property tax payments can be viewed as public school tuition payments for the children of the taxpayers. Taxes on property finance a variety of services which the local political leadership determines to be in the general interest of the community. They are not an indirect sort of purchasing decision.

But if support is not required, may not considerable support be *allowable* as a matter of sound public policy? Drinan also makes this argument, but it was made most pursuasively by the late John Courtney Murray, S. J., longtime Professor of Theology at the Woodstock Seminary.

Murray wrote extensively on the religion clauses of the First Amendment as "articles of peace," intended by the Framers to provide for the coexistence of a number of potentially antagonistic religious groups. So far so good. But Murray further asserted that for the state to impose upon itself the rule that it cannot aid religious institutions impartially is for the state to establish the religion of "secularism." In a famous passage he wrote:

> In the name of freedom of religion it [the Court] decrees that the relations of government to religion are to be controlled by the fundamental tenet of secularism—the social irrelevance of religion, its exclusion from the secular affairs of the City and its educational system, its segregation to the private forum of conscience or at best to the hushed confines of the sacristy. Justice Jackson thought up an apt allusion, but he got its reference wrong; actually it is the philosophizing of the whole Court that reminds one of Byron's Julia, who, in momentary disregard of the original lines and the exigencies of metre, "screaming, 'I will ne'er consent to an establishment of religion,' imposed on the American people."[10]

More is wrong here, however, than mangled metre. The argument that for government to refrain from aid to religion is to establish the religion of secularism is obscurantist. Either it reflects intellectual fundamentalism (if you are not with me you are of the enemy), or a play on words ("religion" used in a way which destroys its essential core of meaning). As Paul Freund has remarked "to say that Americans worship what William James called the bitch-goddess, success, is not to assert anything relevant to the usage of the word 'religion' in the First Amendment."[11]

"NO-IMPOSITION"

A number of commentators have developed variations on the approach championed in the Court by Justice Stewart—that if there was no coercion of individual conscience—in other words, no free-exercise problem—then no establishment problem can exist.[12] This assumes the two religion clauses to safeguard only one value, that of freedom of worship. Howe believed this but never argued it explicitly; others have made elaborate arguments.

One such writer, Professor Alan Schwartz of the Ohio State University College of Law, has suggested that the establishment clause should not be considered breached unless the state action in question has the effect of "imposing" on someone a religious belief or practice.[13] As for other possible establishment clause values which might be disserved by such an approach, there was no need to worry because there were none of importance.

The Madisonian notion that the establishment clause has the independent purpose (value) of precluding civil strife is dismissed with particular élan.

> The strife to be avoided is apparently supposed to be caused by the antagonism of religious or irreligious groups who are not aided or who feel the others have received a disproportionate share. Since inequality in aid could, presumably, be remedied by a constitutional requirement of equality and since it is not suggested that unavoidable inequalities in aids to religion present peculiar constitutional dangers, proponents of this view apparently regard the bona fides of the grievance to be irrelevant. It is sufficient that aid does cause strife, whether or not that strife is rational. To state this proposition is to ridicule it.[14]

But the strife-avoidance argument is more complicated than

that. First, it is not the constitutional requirement of equality which is doubted by strict separationists, but the possibility of the allocative process of political bargaining working to produce a tolerable level of satisfaction among the claimants.[15] Second, it is not that religion is asserted to possess peculiar *constitutional* dangers (whatever this may mean), but that religion presents peculiarly explosive *political* dangers.[16]

A more persuasive rationale for dismissing strife avoidance from our concern has come from Jesse Choper, Professor of Law at the University of California at Berkeley. He would allow aid to church-related institutions as long as the amount of the aid did not exceed the value of the secular service which the state wishes, in effect, to purchase. While granting the peculiarly divisive quality of religion as a political issue, Choper asks why it is so easily assumed that a no-aid rule will result in less such religious-political strife than an effort (however awkward) to allocate fairly. In other words, with Catholic parochial schools increasingly straited and forced to close in many instances, will the no-aid principle or the equal-aid principle be more productive of conflict? Choper has no way of answering with certainty, but neither do those who advance strife avoidance as an independent purpose for the establishment clause.[17]

EDUCATIONAL REFORMERS

Perhaps the most cogent criticism of the Court's establishment decisions have come from those who, cutting loose from the old debates over use of history, distributive justice, strife avoidance, and so on, have based their arguments squarely on public policy. And since in talking of establishment we are talking principally about schools, this means on what is sound educational policy for America in the 1970's.

Some of these commentators have been content simply to point to the number of children in church-related schools and suggest that government must concern itself more actively with the quality of their experience there.[18] Others have focused on the ills of the public schools (especially those of the decaying inner cities), and argued that these schools and their students would benefit from brisk non-public educational competition—which must be stimulated and sustained by governmental aids of various sorts.[19] A particularly cogent version of the education reform critique has come from Alexander Bickel of the Yale Law School.

In October of 1969, Bickel delivered the Holmes lectures at the Harvard Law School. This lectureship, so often the occasion for important comments on American constitutional law, proved so again. The lectures, published as *The Supreme Court and the Idea of Progress,*[20] reviewed the recent performance of the Supreme Court and found it wanting. The Justices, Bickel suggested, imbued with an engaging but undiscriminating egalitarianism, had overextended themselves in shaping new uniform legal rules in a number of areas of national life. The full argument is complex and beyond our present concern, but one difficulty Bickel foresaw for the Court concerned the establishment decisions.

All of the Court's decisions touching on schools have been of a piece, Bickel argued—whether they involved religion and the establishment clause or race and the equal protection clause. The Justices have seen the American public school as charged with a critical assimilationist mission. Nothing would do but that the schools be, as a matter of constitutional law, as socially uniform, and as comprehensive, and as secular as possible. To this end, successive decisions have extended *Brown* v. *Board of Education* well beyond prohibiting state enforced segregation to include the requirement of a "unitary" school system. And as Southern states have sought to provide escape hatches for their middle classes into private schools—through the device of the tuition grant—the Court has aggressively asserted the assimilationist mission of the public schools by striking down these arrangements as transparent efforts to perpetuate the state enforced school segregation proscribed by *Brown.*[21]

The difficulty with this line of constitutional policy, according to Bickel, is that it will, in the very short run, have just the opposite effect from that desired by the egalitarian justices who authored it. This will be true because there is no practical way of keeping middle class white children in integrated urban schools. They will make their ways into private schools or into the parent-dominated "private public schools" of the suburbs. Blacks in the cities will be left with highly centralized, unresponsive school systems over which they have little control and which they perceive increasingly as disserving their children.

Such a social result, Bickel held, can only be avoided in one of two ways. First, by creating giant centralized school administrative districts (cutting across present city, county, and even state lines) which, even if politically possible, would hardly respond to the desires of parents, white and black, to have a strong voice in the education of their children. Or, second, by decentralization of urban public school systems, to provide for extensive community (read subcultural) control, and coupling this with state tuition grant programs which would allow the poor as well as the affluent to have access to a variety of different sorts of schools for their children.

Bickel thinks the latter course obviously desirable.

> Under pressure, the insistence on the assimilationist mission of the public schools which are unable to perform it cannot be maintained, and it should not be. When it is abandoned, decisions forbidding religious exercises in the schools, or financial support by the state to church-connected schools must also go. To attach the [present] law of the Constitution to tuition grants, and to hold the private schools predominantly supported by grants are in effect public and may not sponsor religious exercises would defeat the essence of the policy of a tuition grant scheme. . . . If schools supported by the state in indirect fashion may sponsor religious exercises, what good reason would there be for holding that schools directly financed by the state, but relegated to parent and community control, may not?[22]

In short, America is shortly to experience a sea change in educational policy which will render irrelevant much previous constitutional law, law crafted by Justices with an obsolete model of "the school" in mind. New constitutional law must follow the new social imperative. When Dickel wrote, it was easy to believe that this was happening—*Allen* was heard as the bellwether. *Lemon–Di Censo* dimmed this prospect for change, and it is a fair guess that Dickel would view Burger's "no-entanglement" test with distaste.

The secular public school, of course, does not even now lack defenders,[23] and perhaps the most sensitive critique of *Allen*, and by implication of Bickel, has come from Paul Freund of the Harvard Law School. Freund found *Allen* a worrying retreat from the principles of *Everson*. "It is hardly surprising," he pointed out, "that Justice Black, the author of the bus decision, was a fierce dissenter in the textbook case. Of course a bridge that carries you to the verge is apt to be burned behind you. . . ."[24] The textbooks under the New York program were actually selected and ordered by the private school authorities (albeit from lists approved by the state and with the bill sent to the local school authorities), and this comes too close, for Freund, to using the taxes of unbelievers to support religious activity. The key establishment value for Freund is that of religious voluntarism, and only a clear constitutional rule can safeguard it. "Ordinarily," he remarked,

> I am disposed, in grey-area cases of constitutional law, to let the political process function. . . . The religious guarantees, however, are of a different order. While political division is normally a wholesome process for reaching viable accommodations, political division along religious lines is one of the principal evils the First Amendment sought to forestall. . . . Although great issues of constitutional law are never settled until they are settled right, still as between open-ended, on going political warfare and such binding quality as judicial decisions possess, I would choose the latter in the field of God and Caesar and the public treasury.[25]

Only against the background of Freund's lifelong commitment to judicial self-restraint and deference to popularly elected branches can the conviction behind this statement be properly appreciated. As with Frankfurter before him, the religion clauses (and more particularly the establishment clause) are of a "different order."[26]

CONSTITUTIONALIZATION OF CONSCIENCE

Turning to the free-exercise area, typical of commentators who have urged reading the free-exercise clause as a general protection of conscientious objection is Milton Konvitz, Professor at Cornell, and one of the most prolific and passionate students of civil rights and liberties in America. In a little book entitled *Religious Liberty and Conscience: A Constitutional Inquiry,*[27] Konvitz made his case.

Relying on precisely that aspect of the craftsmanship of the "Warren Court" which has aggravated commentators such as Bickel—its tendency to express itself in delphic and unexplained terms—Konvitz noted the reliance of some Justices (e.g., Goldberg in *Griswold* v. *Connecticut*) on "emenations" and "penumbra" of meaning which surround the specific statements of the Bill of Rights.[28] Surely, Konvitz suggested, if a right to privacy could be found to be implied by the First, Fourth, and Ninth Amendments, it was not too much to suggest that the free-exercise clause implied a protection of individual conscience, whether colorably religious or not.

Furthermore, Konvitz would allow no definition of religion. Nor, indeed, would he allow any testing of sincerity. Adopting the argument of Jackson's *Ballard* dissent, he viewed the question of sincerity as part and parcel of the question of what is believed, and thus beyond the competence of courts. Courts must, as a free-exercise requirement, take the drug cultists and the selective objectors to military service at their words; to do less would involve judges in making discriminations among claimants which would run counter to the spirit of both religion clauses, and would be distinctly unegalitarian.

The argument was made with great verve and goodwill. Konvitz appealed, in impeccably liberal terms, for protection of human sensibilities from interference by the state—even to the state's refraining from examining the extent of the bona fides of the sensibilities asserted. But there are degrees of consideration and privacy no legal system can grant and survive. As one reviewer of Konvitz's book noted,

> A legal system cannot accord special treatment to religious claims and also accept without any scrutiny every assertion of such a claim, and unavoidable corollory of recognizing such claims is some test of sincerity.[29]

In short, it is not really helpful to exhort the judiciary concerning the value of human conscience without suggesting how judges are to go about the job of line drawing. Other commentators over the years labored to suggest the sorts of tests and limiting cases which Konvitz neglected, and several of these attempts are noteworthy.

Giannella

In the May 1967 issue of the *Harvard Law Review,*[30] Donald Giannella, Executive Director of the Institute of Church and State of the Villanova Law School, addressed himself to the task of specifying limits on free-exercise exemptions, and discovered one in the ancient distinction between *mala prohibita* and *mala in se*. In Giannella's version, offenses "designed to serve only the ends of public health, safety, or welfare by the imposition of fines and imprisonment" are *mala prohibita,* while "true crimes," "those based on the moral censure of society," are *mala in se*.

Society can tolerate, Giannella suggested, exempting religious objectors from certain sorts of health and safety regulations, but must insist that its moral judgments be respected regardless of religious scruple. Where things *mala prohibita* are concerned, a balancing would be appropriate in which the interest which the regulation protects is weighed against the extent of the free-exercise deprivation. Really important health and safety regulations presumably would be enforced, while those of a more marginal character would give way to free-exercise claims.

But how are we to know which is which? Is, for instance, refusal of military service *malum prohibitum* or *malum in se?* Does it make a difference whether the nation is at war or peace?

Might it depend on the character of the threat to the nation? And what of drug crimes? Are legal proscriptions of narcotics and hallucinogens health and safety regulations or expressions of the moral sense of the community?

Nor does Giannella offer much comfort in the matter of defining religion for constitutional purposes. He would extend the increased protection of the free-exercise clause to (1) conventional, theistic believers, and (2) "those nontheistic conscientious objections that are based on an intensely felt, selfless, and thoroughgoing personal commitment to the brotherhood of man. . . ."[31] The attempt here was to exclude mystic and drug cultists, and suffered, at the same time, from the flaws of constitutionalizing the conventional (part one), and forcing courts tc a fervency test (part two).

Clark

Two years later, also writing in the *Harvard Law Review,* J. Morris Clark took up the tasks of limiting and defining.[32] Rather than the slippery distinction between *mala prohibita* and *mala in se,* Clark distinguished between those laws which command the individual to perform a "duty" and those laws which command that he refrain from doing something. Clark's assumption here was that it is less important for society to require people to do things than to stop them from doing things. The former sort of regulation is likely to be designed to further some scheme of social improvement, while the latter is characteristically directed at supressing anti-social acts. In the case of individuals refusing to *perform* acts on grounds of religion or conscience, the presumption would favor the individual, and the state would have to show a compelling interest in order for it to prevail against such a refusal. Where a prohibition of action is concerned, the regulation would prevail against a free-exercise objection—except where the individual's refusal resulted from what he believed an "inexcusable duty" and where only the individual and other fully consenting persons were involved. In this latter class of cases, the presumption would, again, favor the individual.

In defining religion (specifying to whom free-exercise protection is available), Clark chose the "parallel function" approach employed by the Court in *Seeger* and, in modified form, in *Welsh*. The majority opinions in both these cases, as we have seen, contained a partially suppressed psychological argument: that beliefs could be classified in terms of the functions they performed in the system of the personality rather than classified in terms of their contents or intrinsic characters. Thus "parallel" as used by Justice Clark and Justice Black meant psychologically and functionally parallel. Mr. Clark attempted to make the psychological theory explicit. "The most important interest protected by the free-exercise clause," he suggested, "is the prevention of severe psychic turmoil that can be brought about by compelled violations of conscience." For this reason, "a psychological definition of religious belief seems appropriate."[33] Clark admitted that it is either difficult or impossible, following a psychological approach, to distinguish theistic from nontheistic beliefs, or to distinguish either of these from essentially political or sociological views, or even, perhaps, to distinguish conscience from self-interest! Nevertheless, he contended, there is nothing better than letting the jury or other trier of fact struggle with this hard judgment. And there are, Mr. Clark concluded, some indicia of "intensity of compulsion" (sincerity?) which are manifest to those who must decide individual cases—duration and expression of views to others being among the most important.

This statement of the parallel role approach is considerably clearer than any judges have thus far produced, but before courts accept it, they should be clear that, in Mr. Clark's version, it is absolutely comprehensive. Any belief, the violation of which would cause "psychic turmoil" would, if found "intense and compelling," qualify the holder for free-exercise protection. It is tempting to suppose that judges have not achieved the clarity of Mr. Clark's expression precisely because they recoil from the full implications of the approach. Like Mr. Justice Clark in *Seeger* they are attracted to the parallel role approach as a way of overcoming the theistic-nontheistic distinction, but covertly they wish to continue to exclude "merely" political, social, and moral views.

Mansfield

Finally, an elegant argument for reading a conscientious objection principle into the free-exercise clause came from Professor John H. Mansfield, of the Harvard Law School. Restricting himself to the single issue of exemption from required military service, Mansfield attempted to limit the category of the exempted by returning to an intrinsic definition of religion and conscientious interest; that is, by designing a test of the content of what is believed. "A religious belief," Mansfield argued,

> is first of all a belief, that is to say the affirmation of some truth, reality or value. In addition it addresses itself to basic questions about the meaning of human existence, the origin of being, the meaning of suffering and death, and the existence of a spiritual reality.[34]

It is quite proper, Mansfield suggested, for government to prefer those (whether conventionally religious or unconventionally conscientious) whose objections arise out of grappling with "fundamental" religious-type questions over those whose opinions are not derived from a consideration of such fundamentals. Thus Mansfield overcame the theistic-nontheistic distinction without including everybody. Special consideration was accorded beliefs both strictly religious and religious-like. Yet the exemption was not to extend to the infinity of opinion.

But Mansfield's content test of belief is really no less unsatisfactory than intrinsic definitions of religion already available in the literature and found wanting. Augustus Hand, in *Kauton,* had said that "religious belief arises from a sense of the inadequacy of reason as a means of relating the individual to his fellow-men and the universe."[35] Charles Evans Hughes, in *Macintosh,* had said that "the essence of religion is belief in a relation to God involving duties superior to those arising from any human relation."[36] While Mansfield does employ somewhat less conventional terms, his approach invites discrimination in favor of the familiar over the novel, the articulate over the garbled, the principled statement over the reiterated intuition. Mansfield succeeds in extending his exemption beyond the conventionally religious, but only to include the *conventionally* conscientious.

And here we are back again at the familiar question of whether such discrimination can be justified. No one has doubted this justification more eloquently than John P. Roche. Reviewing David Manwaring's discussion of the decline of the secular regulation rule in *Render Unto Caesar,* Roche scouted the notion that one sort of belief may be preferred to another:

> In a society founded upon secular principles there can be no favoritism of this sort: "glib" political objection to war can be no worse, or better, than tormented and perhaps incoherent religious views. A jury may take sincerity into consideration in its meditations; a Judge can evaluate it before sentencing; and the executive can take notice of it in his employment of the pardoning power; but it has no place in the objective legal structure.[37]

It is on this point, ultimately, that Mansfield and Giannella, along with the judges, come to grief. If, on the other hand, like J. Morris Clark, one adopts a thoroughgoing functional, or parallel, approach, one risks creating an exemption for the asking, limited only by a jury's impression of sincerity. Milton Konvitz would not even leave us that.

THE "SINGLE PRINCIPLE" APPROACH

Thus far, the academics do not seem to have helped the Justices very much. A few nice points have been clarified, but the dialogue does not seem much advanced over what we found in the opinions. One further item of academic advice remains, however, and that is altogether more interesting.

In 1961 Professor Philip B. Kurland, of the University of Chicago Law School, published an article titled "Religion and the Law: of Church and State and the Supreme Court."[38] The following year a revised version was issued in book form.[39] Professor Kurland's effort was noteworthy for its mordant criticism of many of the conventional arguments which swirl around the religion clauses. But it offered something even rarer and more important: an easily understood, intellectually parsimonious principle which promised to allow for a logical and integrated interpretation of the religion clauses. In short, Kurland staked out a high road to doctrinal coherence.

Kurland noted the failure of others to integrate the two clauses so as to eliminate the contradiction between establishment and free-exercise, and promised to do better.

> The utilization or application of these clauses in conjunction is difficult. For if the command is that inhibitions not be placed by the state on religious activity, it is equally forbidden that the state confer favors upon religious activity. These commands would be impossible of effectuation unless they are read together as creating a doctrine more akin to the reading of the equal protection clause [of the Fourteenth Amendment] i.e., they must be read to mean that religion may not be used as a basis for classification for purposes of governmental action, whether that action be the conferring of rights or privileges or the imposition of obligations.[40]

At first blush, the potential of this approach appears breathtaking: government will act to secure its otherwise legitimate ends, and religion simply will not be taken into account. This, truly, is a neutral principle of constitutional law. Incredible that it could have eluded us until 1961! But the bloom of enthusiasm fades when one begins to think out the policy consequences of the principle.

In the establishment area it would mean that any religious institution was eligible for participation in any governmental program which was not specifically designed to advantage religious institutions. Thus a program to aid all private schools—even to the extent of facilities construction, maintenance, and teachers' salaries—would be open to religious schools without restriction on sectarian overtones as long as the religious schools met all of the criteria of qualification established for all schools wishing to participate. It would *not* be possible for the governmental granting authority to establish additional criteria to limit the religious character of participant schools, for this would be to employ religion as a basis of classification.

In the free-exercise area the Kurland approach requires a return to something close to the old secular regulation rule. Legislatures might regulate citizen behavior in furtherance of any otherwise proper objective, and religious belief would not be ground for exemption to the operation of such regulation. Only if the regulation was aimed directly at the religious exercise itself (religion becoming the basis of classification) would the First Amendment question arise.

The trouble is that these policy outcomes are unacceptable to major segments of the Supreme Court's constituency, and to major segments of general public opinion. There remain too many highly articulate interest group spokesmen who are deeply troubled by the extensive participation of religious institutions—institutions actively striving to advance sectarian doctrine—in public programs. And there are also too many people who would bitterly regret seeing the free-exercise clause restricted once again so as to protect religiously motivated behavior only when government specifically legislates against it.

CONCLUSION

Throughout this tracing of academic comment and criticism (and throughout this book), there has recurred a nagging concern for doctrinal coherence—or, in the currently popular phrase, "judicial craftsmanship." This concern comes naturally to those working in the scholarly tradition, and it is not misplaced. Only the most perverse of result-oriented critics of the Court pretend not to understand the importance of craftsmanship to the continued performance of the Court's various functions within the American political system.[41]

But, and this is the lesson to be learned from Professor Kurland's effort, it is too much to ask that an approach be accepted because it will lead to greater coherence. Craftsmanship is necessarily an important consideration to a constitutional court, and to say that fewer conceptual problems will be presented in adopting one approach to a constitutional provision rather than another is to say something of consequence. But tidiness and symmetry and coherence are not ultimate values; they are only *among* the values which the Justices must strive to serve. The value of doctrinal consistency may be *properly* jostled by the demands of political adjustment. While it might be a triumph of craftsmanship for the Court to follow Professor Kurland, a sufficient policy consensus does not exist. Should the Justices adopt the Kurland principle almost every one of the Court's attentive public would be upset with some aspect of the policy outcomes. Surely the Court can lead "public opinion" and attempt to stimulate consensus from time to time, but before Justices embark on such trail-blazing they had better assure themselves that the opinions of the various opinion-making elites which are particularly attentive to constitutional law are at least *moving in the direction* the Justices wish to take. The Supreme Court may be able, indeed, it may be one of its important functions, to set the pace of national policy change from time to time. But there are limits. For the Court to attempt to swim across powerfully moving tides in search of doctrinal consistency would be to risk the long-run political position of the institution just as surely as continued slighting of the value of doctrinal consistency would risk that position. Constitutional "principles" are meaningless unless the values they are meant to serve are made explicit, and the whole attempt is bootless if the values are not widely shared.

NOTES

1. Precisely how extra-judicial writing affects the performance of courts has not yet been carefully detailed. The fact that little work of a systematic or imaginative sort has been done should not, however, embarrass us in our intuitive conviction that it *is* important. See for historical treatments Benjamin R. Twiss, *Lawyers and the Constitution* (Princeton: Princeton University Press, 1942); and Arnold M. Paul, *Conservative Crisis and the Rule of Law* (Ithaca: Cornell University Press, 1960).

2. Edward S. Corwin, "The Supreme Court as National School Board," 14 *Law and Contemporary Problems* 3 (1949).

3. Erwin N. Griswold, "Absolute is in the Dark," 8 *Utah Law Review* 167 (1963).

4. Howe, *op. cit.*, pp. 9–23.

5. For alternative views on this matter see Charles A. Miller, *The Supreme Court and the Uses of History* (Cambridge: Harvard University Press, 1969); and Alfred H. Kelly, "Clio and the Court: An Illicit Love Affair," 1965 *Supreme Court Review* 119.

6. See this writer's review of *The Garden and the Wilderness,* 9 *Church and State* 129 (1967).

7. Non-Catholic spokesmen for aid to Church-related schools are treated in Morgan, *op. cit.*, pp. 64–67.

8. (New York: McGraw-Hill, 1963). See also "Aid to Parochial Schools—Constitutional," in Oaks, ed., *op. cit.*, pp. 55–72.

9. *Ibid.*, pp. 119–135. As Jesse Choper notes (see note 17 below), *Sherbert* v. *Verner* has given the old argument a new lease on life.

10. "Law or Prepossessions?," 14 *Law and Contemporary Problems* 23 (1949).

11. "Public Aid to Parochial Schools," 82 *Harvard Law Review* 1680 (1969).

12. See, for instance, the brief prepared in the legal department of the former National Catholic Welfare Conference at the time of the first Kennedy aid-to-education battle: "The Constitutionality of the Inclusion of Church-Related Schools in Federal Aid To Education," 50 *Georgetown Law Journal* 399 (1961).

13. "No Imposition of Religion: The Establishment Clause Value," 77 *Yale Law Journal* 692 (1968). See also "The Non-Establishment Principle: A Reply to Professor Giannella," 81 *Harvard Law Review* 1465 (1968).

14. *Ibid.*, p. 711.

15. One obvious problem is that churches minister in very different ways. To aid all religious schools equally is to treat equally only those groups which consider schools an important part of their mission. Those groups which have no schools but rely rather on evangelical preaching are not apt to feel fairly dealt with. Is the answer to subsidize some preaching along with some schools?

16. Schwartz, *op. cit.,* p. 711. Schwartz also mentions and dismisses several other possible establishment values, but since none of these has been as central to the debate as "strife avoidance," they may safely be passed over.

17. "The Establishment Clause and Aid to Parochial Schools," 56 *California Law Review* 260 (1968).

18. See, for instance, Jacob W. Landynski, "Governmental Aid to Non-Public Schools: The Constitutional Conflict Sharpens," 36 *Social Research* 333 (1969).

19. For a discussion of such proposals see Morgan, *op. cit.,* pp. 46–47. More recently we have had Christopher Jencks' defense of his education voucher plan. This proposal, adopted by OEO, was discussed in Chapter 4: the recent defense approved in *The New Republic,* July 4, 1970.

20. (New York: Harper and Row, 1970).

21. For decisions on Southern tuition payment programs see *ibid.,* pp. 141–154.

22. *Ibid.,* p. 149.

23. An example of the persistence of what might be called "public school fundamentalism" comes from Sidney Hook: "The public school system—which one defender of the parochial school system once characterized as *'Our Public Enemy Number One'*—helped to forge a united nation. Anything which weakens it weakens the nation." *Religion in a Free Society* (Lincoln, Nebraska: University of Nebraska Press, 1967), pp. 110–111.

24. Freund, *op. cit.,* p. 1683.

25. *Ibid.,* pp. 1691–1692.

26. Another attempt has been made recently to give precise statement to the Freund-Frankfurther "preferred position" theory of the religion clauses. See Stephen Shapiro, "Toward a Uniform Valuation of the Religion Guarantees," 80 *Yale Law Journal* 77 (1970). This effort seems to sacrifice the parsimony achieved by Freund's "voluntarism." Shapiro's suggested value was "free adoption, observance, and propagation of belief."

27. (New York: The Viking Press, 1968). Another writer who argues that religion must mean conscience because there is no core meaning left to the word "religion" is Harold Stahmar. See 1963 *Religion and the Public Order,* 116.

28. *Griswold* v. *Connecticut,* 381 U.S. 479.

29. Kent Greenawalt, 70 *Columbia Law Review* 1133 (1970).

30. "Religious Liberty, Non-establishment, and Doctrinal Development: Part I. The Religious Liberty Guarantee," 80 *Harvard Law Review* 1381 (1967).

31. *Ibid.,* p. 1431. On the difficulties of a "balancing test" see Charles Fried, "Two Concepts of Interests: Some Reflections on the Supreme Court's Balancing Test," 76 *Harvard Law Review* 755 (1963).

32. "Guidelines for the Free-Exercise Clause," 83 *Harvard Law Review 327* (1969).

33. *Ibid.,* p. 342.

34. Mansfield, *op. cit.,* p. 10.
35. 133 F. 2d. 703, 708 (2d. Cir. 1943).
36. 283 U.S. 605, 633, 634 (1931).
37. John P. Roche, *Shadow and Substance* (New York: Macmillan, 1964), p. 235.
38. 29 *The University of Chicago Law Review* 1 (1961).
39. Philip B. Kurland, *Religion and the Law* (Chicago: Aldine, 1962).
40. *Ibid.,* pp. 17–18.
41. See, for instance, J. Skelly Wright, "Professor Bickel, the Scholarly Tradition, and the Supreme Court," 84 *Harvard Law Review* 769 (1971).

Conclusion

This author's views on the merits of the various issues treated in the preceding pages should now be clear, perhaps painfully clear. But to avoid any lingering ambiguity, and to forestall charges of urging by implication what one is unprepared to argue, let me summarize where I think the Court has done well and where it has done ill.

The Court has done well to the extent it has retreated from the quite sweeping theory of separation articulated by Black in the early pages of his *Everson* opinion. Perhaps in the coming decade sufficient support may develop for going as far as Kurland, to hold that providing the primary purpose of the governmental program be secular and the legislative ends satisfy the public purpose requirement of the due process clause, governmental programs which provide substantial support to religious institutions are constitutional. *Lemon* was a step backward.

It is now a commonplace that Americans are coming to care less about church affiliation and, thus, the argument for strict separation based on creeded divisiveness is weakening. At the same time the conviction grows that in an increasingly urbanized or "mass" society it is important to encourage the development of a variety of private charitable and educational styles. And religious schools themselves are secularizing at such a rapid rate that talk of the dangers of proselytizing and imposition of faith is losing force. Nor does the overriding concern for racial justice require excluding church-related schools from public programs. Far from regarding religious schools as a menace, many minority parents are enthusiastic about them, and only wish more were available. The American public schools simply do not need a monopoly position. They can profit from "public-private" competition, and the stock reasons for keeping parochial schools out of the programs cease to compel.

Publicly sponsored religious exercises may continue to be capable of generating disharmonies at the community level—especially as skepticism toward conventional observances spreads in the population. To this extent the hard constitutional line of *Engle-Schempp* still commends itself as policy. In addition, it is quite possible to coherently adopt a permissive posture toward monies for church-related schools while at the same time strictly proscribing liturgical invocations in public schools. Again Kurland is handy on the point: aid to all independent schools does not involve a religious classification but teacher-organized praying and Bible reading surely does.

In the area of government support a much more accommodationist posture will be as suited to the America of the 1980's as it would have been unsuited to the America of fifty or one hundred years ago. We have reached a point in the matter of governmental involvement with church-related institutions where some new constitutional law (already developing) is worth the risk of an historical disjunction. The Court should proceed to turn the old Protestant-tinged separationism of the nineteenth century (soft on prayers hard on money) inside out. On reflection, there is no anomaly in banning even modest prayers in the common schools, while aiding specialized independent schools where sectarian prayer is routine.

The Court has done ill to retreat from the secular regulation rule as it did in *Sherbert*. The free-exercise clause should not be expanded into a general protection of unorthodox (otherwise proscribable) behavior, ringed about by "compelling interest" and "alternative means" tests. But here it is quite doubtful that a sufficient consensus will develop to support the crispness of Kurland's rule—that as long as government does not use religion as a criterion of classification, and as long as the initiative is an otherwise valid secular regulation, it may be enforced against claims of religious scruple.

The expression of ideas is properly, if not sufficiently, protected by the speech, press, and association clauses. The Justices are having a difficult enough time adjusting the boundaries of these guarantees in a complex and restless society. To add another dimension to the problem involving religiously motivated behavior would be needless and possibly mischievous.

In a period of decline in traditional religions and rise of a welter of "fad faiths" it is extremely unwise to begin admitting exceptions to otherwise proper health, welfare, and criminal regulations. The almost certain result will be unfairness which will bring the legal system into contempt. The preferring of religious over non-religious reasons for non-compliance with the law is troublesome enough, and the impossibility of satisfactorily limiting the category ("religious") would seem a conclusively negative argument.

While the Court's adopting the full Kurland approach is not at all likely, it is by no means clear that the secular regulation notion will be wholly abandoned, and we seem in for a prolonged period of "decisional ricochet" between irreconcilable theories of the free-exercise clause which the Justices will insist can be reconciled. What may be sound judicial politics in the short run will result in bad doctrine and bad public policy. The civil libertarians (a rapidly multiplying species we are often told) are eager for any weapon, however internally faulty, to protect individuals against the state, and the Supreme Court is not—and properly is not—immune from the necessity of embracing a bad idea whose time is come.

The Court, finally, has done well to refuse to be moved in the direction of a general constitutional right of conscientious objection to otherwise valid requirements. A *Sherbert*-type exemption for religious reasons is difficult enough to support, but a First-Amendment-based right not to have to do things which the state commands cuts at the moral foundation of civil government.

Perhaps the most sophisticated argument for exempting conscientious objectors from military service is Michael Walzer's *Obligations,*[1] Chapter 8. Walzer suggests that a state should pursue a liberal policy of exemptions for conscientious objectors —not because objectors can be understood to have any *right* to exemption, but because the *state itself* will be better (the quality of governance more civilized) to the extent it finds itself able to relieve individuals, as a matter of grace, from performing a task which is in some very basic sense distasteful.

This approach, of course, raises many of those problems of fairness and proper criteria with which we have become familiar in these pages. And it is quite clear that the criterion of religiosity cannot be employed in America as Congress has attempted to employ it without dramatically altering the prevailing theory of the establishment clause. The difficulties and dangers and necessity of sincerity tests abide, and any standards and rules legislatures develop for dispensing grace must meet at least the constitutional standards of due process and equal protection. But with all this, leaving exemptions to the political process as a matter of "ordinary" policy, is far to be preferred to constitutionalizing conscience. The legislature can create exemptions with at least some selectivity; it can fall back on reasons of practicality and expediency which would create scandal coming from a constitutional Court. The legislature, in short, is not as vulnerable to the arguments by analogy and the demands of doctrinal symmetry as the Justices. It is precisely the striving toward doctrinal coherence —the distinctive, legitimatizing characteristic of the American Supreme Court—whch renders it unwise to attempt to handle conscientious objection constitutionally. Either the exemptions will be extended into areas where they are politically unacceptable, or they will not be so extended and the Court will not be able to explain why. Legislatures do not labor under the same obligation to explain, and they have a great deal more room for policy maneuvering before running into constitutional restraints. That the national Congress has not done very well in avoiding constitutional constraints is an unhappy but not a necessary outcome.

These views may strike some readers as illiberal. I have plumped for aiding schools run by myth-ridden priesthoods, traditionally the enemies of liberalism. I have opposed expanding greatly the protection of religiously motivated behavior and the elevation of conscience into a constitutional right to disobey. Such an impression of illiberality is, in one sense, quite correct. I believe that the conventional liberal positions on the religion clauses (as reflected, let us say, by the ACLU) are obsolescent—that they no longer serve the liberal goal of maximum diversity and individualism consistent with a decently ordered government and society.

It is not the proper part of liberalism in post-industrial America to favor a state monopoly in education or to favor "religious" motivations over "merely" secular reasons in applying laws to the affairs of men.

NOTES

1. Michael Walzer, *Obligations* (Cambridge: Harvard University Press, 1970), pp. 120–145.

Index